D0946348

Ragged But Right
The Life & Times of George Jones

Ragged But Right

THE LIFE & TIMES OF George Jones

BY DOLLY CARLISLE

Contemporary Books, Inc.
Chicago

Library of Congress Cataloging in Publication Data

Carlisle, Dolly.
  Ragged but right.

  Includes index.
    1. Jones, George, 1931–   2. Country musicians—United States—
Biography.   I. Title.
ML420.J756C4   1984   784.5′2′00924   [B]   84-1826
ISBN 0-8092-5537-5

Copyright © 1984 by Dolly Carlisle
All rights reserved
Published by Contemporary Books, Inc.
180 North Michigan Avenue, Chicago, Illinois 60601
Manufactured in the United States of America
Library of Congress Catalog Card Number: 84-1826
International Standard Book Number: 0-8092-5537-5

Published simultaneously in Canada by Beaverbooks, Ltd.
195 Allstate Parkway, Valleywood Business Park
Markham, Ontario L3R 4T8 Canada

To my husband,
Floyd W. Kephart, Jr.

Contents

Acknowledgments

MANY SHOULD BE THANKED; only a few will be mentioned. The staffs of both the Country Music Association and the Country Music Hall of Fame in Nashville were generous with their time and their files.

There is no way to adequately thank the staff of CBS Records in Nashville, who gave beyond the call of duty. I appreciate their gracious support.

Yvonne Norman, who transcribed my interview tapes and who helped to keep my records in some kind of order, was wonderful.

I have to thank my editors, who guided this poor writer on her first outing of writing a book. Their hard work and patience compensated for my stumbling.

Above all, I'm grateful to W. T. and Helen Scroggins, who gave hours upon hours of their time. This book could not have been written without their help. I am grateful that I had the pleasure of sharing the company of these dear people.

Last, but certainly not least, I wish to thank my husband and best friend, Floyd W. Kephart, Jr., who gave me the greatest gift of all—the faith that I could write a book.

RAGGED BUT RIGHT
THE LIFE & TIMES OF
GEORGE JONES

"Writing a life story of me would be very, very important. [It wouldn't be] for money, not for fame and glory. My life story, if I was ever lucky for somebody to write it, is for truth only. That would mean more to me than all the fortune and fame, money, and gold in the world. Other than having Christ in my life."

—George Jones, as spoken
  to the author on
  December 28, 1978

I'M RAGGED BUT I'M RIGHT

by George Jones

Well, I've come here to tell you folks, I'm rag-ged but I'm right, I'm a tramp and a round-er I stay out late at night, Por-ter-house steak three times a day for my board— That's more than a-ny loaf-er in this big town can af-ford. Well, a big e-lec-tric fan to keep me cool when I sleep.— A lit-tle ba-by boy to play a-round Dad-dy's feet, I'm a ram-bler, I'm a gam-bler, and I lead ev'-ry life, 'cause I tell you folks, I'm rag-ged but I'm right.—

Now, — when I got mar-ried — I knew I'd set-tle down, and build a lit-tle love nest right here in my home town, So now I've got a fam-i-ly, one that I'm proud of— I know that I'll be hap-py 'cause they're the ones I love.

© Copyright 1956-Starrite Publishing Co., All rights assigned to Fort Knox Music Co., Reprinted by permission. All rights reserved.

CHAPTER

1

Some Day My Day Will Come

THE OMENS of winter were plainly evident on that grey, damp October day in 1981. The once brightly hued colors of autumn had already turned into the muted, drab shades of winter. Leaves hung listlessly from the massive oak trees. Dank piles of faded foliage lay in ever-changing patterns of kaleidoscopic design on the cold ground as the chilled winds blew across the open spaces. The trees, once caressed with varying forms of life, were now barren. Even the sky, pregnant with one of winter's cold rains, cast a dreary, gloomy spell over the countryside.

Nashville's monolithic Opryhouse stood tall, majestic, remote, and imposing near the banks of the Cumberland River. A visitor seeing the structure for the first time is usually overwhelmed with its immensity, its larger-than-life grand architectural lines. The twelve-foot doors and the skyward slanted beams hint that its occupants are giants, titans descended from the gods themselves. Everything about the place defies the laws that govern the ordinary. In contrast to the drab surroundings, the grounds encasing

1

the Opryhouse were abloom with the fresh, dewy colors of spring. Pinks, reds, yellows, and lavenders sang from a chorus of well-manicured gardens, resplendent with life and freshness as though the grounds were once removed by an invisible glass shield from the otherwise ordinary world.

If it had been built in another age, the Opryhouse might have housed the Greek mythological god Apollo. He could have wished for no grander nor more magnificent structure. And the place would have been an appropriate setting for inviting the other gods to come over while he strummed on his lyre and imparted wisdom through his magical use of oracles and signs of what would be.

But as it is, the Opryhouse is home to the Grand Ole Opry, the symbolic birthplace and womb of country music. Every week, on Friday and Saturday night, its stage is bustling with the activity of what has become radio's longest-running live show and has affectionately been dubbed "The Opry." Once marooned in a dilapidated wood building in downtown Nashville, the Opry's base of operation moved to its current home in 1972. A circular piece of the original floor was saved and meticulously placed in the stage's center as the only vestige of its former life. To this day it serves as the symbolic focus of what has now turned out to be a $270-million complex, complete with a sprawling 614-room hotel (Opryland Hotel) with an old-fashioned colonial architectural design, television studios, a nationally recognized theme park (Opryland), and Nashville Network, an independent cable station that features country music and its stars.

The Opryhouse was an appropriate place for the showcasing of the Country Music Association's Awards Show, where the brightest and the best of country music's entertainers are anointed with awards and adulations during a live telecast seen each year by some 48 million viewers. And now, as the last remnants of the day's sunlight filtered through the overcast skies, the structure blazed in the glow of dozens of ground lights. And as the hour approached for the eight o'clock telecast to begin, hundreds of gaily attired people passed through the oversized doors. Massive chandeliers cast shimmering light beams on the assemblage as it passed through the foyer, creating a fairyland effect. A magical aura permeated the air as well as a charged excitement that is commonplace anytime a live television show is about to begin. CBS operatives were already gearing up for the network's nationwide coverage of the event. The auditorium was abuzz with activity. Stagehands—workmen dressed in faded blue jeans and scuffed sneakers—were busy making their last-minute checks of props and equipment. A lighting technician lifted up a long aluminum pole with a hook on its tip to adjust a high hanging ceiling spotlight.

The evening's celebrities had on their coming-out clothes. Conscious of perpetuating their individual images to the millions of viewers who would soon be watching, all had on their identifiable attire. Charlie Daniels lumbered down the aisle dressed in his customary dry-cleaned blue jeans and cowboy hat pulled down low so that his eyes could barely be seen. In contrast, petite Lynn Anderson glided into the auditorium ensconced in a coral chiffon floor-length formal gown that fit tightly in the bodice and then billowed out at the skirt. Her strawberry blonde hair had purposefully been combed to flow down her back. She was cognizant that her hair was a trademark. Dottie West strutted in, proudly displaying her latest Bob Mackie creation—a gold lamé variation of her usual form-fitting outfits. Johnny Lee, country music's reputed womanizer, characteristically pranced in, donning his latest custom-made cowboy hat. He was accompanied by his future wife, "Dallas" television starlet Charlene Tilton. Chet Atkins, the legendary guitar player and record producer, sheepishly strolled in, wearing a simple black tuxedo.

Like butterflies fluttering from one flower blossom to another, the luminaries paused only momentarily in their movements about the auditorium. The Country Music Awards Show is as much a social affair as it is a coronation. Surprisingly, the entertainers see little of one another through the year. Most are too busy developing their individual careers to have time to chitchat or socialize with one another. On such an occasion as an award show it is their perfunctory duty to see as many of their compatriots as possible.

The flutterings grew more frantic and hurried as the time neared for the show's airing to begin. Anticipation built as celebrities rushed to their dressing rooms to add a final puff of powder and give their coiffeured hairstyles one last spurt of hairspray. Show hostess Barbara Mandrell paused to take a few deep breaths of air to calm her nerves. Her co-host, Mac Davis, gave himself one last glance-over in his dressing room mirror. Although both were veterans of network television appearances, the CMA Award Show embodied added challenges. It was live. Any error would be obvious and uncorrectable. The show was popular, usually drawing the evening's largest share of the TV-watching audience. And their performance would be compared to that of their many cohorts. The hosts, along with all those entertainers who were to appear, wanted to perform at their very best.

Meanwhile, singer George Glenn Jones was standing in the foyer nervously chain-smoking Vantage cigarettes. He was uncomfortable in his three-piece chocolate-brown polyester suit and ruffled shirt, which he had conspicuously unbuttoned at the neckline. He had little interest in these glittery, tinsel-town affairs and had not wanted to come. And would not have attended if he had not been held captive in an Opryland hotel room all afternoon. Just minutes before, Wayne Oliver, George's would-be manager, and Rick Blackburn, vice-president of CBS Records, had come to fetch him in a black limousine. They now stood on either side of him, as guards might stand, making small talk.

George had been nominated for four CMA awards and, along with the young, vibrant group Alabama, was thought to be the odds-on favorite to clinch the evening's accolades. Many, like Johnny Cash, Emmylou Harris, and others, believed George to be the king of country music. "I can say, without hesitation, that George Jones is the greatest country music singer who has ever lived," declared Buddy Killen, president of Tree International Publishing, the world's largest music publishing company. But ironically George saw himself as a simple singer who wanted nothing more than to "sing my songs." He did not feel comfortable in the midst of stars because he didn't view himself as one of them. Instead, he would have preferred to have been in East Texas, settling down to a country supper of green beans and cornbread prepared by a good woman. If his evening had been ideal, he would have moved into the living room after supper where he would have stretched out before the TV set for an evening of entertainment. His woman would join him after clearing up the dishes, and they would doze off together in the quiet of their home with the bright lights and hubbub of the evening's events confined to a TV set.

Few understood George. To most, he was an enigma. Certainly his on-and-off girlfriend of several years, Linda Welborn, had not figured him out. The dark-haired, quiet, mousy young woman had accompanied George to Nashville. Unlike George, she revelled in the bright lights. But George had stolen her thunder when he ordered her to sit in the balcony, far away from where he would be sitting on the main level in the designated section for the entertainers. They had had another spat. Even though George had continued to let Linda live with him, he regarded her much like an old suit. He hesitated to throw her out until he found someone with whom to replace her. As it turned out, Linda and George's date for the Country Music Awards Show was to be one of their last. "George is real particular about his looks," once observed George's hairdresser, Jimmie Hills. "And he's just as particular about how his girlfriend looks." "Linda dressed real gaudy sometimes," continued Ann, Jimmie's wife and hairdressing partner. "And George would get embarrassed about what she had on. Sometimes she'd put on things you'd expect to see on a prostitute," Ann added.

Another woman was already on the horizon, Nancy Sepulvada. She was a Shreveport, Louisiana, lass in whom, of late, George had displayed an increasing trust and admiration. Time would prove that Nancy would better understand George than any of his three wives, including his most famous wife, Tammy Wynette, who, contrary to her theme song, had failed to "stand by her man."

Actually, George was a simple man but one with conflicting goals. He valued above all else his privacy and coveted a simple, but secure home life. He probably could have had either if he had been willing to give up his singing profession. But that alternative was unacceptable to George, who had grown accustomed to earning a six-figure yearly income. Unfortunately, George had refused to accept that loss of privacy was part of the price he had to pay in order to merit a big income. Other entertainers, like the group Alabama or Barbara Mandrell, had long since willingly made that sacrifice. For them, the benefits far outweighed the loss. "I'd be disappointed if the fans didn't come up," Barbara once remarked. "That recognition is what I've worked so hard for all these years." Conversely, George felt uneasy and unworthy of the public's anointments and bitterly resented being made to attend these flowerly fanfares.

So, while others excitedly rushed to their seats in great anticipation of what was to come, George lingered in the hallway for as long as was possible, hoping to postpone the inevitable. The more he thought about going in, the sadder and more forlorn he became. He fidgeted, first with his hair, patting the top of his head as he might have a dog. He frequently adjusted his vest and pulled at his sleeves. Occasionally he scratched his face and neck, as though attacking an annoying flea. But in spite of his obvious discomfort, George's destiny, at least for the next two hours, was foreordained. Rick Blackburn had long before decided that George was going to be present to pick up his awards if George was lucky enough to win any.

George's conflict was ·not new. His reputation for feigning illnesses and drunken stupors to avoid such appearances was so well-established that he had been affectionately nicknamed "the possum" years earlier. In more recent times, however, his antics had adopted a more self-destructive edge. In 1979, he had nearly died from drinking too much alcohol and snorting too much cocaine. He had been so strung out that a close friend, songwriter Peanut Montgomery, had described George as "destructive both to himself and others," and checked George into an Alabama hospital. In 1979 George had sunk so low that he had been declared a ward of the state. Now, two years later, although still struggling with his addiction to cocaine, George was back, his voice miraculously as strong as ever. In the previous year he had recorded his most successful song to date, "He Stopped Loving Her Today." It had been his first gold record and was on its way to becoming his first platinum record. The country music industry had never been known to rally around an artist the way it had supported George. But then, no one else could sing like George. It was with a spirit of appreciation for his talents that the CMA had bestowed more award nominations on the frail, worn singer than ever before in his thirty-year career.

George was back, but Rick Blackburn, as well as most of those who befriended the singer, knew his future, at best, was undecided. "It would not surprise me to get a phone call any day saying that George had been found dead or had had a fatal car accident," Blackburn reflected some months later. Even though George had been in and out of hospitals to overcome his drug problem, the man still had no family life and therefore no anchor from which George's traumatized, insecure personality could be buoyed up. Blackburn's fears were all the more reason he had wanted George to be at this award show.

But George had no such insight, even though, when asked, he admitted that he was surprised to still be living. He had imagined dying young in the style of his hero, the legendary Hank Williams. True to form, George had lived just as fast, loved just as hard, and therefore was expecting to die young like Hank. But an early exit from his earthly life had not been George's fate.

Instead, he was an old-looking fifty-year-old. His years of reckless living were reflected on his lined, haggard face like a road map. A long-term excessive drinking problem had left his skin grey and as parched as papyrus paper. But other indulgences had contributed to his timeworn appearance. Cocaine had burnt his sinuses. For days at a stretch, he was too drugged to eat or sleep. For a while he had cared about neither as long as he had his snort. The neglect of his personal well-being was evidenced in his rounded, stooped shoulders that looked as though they were supporting the weight of the world and in his sad, basset hound facial expression that said that for every time he had overindulged in life's temptations he had suffered an equal misery.

As the time drew near for the threesome to leave the lighted foyer and enter the dark auditorium where they would take their seats, George looked longingly at the open door that led to the outside and to what he interpreted as his freedom. But he knew he was trapped. Both Rick and Wayne were familiar with George's escape schemes. They had either directly experienced or heard of the times George had climbed out of bathroom windows or suddenly disappeared in a crowded airport. They were not about to let George out of their sight. So when the cue came from Blackburn that it was time to go in, George shrugged his reluctance but obediently stubbed out his cigarette in a nearby ashtray stand and took his place between the two men. As they entered the 4,220-seat hall, George made no attempt to mask his unhappiness. He moved begrudgingly, with stiff, stilted motions like those of a wound-up doll.

The threesome took their seats just in time. The lights went low, the orchestra started playing, and a stagehand gave the tuxedo-attired hosts—Barbara Mandrell and Mac Davis—the cue to let them know they were now live on the air. The knowledge that some 48 million viewers were fixed to their seats in their respective homes gazing at them did not fluster them. Both were accustomed to such intense pressures. Barbara had flown in from California during a break from taping her weekly NBC variety show, "Barbara Mandrell and the Mandrell Sisters." Mac was a veteran at hosting network specials and had already starred in two successful motion pictures. They were professionals in the fullest definition of the word.

The show began with the presentation of the industry's Female Vocalist of the Year award to Barbara Mandrell. It was to be her night. She had always been one of country music's most disciplined and hardest-working members, and at thirty-two years of age her determination and hard work had earned her a successful network series. The industry was usually generous in its recognition of such extraordinary effort. And tonight Barbara's cohorts were not going to disappoint her. She accepted the bullet-shaped award with aplomb and then quickly resumed her co-hosting duties.

"My next guest, Dolly Parton, has a problem," Barbara teasingly said. "She's in Austin, Texas, filming a movie [*The Best Little Whorehouse in Texas*] with Burt Reynolds. Big problem, right?" By way of a closed-circuit television line, Dolly responded in a similar manner. "You know, it's really hard for me to be down here in Austin and see you win and me just stuck here doing these passionate love scenes with that ugly old Burt Reynolds. Can you imagine that?" said Dolly with a coquettish giggle. Barbara retorted good-naturedly, "Well, nobody said show business was easy, Dolly."

While the audience burst out with laughter and applause,

George squirmed in his seat as a child might during a long, boring church service. He perfunctorily clapped his hands with the rest of the audience, but his thoughts were elsewhere. He was wondering' if girlfriend, Nancy Sepulvada, or his sons, Bryan and Jeffrey, were watching. He didn't want to disappoint them by not winning if they were.

But other awards were to be announced and accepted before George would be called up. The group Alabama won awards in three categories—Group of the Year, Single of the Year, and Album of the Year. Charlie Daniels and his band went up to receive Instrumental Group of the Year, and newcomers David Frizzell and Shelly West were honored with the Duo of the Year award. That award, in particular, brought back visions of earlier years to George when he and his third wife and singing partner, Tammy Wynette, had been nominated in that category. Ironically, they had never won the award, even though they had enjoyed a succession of duet hits and had been slugged "Mr. and Mrs. Country Music." Their marriage, unlike their music, had been turbulent. But strangely enough, George still thought of their time together "as the happiest of my life." From its inception their relationship had been a whirlwind affair. They met in 1968, married in 1969, produced a child in 1971, separated briefly in 1973, split in 1974, and then divorced in 1975. During that time they had garnered six top-twenty country hits and headlined an array of newspaper stories. Six years had passed since he had last been nominated with his Tammy. And during that time he had proven to be the stronger talent of the two. Tammy had failed to regain her popularity of the early 1970s. Conversely, George was at the peak of his career, in spite of his frequent no-shows, alcohol and drug problems, and poor management. But he had not found the true love that Tammy claimed she had discovered in her current husband, songwriter George Richey. The couple sat just a few seats away from George.

Finally George's name was announced as the recipient of the Male Vocalist of the Year award. George took a deep breath and bolted up the steps onto the brightly lit stage. "I just want to say one thing," he mumbled to the camera through clinched teeth. "I'm very proud and I still love Johnny Wright and Kitty Wells.

Thank you very much, and we love that country music is finally back in Nashville." As he turned to walk off the stage he breathed a great sigh of relief and winked at a pretty young dark-haired woman standing on the side of the stage. George figured he could now relax. And as he slid back into his seat next to Wayne, he motioned for the white Styrofoam cup hidden underneath the pew seat to be handed to him. Wayne obliged. George took a long swallow of his Jack Daniels whiskey. He may as well have been taking a slug of life itself.

But George's participation in the evening's events was far from over. "He Stopped Loving Her Today" won in the Song of the Year category. George's tear-wrenching song won for the second time in two years, an unusual occurrence. The audience gasped their surprise but quickly clapped their approval. When Curly Putman and Bobby Braddock, the song's creators, went onstage they thanked the man who had so magnificently delivered the song to the public. "We couldn't have won without you, George," they said across the room as they toasted George with their award, as they might have done with a glass of wine. George smiled and dropped his eyes to the floor. Ironically, the song that had come to symbolize his amazing comeback and which was his largest-selling record ever was also the song that told the sad tale of a man's unrequited love for a woman.

The nondescript cameraman approached unexpectedly, breaking George's melancholy mood. He whispered to Wayne that Barbara Mandrell had requested that George join her in singing her hit, "I Was Country When Country Wasn't Cool." "I'm hoarse," responded George frantically. "It's been set up," the cameraman replied. "No," said George, assuming his point had been made. But a moment later, with the full glare of the cameras and the audience's eyes on him, she made the request. "Oh George, are you out there, George?" Barbara cooed, standing up on her tiptoes. George sat frozen in his seat with a sick grin plastered on his face. He said nothing. "I'll meet you halfway, George," she finally said. Then, skipping down the steps, she walked halfway down the aisle. Realizing he was not going to meet her, she yanked the microphone cord and walked the rest of the distance to George's seat. Now he had to sing. "I'm a little hoarse," he apologized to the viewers and cleared his throat. His voice was raspy; so much so that he could barely hold the notes. George showed his embarrassment. His inability to sing in full regalia further frustrated and depressed him and reminded him yet again that he had lost control of his life.

The moment passed quickly. Soon the blaring lights went to highlight another famous country music face. George was again washed in darkness. Now he was itching to get out. He didn't hear the announcement that Terry Gibbs had been voted the industry's most promising newcomer. He didn't even recollect later that Barbara Mandrell was declared the Entertainer of the Year, country music's most prestigious award. He was too preoccupied with getting out of the side door to pay attention.

Barbara accepted the award with tears rolling down her cheeks. But her eyes were happy. "Thank you so much," she said to the crowd with feeling. "I was standing in the back praying to God that I could win this award, and I'm so thankful that He saw fit to grant me my wish. This makes me happier than you can ever imagine."

As Mac came over to give Barbara a hug and the credits began to roll over the television screen, George hurried out a side door. He moved swiftly, with long and deliberate strides. Before the last of the credits had rolled over the nation's screens, George's frail outline had been engulfed by the night's blackness. He didn't even so much as give a backward glance at the magnificence of the Grand Ole Opryhouse. George Jones, the country music legend and the industry's best singer, did not tarry long enough to voice his congratulations to Barbara Mandrell, a woman he genuinely liked. Nor did he give other acknowledgments. He was far too preoccupied with escaping into an environment in which he felt comfortable. By the time the long lines were forming outside the exit doors and before the orchestra could pack their instruments, George Jones was long gone.

Poor Man's Riches

INETEEN THIRTY-ONE was a dark and cheer-less year; miserable by most accounts. The world was in the depths of the Great Depression. A thick veil of quiet desperation had blanketed the United States like a layer of damp, heavy snow. Pleas of panic had been silenced by a loss of hope. It was to be another year before Franklin D. Roosevelt would challenge the fear of the people.

The George Washington Jones family was in the same predicament as the population as a whole. Times for them were hard, painful, and difficult. Looking back, however, they described the year as one of fulfilled dreams. Their last child, a surprise pregnancy, was their good fortune. In a poor family such as theirs, where material riches are practically nonexistent, a baby becomes a family's treasure. And on September 12 of that otherwise black and cheerless year, Clara Patterson Jones gave birth to George Glenn Jones, her second son, a child who would one day become both rich and famous and as disturbed as the times into which he was born.

"The desert years of the human spirit" is how the then Secretary of State, Dean Acheson, described the early 1930s. John Kenneth Galbraith painted the mood of the nation's people by stating, "Some people were hungry in 1930, 1931, and 1932. Others were tortured by the fear that they might go hungry. Yet others suffered the agony of the descent from the honor and respectability that goes with income into poverty. And still others feared they would be next. Meanwhile everyone suffered a sense of utter hopelessness. Nothing, it seemed, could be done."

The Jones clan was accustomed to hard times. "Poor folks" is how they described their status. But the Depression years called for them to "tighten the belt" on an already lean torso. Still, they were lucky. Hunger may have knocked at their door, but it never entered. "We was hard up," recalled George Glenn Jones some fifty years later with a wince at the memory. "We didn't know how hard up. But we had enough to eat. We didn't go hungry. Those's the ones that had a really hard life. You don't forget if you ever go hungry for very long."

The Jones family avoided famine because they could grow their own food. However, the earth upon which they built a house, planted a crop, and raised their children was not theirs. They were squatters in the old-fashioned definition of the word. Living on undeveloped land owned by the large oil companies, they were allowed, like their neighbors, to squat with the understanding they could never gain rightful title. As long as they lived quietly and didn't cause problems, they were free to develop and cultivate the land for free. It was a major advantage because elsewhere poor people were starving literally to death. William Manchester describes, in his brilliant book *The Glory and the Dream*, how the Jones family counterparts existed.

> Millions stayed alive by living like animals. In the Pennsylvania countryside they were eating wild weed-roots and dandelions; in Kentucky they chewed violet tops, wild onions, forget-me-nots, wild lettuce, and weeds which heretofore had been left to grazing cattle. City mothers hung around docks, waiting for spoiled produce to be discarded and then fighting homeless dogs for possession of it. After the vegetables had

been loaded on trucks they would run alongside ready to snatch up anything that fell off. A cook in a midwestern hotel put a pail of leftovers into the alley outside the kitchen; immediately a dozen men loomed out of the darkness to fight over it. In Long Beach, California, a sixty-two-year-old physician named Francis Everett Townsend glanced out his window while shaving and saw, among a group of refuse barrels, "three haggard very old women," as he later called them. "Stooped with great age, bending over the barrels, gnawing at bones and watermelon rinds." A Chicago widow recalls always removing her glasses so she wouldn't see the maggots.

Thirty percent of the population had no income at all during the early 1930s. George Washington Jones was luckier than those. He was usually able to find something to do that would bring in a few dollars. Helen Scroggins, George's oldest sister, recalls, "He was a real hard-working man." He delivered ice for the small East Texas community of Saratoga where he lived, and when the community didn't have enough money to buy ice George Washington went to sawing barrel stays. To do this, he needed a partner, so his oldest son, Herman, was obliged to help out. Not yet a teenager, Herman quit school and joined his dad in hard labor. "He [George Washington] wouldn't have made enough money to live on if Herman hadn't of [quit], cause [sawing barrel stays] didn't pay but $2 a day," recalls a Jones neighbor at the time, Katy Hooks. "When that little old job played out, they sawed wood. He was bringing in just enough to buy a little bread and that was all."

Their meals were meager and oftentimes provided bulk rather than nutritional sustenance. "A lot of times they [the Jones family] had gravy and bread for breakfast," stated W. T. Scroggins, George Jones's brother-in-law. "A lot of time when they didn't have flour, then they had cornmeal bread. They took cornmeal and made mush out of it. Now they call it grits. Many a time, that's all they had for breakfast." Helen Scroggins concurs: "We had biscuits and gravy every day. I can't remember having too many eggs in the morning. That's one thing we never had, was chicken too much. Daddy always had a big garden. We always had plenty of vegetables. In the winter Mama would fix a big pot of beans in a big iron pot and a big pan of biscuits, and that was a meal. I remember going to town a lot of times and getting twenty-five cents worth of lima beans. Daddy loved them. Mama would put them on in a big iron pot with maybe some fried potatoes. We didn't have meat too much. They killed hogs on the farms, but we didn't have too much of that then."

As bad as it was, W. T. Scroggins characterizes the Jones family as getting along better than his. Only twelve years old in 1930, W. T. already had the responsibility of earning a living to support his mother and two sisters. His father had abandoned the family. "The Depression began to hurt us in 1930," recollects W. T. "We borrowed to make a crop like all farmers did. We borrowed thinking we would get a high price for our crops. Then, at the end of that year, we didn't get nothing for our crops. It got down to five cents a pound. When we planted it, crops had been forty cents a pound. We couldn't pay out of debt. The next year, 1931, we lost everything we had. The farm was lost. A lot of people went on the soup lines.

"I never did get on the soup lines," W. T. continued with a note of pride in his voice. "I got out and I worked for fifty cents a day a-taking care of my mother and my two sisters and brother. I would follow cotton picking, and in 1932 I remember I stopped over in Dallas on my way back [from picking cotton]. I seen little kids eating anything they could find. Didn't make no difference if it was from a garbage can. I seen them little kids had a straight pin and had made a fish hook out of it. They would catch them little perch and put them in a pan without a drop of grease and fry them. They was eatin' them fish bones and all. Some of them were so poor they could hardly get around.

"Down in this part of the country, where Helen and them was, they all depended on the timber to make them a living such as sawmills and all such stuff as logging. When the Depression hit, it hit the sawmills and everything. They had to close down. There wasn't no money for lumber or nothing. They started a WPA, and most of the men that had families got on it to let them work about three days a week, and they would give them so many groceries and such as that. George's daddy never got on WPA. I never heard him talk about it. He always had lots of get-up and pride about him, and he always tried to find something he could make a grocery bill out of it."

Rudimentary food and shelter is all the Jones family had, however. Excess was nonexistent, and what there was came in the barest form. Their wood two-room shack was a do-it-your-selfer built from the bottom up by Mr. Jones. "He even built all our furniture," reflected Helen. Herman recollects that "Mama made clothes a lot out of flour sacks, out of them feed sacks. They was blue and checked." "Helen didn't have her first store-bought dress until she was ten years old," notes W. T. Scroggins.

Because he was so young, George Glenn remembers little of the desperation of the Great Depression years. By the time he started school in 1937 the worst of the economic survival battles were over. In 1932 Franklin D. Roosevelt had been elected, and he was to ease the plight of the American people. W. T. recalls, "After Roosevelt got elected, he went to giving each family a big 48-pound sack of Robin Hood flour once a month. I think if Roosevelt hadn't got elected the year that he was, there would have been fifty percent of the people in the United States that would have starved to death. Roosevelt was the one that saved the world. I was just about to my row's end when they elected Roosevelt. It had gotten to where you couldn't get nothing and they weren't giving you nothing. They didn't even start no kind of relief until after Roosevelt was in. He tried to help the people. Then it took him several years to pull it out. But things were alightin' up considerably by '38 and '39."

George Glenn may have been too young to remember the gruesome details, but nevertheless the Great Depression left its seal on him. He grew up a poor country boy and was proud of it. The times and his environment left him with little else to boast about.

Traditionally, poor people are suspicious of the rich. But during the Great Depression that doubt turned into disdain. George Washington Jones worked hard, gave his all to make enough money to keep his family fed and sheltered. But no matter how hard-working and persevering he was, he could not aggregate anything more than the bare essentials. He was cocky and self-assured, a kind of jack-of-all-trades fellow who had the talent to handle almost any task. Yet, for all his smarts and tenacity, he was a poor man who had little hope of rising above poverty. He assumed, as did many of the nation's poor during that time, that the rich were stealers, liars, and crooks. Otherwise they wouldn't be rich. George Washington Jones felt that a fellow had to sell his soul to acquire wealth.

The rich at the time of the Great Depression did little to dissipate such beliefs. In truth, their actions were what generated those conclusions. The indifference of the rich toward the plight of the poor was appalling. Evidence of their haughty attitudes was pervasive. In *The Glory and the Dream*, William Manchester cites the indictment. A member of the DuPont family was reported to have rejected a suggestion that he sponsor a Sunday afternoon program on the grounds that "at three o'clock on Sunday afternoons everybody is playing polo." A Republican candidate for governor in New Jersey exclaimed to the people that "there is something about too much prosperity that ruins the moral fiber of the people."

As the Depression worsened and the resentments of the poor intensified, the rich grew fearful of the very people toward whom they showed such little regard. Thus the chasm between the haves and the have-nots deepened. In the eyes of the poor the rich looked increasingly wicked, and in the eyes of the rich the poor appeared more and more tattered, disgusting, and threatening. Manchester continued with a description of the emerging American caste system:

> . . . the well-fed were edgy. Company men in employment offices became curt, bank tellers nervous, elected officials were quicker to call the police, policemen faster with the nightstick. Henry Ford had always been a pacifist. Now he carried a gun. . . . New York hotels discovered that wealthy guests who usually leased suites for the winter were holing up in their country homes. Some had mounted machine guns on their roofs.

Almost overnight, once-upon-a-time heroes like J. P. Morgan and Andrew Mellon became monsters.

At an age too young to formulate his own thoughts, George Glenn learned by osmosis the description of his antithesis. As some children unknowingly grow up to be bigots, George Glenn reached adulthood despising the rich. He never knew exactly why he disliked and distrusted the well-off so. But the skepticism ran deep and wide. After becoming a millionaire himself thirty years later George would sometimes look into a reflecting mirror to discover he had become what he had been taught to hate. Horrified at his own success, he would subconsciously reach back, grab for a damaging stone, and throw it long and hard into the reflected image. Unable to separate his own success from the prosperity that he had been so well ingrained to spurn, George Glenn was trapped in a never-ending swing of the success-to-self-punishment syndrome. No sooner had he accumulated wealth than he unconsciously, deliberately went about liquidating it.

"George grew up real countrified," explained Helen. "You couldn't hardly get a sock on him. Half the time he would have his shoes on him and no socks. He would put on the slouchiest britches he had; the shortest ones. Daddy was always such a neat man. But George loved to go just like a country boy, 'cause he loved that. Years later I think it really tore him up when people thought he thought he was better than the family or something. That tore him up real bad. He didn't want nobody to think that he was better than them."

The Depression had a second and contradictory effect on people. It left a strong craving in its victims' psyches for what it had denied them. "After the Depression, when people started having a little money, they just kind of went berserk," recalls Annie Stephens, little George's Sunday schoolteacher. George Washington and Clara had had little money to spend on their older children. But in 1948 Mr. Jones took a wartime job in Beaumont working for the shipyard. For the first time during their married lives the Jones had money left over after paying the essential bills. Most of the children were either married and gone or were old enough to be working. George Glenn was the only child left at home. And Clara spent money on him as though to compensate for all the years that her other children had gone without.

For George, the Depression weaved a destructive web of inner conflict. He was to become one of the few of his lot to have the capacity to accumulate wealth. But, in his heart, George was a poor man, bridled with all the natural resentment and distrust that the impoverished harbor toward the rich. Yet one day George was to experience the dilemma of living in the style that his heritage had scorned. The conflict was real and, for most of his life, unresolved. As a result, most of George's attitudes and actions regarding the spending and handling of money were seemingly irrational and sometimes downright foolish.

3

Small-Time Laboring Man

**EORGE GLENN JONES'S** birthplace of Saratoga, Texas, was as much the nucleus of his emotional and spiritual life at fifty as it had been while he was growing up there. That isolated speck of a community in East Texas was more than a place. It was a state of mind. The fiber of Saratogan existence was held together by a creed so conclusive, definite, and irrefutable that the codes were passed along from parent to child with more fervor than they taught the Ten Commandments. Without the codes, the Saratogan way of life would have crumbled. During his life George Glenn lied, committed adultery, became an alcoholic and a drug addict, beat up his wives and girlfriends, mistreated and abused his friends. But rarely did he defy the Saratoga codes. By those standards George Jones was the good ole boy he was supposed to be.

"It was a little oil field town," recalled George Jones. "There was a big boom before I was born. There was a few hundred there for a while. But then, it wasn't just a handful of people and still isn't really. It's a little East Texas town right outside of Beaumont."

Nothing much is left of that once bustling community of George's ancestors. Dilapidated, weather-worn storefront structures line the town's main street, casting a shadow of what was but what will never be again. Today Saratoga has the chill of a ghost town. But at one time its streets thundered with the prosperity of a boom economy.

Saratoga was abundantly blessed with nature's favors. In the late 1800s and the first few years of this century, folks from all over Texas, Louisiana, and Mississippi flocked to Saratoga to benefit from its natural springs. Saratoga's very name was borrowed from its New York counterpart. Both communities seduced hundreds of visitors who wishfully deluded themselves that the bubbling, frothy overflow was somehow going to create a more youthful appearance or a miraculous cure for whatever ailment was afflicting them. Saratoga, Texas, was reported to have had seven or eight different minerals in its springs, and for a while the tiny, tranquil town was a blissful haven for regional holidayers.

All of that began to change in 1901. For in that year another oozing substance was discovered to be flowing out of the Saratoga landscape. Indians who had settled near Saratoga are reported to have been transfixed by the slimy, black substance for years. But not until some prospectors came across the oil literally seeping out of the Saratoga grounds did its discovery transform the dozing little town into a bustling mecca for get-rich-quick stalkers. "Overnight, they came," reveals one historian. "In special trains, on horseback, and in wagons; seamen left their ships in Galveston and New Orleans to rush to the mecca where a man could be broke in the morning and worth a million by night. Thousands of speculators came with maps, brochures, deeds, and abstracts, selling the same lease three times or four times in one day."

The wild activity literally destroyed much of what had been Saratoga. Oil prospectors quickly spoiled and demolished the springs in their insanely blind and hot pursuit of black gold. Few found their pot at the end of the rainbow. But that fact never caused a pause in their zeal. In the meanwhile, farmland was overturned, wildlife was frightened away, and Saratogans watched with dismay as their little town was turned upside down.

Another historian described the rush in this way: "It wasn't long before the word got around and thousands of hopeful drillers flocked into Saratoga, set up camp, and like the golddiggers of the mid-1800s ravaged anything that got in their way from getting what they considered to be their fair share of the black gold. The peaceful serenity of the mineral springs was soon destroyed and the springs were covered up as part of the transformation that took place in Saratoga from 1901 through the 1920s and 1930s." In their own way, Saratogans struck back. "Because of the terrain, the only possible way for the driller and his crew to get to work was on horseback," recounts the historian. "They tied their horses in the shade a distance from the rig and left them all day. One astonished crew found their horses daubed with assorted colors of barn paint by indignant natives who hated oil in any form. Night watchmen were posted on rigs because the natives took a very dim view of this so-called progress."

Try as they might, townsmen had little success in stopping or even slowing the onslaught. Their efforts were comparable to attempting to plug a crack in a dam with the thumb of a hand. Their pranks were only minor obstacles in the oil riggers' paths. Eventually the flood of outsiders totally washed away the little town. Crime and thievery ran rampant. Law and order were practically nonexistent. Each man, woman, and child had to fend for himself in the wild, wooly, and crazed streets. Townspeople took to their homes, closed up their doors and windows, and stayed there, finally retreating totally into the sanction of their wooden shacks, waiting for the bombardment to subside. When it did and the natives eased back out of their shelters, they discovered a town destroyed. By the late 1920s and early 1930s Saratoga was a shell of a town—spent, used up, and beaten. Townspeople who had remained did so because they had nowhere else to go. The once proud little community composed of sustenance farmers was now a disillusioned shadow of its former self. Once again, the rich and the would-be rich had shown their true colors, in the view of the native Saratogan.

Saratoga is a microcosm of a much larger region in East Texas commonly referred to as "the Big Thicket." So unique is this section of territory that numerous books and studies have zeroed in to describe, peruse, and examine both the terrain and its people.

The land is wild, untamed, marshy, thicketed, and dense, descriptions that are fairly suitable for the kind of people who sprang from its depths. "Once a Big Thicketer, always a Big Thicketer" is the region's motto. Few of the natives leave the area voluntarily. Those who do rarely, if ever, escape its lurking and mysterious mental and emotional grasp.

Geographically, the Big Thicket stretches for about fifty miles in the southeasten corner of Texas just northwest of Beaumont. Boundaries are somewhat fluid, but generally the Big Thicket is considered to start where Polk, Liberty, and Hardin county lines meet and run in a southeasterly direction to below and east of Sourlake. Descriptively, the area can be summed up by one word—hostile. History books reveal that "when westward moving pioneers crossed the Sabine River in Southeast Texas they found a forest so thick they could not get through, so they settled on the fringes or went around. It was described as a forest so thick it couldn't be traveled even by foot."

"People in my lifetime have been lost and died in the Big Thicket," verifies Diane Baxter, a native East Texas woman who, along with her radio personality husband, Gordon, has made the Big Thicket a lifelong study. "It's a hostile environment with mosquitoes that will eat you alive and with snakes everywhere. And it's hot, real hot and humid."

"The history of the Big Thicket goes all the way back to when white settlers were putting down their roots in Louisiana and Texas," chimes in her husband, Gordon, a Big Thicket local who had become intrigued by the Big Thicket mentality about twenty years earlier. "The Big Thicket was an unclaimed area. Louisiana was not interested in extending its borders across the Neches River into there. So they kept their border well pulled back. The Louisianans were very civilized. You can go down into that Cajun country with the sweet potato farmers and find opera houses and people who are very civilized and who subscribe to *The New York Times*. By the same token, the Mexican or the Spanish culture came up toward Louisiana, but again they kept their penetration short of the Big Thicket. It was sort of natural not to go in there because the vegetation was so dense. The old Spanish trail, which was the only way to get West, came down south of the Big Thicket through Beaumont. It was what's now Highway 90. The other way was to cross north of it up through Natchez and Nacogdoches, Texas, and Nachitoches, Louisiana. That trail was about a day's horse ride away. But you couldn't get through the Big Thicket if you were traveling east to west as a merchant or a traveler. Even the civil government's and military government's influences ended with the riverbanks because they were not interested in getting in there. So it naturally became a hideout for that element of people who couldn't stay anywhere else, and they originally moved in there. People settled in the Big Thicket because of something they didn't want. Some negative reason brought them into there. It was a spooky, dismal place and still is. It's not a healthy climate; even the Indians shunned it. They didn't live in here and they were every other place around.

"Then the broth got a little bit thicker with the Civil War deserters and in general runaway criminals," he continued. "People who were running away from something began to migrate there. They loved their own legends, so they built a legend in the Big Thicket 'cause nobody could find them in there. They created a whole special culture that's there to this day. The French had their own thing on one side of the river, and the Spanish had the other thing on the other side of the river. And in the Thicket it was your predominately Anglo bad guy. They were mostly the blue-eyed, blond-haired, long heads, better known as your true-blue huns."

Since the territory was lacking an established government, culture, and laws, the Big Thicketers created their own. Nothing was ever written down. Laws were unspoken. But if they were broken, a man or even a woman could pay with his or her life. Each new generation accepted without question the codes; they were simply obeyed. George Glenn Jones was the third generation of his family to live in the Big Thicket. By the time George had come along, many of the reasons for the creation of the codes were passé. Overall, the laws had become illogical and even self-destructive outside the realm of the Big Thicket. Yet George Glenn continued throughout his life to live just like his daddy had taught him.

Big Thicket codes were virtually unadaptable to life outside the

Thicket. All of George Glenn's sisters and his brother either stayed in the Big Thicket area or returned, if they ventured out. Even George Glenn's sons, Bryan and Jeffrey, who were also raised in the Big Thicket confines remained, although George took each one of them for a time to Nashville. Finally, at fifty-two, George completed his own life cycle by returning to the territory from which he had never been able to escape emotionally. Only there in the thick marshes and among the densely populated pine growth could he find peace with himself.

Throughout life George Jones sought familiarity. Persons with unfamiliar lifestyles or perspectives, he avoided. They disturbed him. In their presence he oftentimes began to fidget. Sometimes he would break out in a cold sweat. His discomfort was caused by a perspective steeped in sentimentality. Any sense of logic was overruled by his emotions. In addition, George Jones hated the idea of change. Saratoga had taught him that the Big Thicket way of life was the only way. The trouble was that trying to live in any other place with the peculiar Big Thicket mindset was like trying to fit a square-shaped peg into a round hole.

Living was simple in Saratoga, Texas, back in the thirties and forties. A man had only to provide a roof over his family's heads and food for the table. Little else was required or wanted. Roles were well defined. Men were men and women were women. No one thought to question if his status was fair or right. Birth control wasn't even a concept, much less a practice. Women became pregnant, children were born and raised, and then, when grown, they started the process all over again. Years and decades passed with little change, and the community liked it that way, especially the men.

In Saratoga and the Big Thicket, the white male reigned supreme. "Little boys were and still are raised with the premise that 'at least I'm not a girl,' " observed Diane Baxter. "They think, 'I may be dumb and I may be ignorant, but at least I ain't a nigger and at least I ain't a girl.' That's the prevailing attitude [in the Thicket]." The Thicket men governed their households like kings. Following the examples established by the European aristocracy of their ancestral homelands, each Big Thicket household was structured similarly to a tiny fiefdom. The head of the household provided a place to live and food to eat, and the wife and children, in return, catered to his whims and wants. "Their sovereignty may have extended only to the boundaries of his own household, but within those borders, the man was considered the absolute ruler," continued Diane.

Of course, as kings, the heads of the Big Thicket households were expected to perform certain duties. "It's important to be a good provider," continued Gordon Baxter. "The Big Thicket man brought the meat to the table, and he was never supposed to fail. It was very, very important to be able to do that." Just as inconceivable as it would have been for a King of England to have told the King of Spain how to rule his kingdom, it was inconceivable that one Big Thicket man would have gone to another to advise him on how to rule his familial kingdom. "Each man was given the choice to be a good king and a kind king," emphasizes Baxter. "But we're talking about royalty and the rights of a king."

Still, the Big Thicket community judged each man on his ability to provide for his family. Faults were overlooked; indiscretions were ignored in direct proportion to each man's care of his family. No other standard of conduct was more important. In a community where survival was the focus of each day's activity and where each family was expected to survive on its own, little else was considered important. A man could beat his wife, abuse his children, stay drunk, commit adultery, even kill another man (as long as the killing occurred because the other man was threatening his survival), but as long as he provided for his family, he was acceptable in the eyes of the Big Thicket community.

Also, the Big Thicket creed held that if a man threatened the survival of another, he did so with the understanding that he was leaving himself open to being killed. "You don't mess with anything that has to do with their livelihood," pointed out Gordon. "You never messed with a man's deer dogs, for example. Let me tell you the rules. If you end up outside a Thicket cabin and you're a total stranger with a New York accent, a Big Thicket man couldn't do enough for you. That's part of the code. Now, by the same token, if you cut his fence and let his cows out and he saw you doing it, he would kill you if he had a gun on him.

"In the Thicket, sports hunters are frowned upon because they believe that if you kill it, you should eat it," Gordon continued. "At the same time, if you fish illegally and it's for the table, it's OK because that has to do with survival."

Rules governing the survival issue in the Thicket were rigid and conclusive. Each man provided for his family and did not harm or hinder the ability of his neighbor to do the same for his. On the condition that the men, around whom the Big Thicket society revolved, obeyed the two golden rules, behavioral latitude was practically limitless. "The Big Thicket man believes that the rules weren't made for him. He believes that they were made for the poor ignorants out there but that he can do what he pleases 'cause he is king. He believes that rules were made for others and had nothing to do with him. So there is never any situation that he shouldn't lie out of or fight his way out of. All of this is acceptable behavior in the Big Thicket," observed Gordon.

In the Thicket, fun was difficult to come by and therefore sometimes surfaced in strange ways, according to Baxter. "If a man takes another man's car for a joy ride, that's OK," explained Gordon, "as long as he didn't need the car. If he stole the car and needed the thing, he would be a common thief and looked down upon. But if you didn't need the car and did it, that's great, that's beautiful. A Big Thicket man can do anything just to be outrageous. One night my wife and I were having a party at my daughter's house. I challenged my son-in-law to see who could get on the roof by climbing the chimney first. I did it. So Allen had to do it 'cause I had done it and I'm the old man. So Allen did it and I went inside just for the fun of it and got his 30-30 and fired a couple of shots at him. I'm a good shot, and I knew I wasn't going to hit him, but there was something very impressive about seeing the flame off the end of the rifle at night and hearing the bullet go by his head and seeing Allen hit the roof, flattened out on the other side, cringing. Since there was nothing else to shoot at and everybody had had a real good laugh, I put the rifle back on the rack over the fireplace and Allen came on in the house. I thought that was just a hell of a good stunt. That was shooting at him, more or less, for the fun of it as a friendly gesture."

Such ill regard for a civilized code of behavior condoned and even encouraged the men to behave in an unorthodox manner. "It promotes an absolutely double standard," reflected Gordon. "All the boys want to get all they can as early as they can from the girls, but that ain't the girl they want to marry. The men are always ready to fight, screw, or cry, or whatever, and all of that is considered high style. Driving their cars as fast as they can drive them is admired. The classic Big Thicket accident is a one-car pick-up wreck at one in the morning where it leaves the road and centers on a pine tree. That's considered to be really a great way to go. That is a Viking death."

Another major expectation of the Big Thicket man is that he maintain control over his providence and command obedience from his household. His authority extends not only to his children but also to his wife. "It's a very European-style marriage in which the man is king," explained Gordon. "The wife does not learn to drive the car. She doesn't need to, because the king drives the car. He brings the wife along as baggage. A woman is supposed to speak when spoken to, walk ten paces behind, and carry the baggage. The Big Thicket man is not supposed to beat them unnecessarily or mark them up in public or anything that crude. But if she gets out of line when sitting around at a party and you have to backhand her, nobody would say anything."

The Baxters point out that occasionally a woman does gain the respect of her community in the Thicket. "There are two kinds of women in the Thicket," observed Diane. "The religious, bouffant-hairdo, hysterical lady who never lets you know she's mad, but God help you if she ever does get mad at you. She is very conscious of her clothes and she realizes that there's something else in the world, but she doesn't quite know what it is and doesn't know how to get there. Then there are the practical women—who were wearing dungarees long before blue jeans were popular—who get down and do what has to be done. The second kind will work like a man and have the respect of the men, and the men don't hold them in contempt 'cause some of these women are damn good horsemen and crack shots."

"But, for the most part, the women really have a bad, bad time of it," concluded Gordon. "Social workers who go into the Big

Thicket now on a regular basis report that the biggest crimes there are the social crimes like wife-beating and incest."

As Gordon Baxter discovered in his own life, honest, loving relationships between a man and a woman are practically prohibitive while living by the code of the Big Thicket. Male domination is paramount. Relationships are of secondary importance. "It's important for the Big Thicket men to have control," related Baxter. "So that if a wife doesn't want her husband to do something and she says so, that makes him want to do it more. The ideal sex in the Thicket is after a man really gives his wife a good beating and she's really crying, completely subdued and huddled in terror. Then he goes over and puts his arms around her, and she sheds her warm, hot, salty tears all over him, and he holds her quivering little body, and they step from that to what is considered the greatest sex they've ever had."

The Big Thicket man must prove his masculinity even unto death. He is required to die with gusto. "It's OK for a Big Thicket man to have a heart attack and die or to have a stroke and become a vegetable," informed Baxter. "But to have an ulcer indicates that he didn't let things go far enough. He didn't let himself out. A Big Thicket man ain't ever going to have an ulcer 'cause ulcers happen to city men who have good manners. Those kind of men don't ever shoot roaches off the wall or fire a rifle at their relatives for the fun of it or beat up on their wives."

When George Glenn was ten years old his family moved away from Saratoga, leaving behind its decaying buildings and antiquated social structure. But like Lot's wife in the Bible, George took the backward glance. Her destruction was immediate and total. George's personal collapse was to be much more painful and insidious. Never able to wrench himself out of the Big Thicket mentality, he was destined to see nothing beyond what he had learned in that backward, stagnated swampland. If he could have somehow perceived what Saratoga had become, maybe he would have had enough insight to understand what the town's creeds would have wrought.

But the Big Thicket teachings were all he knew. So he clung to the Big Thicket commandments like a drowning man clasping a rock to his chest, not knowing that if he let go of the dead weight, he could rise to the surface. For all his personal suffering, George never looked inward for the answer to, or understanding of, his problems. Self-examination was not part of his nature. He believed problems to be caused from without rather than from within. As he grew older, his turn-of-the-century, Big Thicket doctrine entrapped him in a cocoon that grew increasingly at odds with the outside world. Finally, George Jones found himself living in an environment that he neither understood nor could handle.

4

Just the Average Couple

ROM THE DAY he was born, George Glenn Jones was a mama's boy. Clara Patterson Jones took to her last and eighth child, her second son, as though he were her only. The bond that grew between them was special, nontransferable, almost holy. "A mother's love is about the closest thing to real love, to God's love, that we have," George Jones theorized fifty years after his birth. "You see, God is love, pure love. He showed us what love is. The word comes from when God's only begotten Son died. That's like a mother's love."

Special feelings between two people can oftentimes be ignited by a spectacular experience mutually shared. Such was the spark that kindled the flame between George and his mother. His birth was a miracle of sorts for more than one reason. After delivering two sets of twins within a three-year period, Clara Patterson was told by her physician not to have any more children. "But people back then didn't know nothing about taking care of themselves to keep from having children," observed Katy Hooks, reminiscing about when she was a babysitter for the Jones clan. At 38, Clara found herself pregnant with no alternative other than to hope for a healthy child and a survivable delivery. She nearly had one at the expense of the other. "He was the healthiest baby she ever had," recalled Katy, who was a ten-year-old child at the time of George's birth. "Glenn weighed twelve pounds, when he was born. It was almost touch-and-go because the doctor had a time trying to deliver him. He broke that baby's arm trying to deliver him. He was that big."

Clara, as well as her husband, had been waiting a long time for another male child. With the delivery of each of their five children after her first son, Herman, they had hoped for another son. Now Herman was practically a young man, and Clara knew the likelihood of having any more children was slim. Before the birth of George Glenn she sent up many an extra late-night prayer that her last child would be a boy. Her prayer was answered.

George Glenn was born in the late afternoon of September 12, 1931. Helen recalls that all the children were shooed away to a cousin's house by their daddy that day. Some time later her daddy arrived with the news. "Daddy come back and got us and told us we had a big baby brother," recalled Helen. "The first thing I remember when I walked in was they had George's arm in a cast. They told me it was broke 'cause he was such a big baby. It seems funny for him to be such a small person now and him weighing so much when he was born."

Naturally, as the last child, George Glenn was to receive more attention than his older brother and sisters. The first and last child of a large family oftentimes reap favors not granted to the middle children. The first child is the sole beneficiary of the parent's affections until the birth of the second. But the last child is oftentimes the focus of the entire family's attentions. "I believe Glenn was spoiled more than the rest of the children," pondered Katy Hooks, " 'cause he was the last and all the others had begun to get up [in age]."

Regardless of the wooing George Glenn received from his five older sisters and brother, his mama was the family member to whom he cleaved. "Clara wouldn't even let that boy sleep in his own bed," reminisces Katy. "She had him right there sleeping in between her and George [Washington]. She toted him on her arm while she did all the cooking. Helen would have to sit and hold him while his mama washed. He was strictly a mama's baby. He didn't turn loose of his mama. They had a porch swing out on the porch, and when he got old enough to stand alone he would stand up there in that swing [right by her]. He made sure she had her arm around him.

"He never wanted anybody but his mama to hold him," Katy continued. "Glenn wouldn't haul off and go to anybody. Herman would. Anybody would hold him. But George [Glenn] wouldn't. He would go to them girls if he had to. But if he didn't have to, he stayed with his mama right on her arm. She cooked with him, washed with him, and cleaned house with him right on her arm. I'd catch him when she didn't have her arm around him. That was the only way you could play with him. He would scream his head off, but sometimes I took him and played with him to give her a little rest from having to hold him. He loved his mama."

If the populace of Saratoga had been so inclined to designate those among themselves as saintly, Clara Patterson Jones would have been one of the titled. She is reported never to have drunk, smoked, or taken the Lord's name in vain. Nor did she wear make-up since that was viewed by some as the practice of hussies. But her sainthood would not have been bestowed for what she didn't do but rather for what she did do. She read her Bible regularly, helped others even when the act was to her own disadvantage, and always had a kind word to share with others. "She had a hard life but never complained," recalled Estelle Lawson, Clara's sister-in-law. "She had all those children, two sets of twins in a row, and lived with a man who had an irregular income. She put up with his drinking, and she still had a good word for everybody else and would help out whenever she could. One time she made me a dress when times were real bad. She didn't have to make me that dress. She just knew I needed one. I never forgot it. She was a Christian all her life. I've never heard her say one bad word, not even *darn*. There wasn't a better woman in the world than Clara Jones."

Annie Stephens, a Big Thicket minister's wife, agreed with Estelle's evaluation of Clara. "If she could help somebody, she would go out of the way to help. Her moral life was high. She didn't believe in anything that was wrong. She didn't approve of a questionable character. Her life was beyond question. Her character was high but not so high that she thought she was self-righteous either. She was just a plain, good, honest person who wanted to raise her children to the same level that she was."

Clara Patterson must have made her deacon daddy feel proud. Exemplary living is what he had taught. While living under his roof, Lite Patterson's fourteen children were allowed to live no other way. An intense, fiercely religious man, he ruled his household with the Bible in one hand and a whipping switch in the other. "We went to church and Sunday school all the time," recollected Josie Marcontell, a younger sister of Clara's. "Papa made us. We had to. He was deacon of the Baptist Church there in White Oak as far back as I can remember," Josie said of her father, whom she described as a tall man with black hair and a quick temper. "He held prayer there at night. He'd say things to people [when he thought they were doing wrong]. I know one day at Honey Island he was there at the drugstore, and this lady come in there to get her hair cut. Papa told her, 'Lady, you know what you're doing?' She said, 'Well, I'm having my hair cut.' He says, 'You're cutting your glory off from your husband. It's in the Bible.' She got so mad she like to have died right there. He didn't intend to make her mad; he just had to say them things."

According to Josie, Clara was her daddy's favorite child even though all fourteen were extraordinarily industrious. " 'Course all the family worked hard; none of them were loafers," says Josie. "We strived for a living. If so many of us hadn't been girls, the boys could have gotten out and helped us. But every one of us girls worked in the field, hoeing and thinning corn, cane, and peanuts." Clara retained a special place because of an ear for music. She became quite an accomplished organist for those parts. She was her daddy's shining glory during Sunday morning services when she'd play the organ for the congregation. Only once, to Josie's recollection, did Clara disappoint her daddy. That was the day she went and married George Washington Jones.

George W. Jones was the only offspring of a short-lived marital union between a child bride and a gentleman farmer. Fourteen-year-old Mary Farris married twenty-year-old J. R. Jones and immediately became pregnant. Physical nubility does not denote emotional or psychological maturity, however. And from the viewpoint of the Jones family members, Mary was not yet a mature enough woman to handle the responsibility of a new husband and a child. The couple squabbled frequently. Oftentimes, when they did, Mary would storm out of the couple's shack and run down the road to stay with her parents. One fateful day, J. R. grew weary of Mary's childish tantrums and gave her an ultimatum. "Her family lived real close," recalls Estelle Lawson, George Washington Jones's stepsister, "and she was still a baby. So when she got good and ready, she'd run to her mama's house. One day he [J. R.] told her that if she left, he wouldn't come and get her no more."

Apparently the young bride, who was approximately four months pregnant at the time of her husband's ultimatum, didn't believe his threat. "One day she throwed a fit when he come in from town," testifies W. T. Scroggins. "He had brought her a new dress and a big old bottle of snuff. She dipped snuff. She got real mad, tore the dress all to pieces, and throwed the snuff up against the wall and broke it and I don't know what all. Then she went to her mama's."

J. R. was true to his word. He didn't fetch her, and she didn't return. When Mary gave birth to a dark-haired, red-skinned baby boy several months later it was only natural that her mother, the baby's maternal grandmother, assumed the parental role. "Grandma Farris and Mary's sisters raised daddy [George Washington] because his mama was still so young," observed W. T. Scroggins. So young, in fact, that in later years he related to Mary more as a brother to a sister than as a son to a mother. In 1896, about a year after her child's birth, Mary married a lumberman named Lee Killingsworth. They met while she was a cook at a boardinghouse near the lumberyard where he worked. When Mary moved out of the Farris home to establish her own with Killingsworth her baby boy stayed with his Grandmother Farris and two spinster aunts. "My daddy never did live with them [the Killingsworth family] very much," cites Helen Scroggins. "He'd go and see them, but he stayed with his grandma and old aunts. They raised him. One of them was a teacher, and they taught him everything he knew."

Grandma Farris was a wiry, sinewy spitfire of a woman. A Cherokee by birth, she was the epitome of Mammy Yokum in the Li'l Abner comic strip. "She'd just as soon run at you with a butcher knife as to look at you straight," says Ivalene Jones with a chuckle. "She was bad. She'd take her clothes off and sell them for something to drink. But she spoiled George Washington rotten. She could say anything to him or about him she wanted. But she wouldn't let nobody else do it. That Mr. Killingsworth knew he better not say anything about him or he might have found himself waking up out in the yard somewhere with a half cup of coffee in his face. She was that kind of person."

George Washington grew up rough-edged and fun-loving. The Farrises worked hard and played hard. By the time he was six he was carrying water for the loggers who worked near his grandmother's house. At ten he was expected to be self-supporting and was. He had a full-time job as a logger. School lessons were taught at night. "They was real poor people," says Ivalene Jones. "When he [George Washington] was a kid I remember him telling about carrying water out on a logging job where the men was working to make a little money to help out his grandparents. I think he pretty well worked ever since he was able all his life to help them make ends meet."

Who knows what attracted Clara Patterson, the daughter of a strict, fiercely religious, God-fearing deacon, to George Washington Jones, the grandson of a rough and tough, hell-raising old woman, or vice versa? Maybe his muscular, lean, dark, striking looks were what caught her eye. Perhaps he was fascinated with Clara's fair, light-haired, buxom appearance. Heaven knows her proper manners and gentle nature were an anomaly to him. Father Time, the perpetrator of lost hopes and broken dreams, would eventually sour their dewy fresh and idealistic love for one another. But so determined and bullheaded were they in the spring of 1915, nobody could tell them a thing. All they knew was that they were in love.

Much to the chagrin of Lite Patterson, they ran off to marry. "It really did hurt him," recalled Josie Marcontell. But the fiery-tempered old man had not approved of Clara's dating the Jones boy. "The Jones family was pretty good people," continued Josie.

"They just wasn't all that religious. They weren't a bit like my daddy." Despite Lite Patterson's misgivings about the Jones boy, Clara continued seeing the strikingly good-looking young lumberman. "Mama and her family lived at Bragg Station," said Helen Scroggins. "He was at Nona hauling pine. He'd started hauling pines about thirteen. He'd catch the old freight train all the time and see her. And boy, Grandpa didn't want Mama to marry Daddy at all." But marry they did. According to family members, Lite Patterson eventually accepted Clara's new husband. But, they refrain, it took awhile.

The newly wed couple initially set up housekeeping in a camp shack furnished by the lumber company. Soon afterward they moved to Sourlake where George W. took an oil rig job. The money was good, better than what he had been making at the lumber camps; but he didn't care for the work. So he quit and moved the family to Saratoga where he resumed his logging trade. To earn a little extra and to carry him through the times when logging jobs were scarce, Jones also delivered ice.

George Washington Jones was quite the handyman, providing the amenities the family would not otherwise have had. "My daddy was smart not to have had more education," observes Helen Scoggins. The two-room log house in which his family lived was hardly anything fancy, but for those times it was comfortable. The floors were wood planks instead of dirt as was common in the Big Thicket, and there was a front porch with a swing for sitting in the summer days and a big black potbelly stove around which the family gathered during the cold winter days. According to Helen, George W. was adept at fixing automobiles and was particularly gifted at caring for the sick. "He could have made a living by being a doctor," she asserts. "Daddy had a good smart mind on medicine. Doctor Roark, our doctor there in Saratoga, used to come and get him anytime he would have a wreck or something. He'd get Daddy to help him sew people up. If we had an accident or anything at the house, Daddy never ran to the doctor. My sister was choking to death one time on a bone and he knew just what to do. She had turned black. But he turned her upside down and dug until he got the bone out of her throat. He knew just what to do for bleeding or anything."

George W. and Clara had their first child, Ethel, in the spring of 1918. She became the apple of her daddy's eye. "He kind of worshipped the ground she walked on," recalls Helen. According to family members, Ethel was an ideal child—bright, gay, well behaved, and devoted to her daddy. She'd go along when possible when he delivered ice or was working in the woods. "It was more or less that he worshipped that kid," recalled Ivalene Jones, Herman's wife. "He'd walk her to school and everything."

During the next seven years Clara Patterson Jones produced four more children—Herman came in 1921, followed by Helen in 1922. The twins, Joyce and Loyce, arrived in 1925. George Washington displayed neither the unabashed affection nor showed the attention to the others that he had toward Ethel. "They had other children," continues Ivalene. "But he didn't care for none of them like he did her."

Childhood illnesses were common in the Big Thicket. Malaria was particularly prevalent because of the heavy infestation of mosquitoes. According to Big Thicket natives, the varmints invaded the swamp like locusts on a field during the wet seasons. Mosquitoes spared none in their ruthless search for prey, not even children, who were usually the most vulnerable to their disease-transmitting bite. Fortunately, the Thicket bred a tough-skinned, lively group of children. Many contracted malaria; most survived. Only a few died. Except for the two babies, all of the Jones children had already had the infection when it struck Ethel in the spring of 1926. "Just a few weeks before, I'd been sick as a dog," recalls Helen. "Then Herman got it."

But Ethel's attack was sudden and vicious. "Ethel got up one morning and told her mama that Helen and Herman would have to help take care of the babies," Katy Hooks said with a forlorn glance. "She was near nine years old then; real cute and little. Then she hung around her mama, and Clara told me she then got in by the heater and yelled out she was cold. So they put her to bed, and George [Washington] run to get the doctor. She died by the time he got back to the house."

Her death was tragic for all the Jones family members. But George Washington Jones was devastated. "It was like he lost one of his possessions," recalls Helen. "I think it was especially bad because she was his first child. He could never accept losing something that had been his."

His mourning and crying continued for months. Then the months turned into years. Helen Scroggins recalls that five years after Ethel's death, George Washington still openly grieved over her passing. Increasingly, his mourning turned to self-punishment, as though he was somehow responsible for her passing. "He cut her hair all the time," recalls Helen. "But that day [the day Ethel died] he must have nipped her ear or something. He made her mad cutting it. She told him, 'Daddy, you ain't never going to cut my hair no more.' He used to say he thought about that all the time 'cause he never did get to cut her hair no more." To ease his guilt, George Washington took to drinking. "He didn't start drinking for quite a while after she died," continued Helen. "When he did he wouldn't drink very much—just enough to sit there and cry and tell things she said. When he started drinking he thought he could blot it out. But all he done for a long time was to cry about her when he was adrinking."

The Jones family was forever scarred by Ethel's untimely death. George Washington never accepted it. Worse, he blamed himself for allowing her death to occur. Instead of permitting her memory to fade as an old picture pales with the passage of time, George Washington insisted that Ethel's ghost live on. His self-pity soured everything around him. It spread like a haunting disease through the family, affecting all of the relationships in its wake.

In their early years of marriage Clara and George Washington displayed a true fondness for one another. According to most accounts, they were devoted to one another. "He was crazy about her," recalled Katy Hooks, who witnessed their mutual affection on numerous occasions. "Mrs. Jones was his special person," related W. T. Scroggins. "When you got a special person in your life, that person comes before anybody; I don't care who they are. Well, Mrs. Jones was that kind of person to Mr. Jones. He was jealous of her in a way; not like he thought she was going to run off and leave him or something like that. But he just thought that she was supposed to come first. If she was sick, she was going to be tended to right then. If the kids were sick, they could play around with it a little. But they didn't with the mama."

Sometime after Ethel's death family members recall a distinct change in George Washington and Clara's relationship, especially when he was drinking. "Before he started drinking and when he wasn't drinking, he was really good to her," observed Ivalene Jones. "He would just wait on her if she was sick, and it seemed he just couldn't be good enough to her. He'd fix her soup. I've seen him just treat her like a baby, waiting on her hand and foot. But then when he'd get to drinking he was mean to her."

George Washington did not beat his wife. "He was just like any drunk person," continued Ivalene. "He was rough when he was drunk, with all that cussing and carrying on and slamming things around. I don't think he ever did hurt her. He might have pushed her around some, but I don't think he ever did, say, just really beat up on her or anything like that." But then physical blows aren't necessary to inflict emotional and spiritual suffering on another.

Clara Patterson Jones was not accustomed to being around drunken individuals. Such behavior was foreign to her and, according to her upbringing, "caused by the devil." She was a gentle, passive individual who frightened easily. More importantly, drinking was sinful and she wanted no part of it. So when George Washington started drinking, Clara started running. Many a time she would gather up the children and run out of the house. "There's something about drinking that really done something to Mama," Helen noted with a plaintive sigh. "She just couldn't stand it. I told her many a time to wait and say something to him when he was sober 'cause I knew [if she said something to him when he was drinking] they were going to end up with a big fight."

The pattern became a regular way of life for the Joneses. George Washington would come home drinking or drunk, then Clara would start nagging. He would proceed to get drunker. "She was a nagger," continued Helen. "Maybe he'd come in drinking just a little bit. Then she'd keep on [nagging] 'til he would go off and get drunk then. She couldn't stand liquor at all. That was the way she was brought up. She probably couldn't help herself."

As the years passed, the love and sincere affection they had once felt for one another faded so that by the time Clara Patterson Jones gave birth to her last child she was a lonely, disillusioned woman. It was only natural that she would elicit from her new child the kind of attention and care that she was beginning to miss so desperately in her withering marital partnership. She showered George Glenn with all the love and affection that she had once freely given to her husband. Little George became the center of her devotion. Their relationship became so intense that as an adult George Glenn Jones would proclaim, "My mama loved me more than anybody ever did."

CHAPTER
5
Tender Years

EORGE GLENN was not raised with a silver spoon in his mouth. Far from it. "It was your basics, you know," observed George. "They [his parents] was just your old country, hard-up type of living. We was raised on plenty of flour, chickens, and our little garden. We had plenty to eat but nothing like steak, caviar, and all that stuff." But all things considered, he was pampered. Or at least that is the view of his brother and sisters.

George enjoyed financial favors about which the older children had only dreamed. The economy was booming. The Great Depression was a bad memory that the nation was boldly trying to forget. In the early forties a war was being fought. Younger men were fighting and dying on the battlefields around the world, but in East Texas, George Washington benefited from the war as did hundreds of other former rural yeomen. It offered him the opportunity to have a steady-paying job at the Beaumont shipyards. In 1942 George Washington packed up his few earthly belongings and moved his family, now consisting of only Clara, little George, and the two younger twins, to a federal government tenant housing in the metropolis. As for hundreds of thousands of other families, the move from the country into the city forever changed their way of living. Initially, they were so glad to be rid of the constant scrounging just to have a meal on the table each day that they were thrilled at their new life. But years later former squatters like George Washington and Clara wistfully wondered from time to time if something precious had been left behind in those jungled, belligerent woods.

"When we were growing up, Daddy was having a hard time making a living," noted Helen Scroggins. "So he couldn't treat us that way [the way George Washington and Clara treated George Glenn]. He made us work and carry our load. But George never had to do that much around the house [after the family moved to Beaumont]. I don't think he ever carried the garbage out."

"George was really the only child who didn't have to live through a little bit of the Depression," W. T. explained further. "The family had it so rough then, the tendency was to make it so much better for George."

Clara Jones just wouldn't listen to her husband and the older children when they told her little George should be made to perform chores and carry his share of responsibility. "It hurts the child when you don't teach them [to do chores]," reflected Helen. "Mama may have thought she was being mean to the children, making them do all those things [back in Saratoga], but she wasn't." But after working most of her life from daybreak to nightfall, Clara was hard-pressed to find ways of occupying her own days, much less give George jobs to do. "There just wasn't that much to do living in an apartment," recalled Helen. "Mama was living in a two-bedroom apartment, and it didn't take much for her to clean it up. He [George Glenn] didn't have nothing to do but just be there. All Mama had to do was see he got his meals. Anything he [little George] wanted to eat, she'd get it. He nearly always had his way of getting things in those days. They'd go places together. If she had a penny and he wanted anything, he'd get it. Nothing was too good for him, in Mama's eyes."

But Clara harbored a more serious and subtle incentive for pampering her youngest son. She was lonely. Estranged from her alcoholic husband and cast into an environment in which she felt uncomfortable, she increasingly clung to George Glenn. She thrived on George Glenn's devotion and attention. "Mama was really overprotective of him," vouched Helen. "When he was little he'd go crawl up in the bed with Mama. Then when he got older he never learned to stand on his own two feet or nothing. The rest of us was taught we were going to have to stand up out there in this world. He never was taught that. Mama overprotected him because he was the baby." Perhaps unconsciously, Mrs. Jones wanted George to remain the dependent personality. She felt she had lost a husband. Certainly she didn't want to lose her favored son.

Through Clara Jones's eyes, her son could do no wrong. His misbehavior was always waved aside as the prank and whimsy of a child. Discipline was not Clara's forte. Annie Stephens, a neighbor and wife of the minister where the Jones family went to church during the family's brief, intermittent stay in Kountze on their path to Beaumont, recalls one incident particularly reflective of Clara's protective, lax disciplinary attitude toward George Glenn. "We were on our way back from a camp meeting where George sang real good," recalled Annie Stephens. "Ruth saw him and she said, 'Glenn, I want you to give Dad this money.' She gave him a five-dollar bill. That was quite a little bit in those days. So, anyway, we came on home. We didn't talk to him about it. That wasn't any of our business. So Glenn the next day went uptown to Kountze and messed around. He spent the five-dollar bill. In the meanwhile Ruth saw her daddy and made mention of the money. Glenn had met a little girl at the camp meeting, and she gave him a picture. So he had the picture in the billfold, and we knew about the money. We had an outdoor toilet, and because Glenn knew his daddy was coming sooner or later, he stuck the billfold down between some cracks in the toilet. My husband went out there and saw a billfold down underneath the cracks. He got it out, and whose was it but Glenn's with that same picture in it? So my husband just stuck it in his pocket.

"Here the old man came. Glenn was still at our house, and the old man came in and said, 'George Glenn, where is my money?' Glenn says, 'Daddy, I don't have it. I lost it.' He said, 'Glenn, you know better. You didn't lose that money.' Glenn said, 'Daddy, so help me God, I'll put my hand on this Bible and swear that I lost that money.'

"We knew better. I figured he spent it uptown, but my husband knew it wasn't in his billfold. So, naturally, we were on Glenn's side 'cause we didn't want him in trouble. So his daddy fussed and argued at that kid. And Glenn would say, 'I hope God strikes me dead right now, Daddy, if I'm lying.' His mama said, 'Glenn, Glenn.' And Mr. and Mrs. Jones argued back and forth all morning. Finally the old man took the boy and said, 'You come outside with me. You're lying and you know you're lying.' "

Having a soft place in her heart for little George, knowing the personal strife that existed in the family, and suspecting that Mr. Jones wanted the money to buy liquor, Mrs. Stephens automatically sided with the mother and son. Mrs. Stephens recalled the day had been long, hot, and arduous. Mr. Jones's temper was flaring; Mrs. Jones was distraught at the prospect of her baby being whipped. The minister's wife recalled finally turning to Mrs. Jones and calling on God to intervene and put an end to that day's turmoil. "I began to cry," told Mrs. Stephens, recalling her feeling of emotional depletion that day. "I said, 'Mrs. Jones, let's pray and ask God not to let him whip Glenn. I said, 'Whatever the kid did with the money I don't know, but let's pray.' So we did.

"So finally the old man came back in the house, and he told her, 'Let's go. But that boy is lying to me.' She said, 'Well, George, leave him alone. Let him find it or whatever.' So they finally left. After they left my husband reached in his pocket and pulled out that billfold and said, 'Glenn, who does this belong to?' 'Why, I lost that, Brother Byrle,' Glenn said. My husband said, 'Now you know better than that.' He said, 'Where did you lose it?' Glenn said, 'I don't know.' He said, 'Glenn, you do know where you lost that.' He said, 'I saw that under the toilet.' Then the kid began to laugh. We knew he spent that money. He told us he spent it on jukeboxes and hamburgers." Mrs. Stephens rationalized as Clara often did in those days that, whatever little George did wrong, his father's transgression of drinking was much worse. "George didn't mean any harm," reflected Mrs. Stephens, when asked about little George's lying.

The financially better times did not make for a happier home

Clara Patterson (George's mother) as a young woman, standing with two of her sisters. (Courtesy of Jones family)

George Washington Jones (George's daddy) standing behind the table with his Grandma Farris and two aunts, Aunt Betty and Aunt Eula, in about 1900. The man is unidentified. (Courtesy of Jones family)

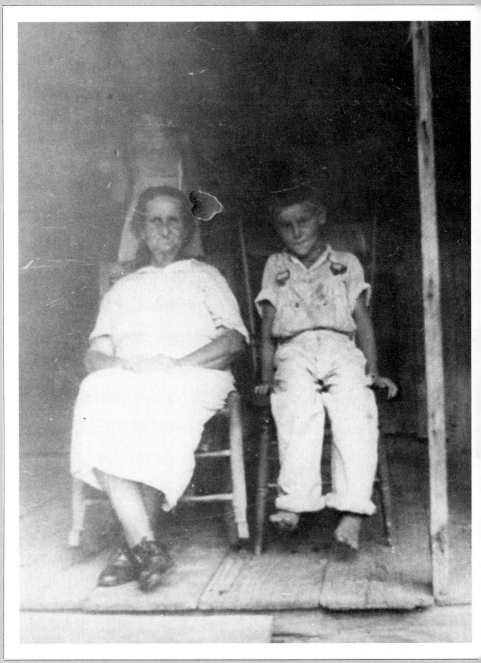

George Glenn sitting with neighbor Mrs. Hodge (Katie Hook's mother) on her front porch. George Glenn liked to go to her house because she fixed him candy and cakes. (Courtesy of Jones family)

George Glenn (second from left on front row) with the other children who attended the Full Gospel Tabernacle Church in Kountze, Texas. George began singing publicly at this church. (Courtesy of Mrs. Annie Stephens)

Where George attended church, First Gospel Tabernacle, in Kountze, Texas, as a child. (Courtesy of Mrs. Annie Stephens)

George's mama and daddy, George Washington and Clara Jones, walking down a Houston sidewalk in the 1950s. (Courtesy of Jones family)

George Glenn walking down the street of Beaumont, Texas, playing the guitar his daddy had purchased for him. (Courtesy of Jones family)

George is standing next to his new wife, Dorothy, on their wedding day in 1950. Dorothy's mother, Mrs. Bonvillian, and George's mother, Clara, are on either side of the newly wed couple. (Courtesy of Jones family)

George returned to Texas in late 1952 after getting out of the Marines and met 18-year-old Shirley Corley, standing here on a Beaumont sidewalk. (Courtesy of Jones family)

George at 19, dressed to perform at Playground Park in Beaumont with husband-and-wife singing team, Eddie and Pearl. (Courtesy of Jones family)

In late 1950, George joined the United States Marines. Here he is in uniform. (Courtesy of Jones family)

This is a publicity shot of George in the late 1950s about the time his career was beginning to take off. (Courtesy of Jones family)

George Jones and Melba Montgomery in the early 1960s. (Courtesy of Jones family)

George with his mama, Clara, and daddy, George Washington, not long before his daddy died. (Courtesy of Jones family)

One of the last pictures taken of George Washington and Clara together after they had reunited. (Courtesy of Jones family)

George sitting atop a wood fence built on his Beaumont ranch in the mid-1960s. (Courtesy of Jones family)

George's customized Pontiac Bonneville convertible with over 4,000 silver dollars embedded in the upholstery. The car, along with an array of antique automobiles, was on display at the Old Plantation Music Park. (Courtesy of Jones family)

The Plantation Park homeplace, where George spent some of his
happiest days. (Courtesy of Jones family)

George had been nervous about the success of his Plantation Park. He had little to worry about. Over 5,000 fans turned out for the first show. (Courtesy of Jones family)

George and Tammy dressed up in typical attire for a show at their Old Plantation Music Park in Florida. (Courtesy of Jones family)

George and Tammy presenting birthday cake to Georgette on her first birthday. (Courtesy of Jones family)

George Jones with his producer, Billy Sherrill. (Photo by Slick Lawson)

All of George's children, including Tammy's three girls. From left to right are Denise (Tammy's daughter), Jacquelyn Fay (Tammy's), Susan (George's oldest child), Jeffrey holding Georgette, Gwendolyn Lee (Tammy's), and Bryan. Photo taken in Florida in early 1971. (Courtesy of Jones family)

George with Waylon Jennings. (Photo by Slick Lawson)

life in the Jones household. George Washington and Clara were in a constant broil about his drinking. He drank and she nagged. Their alienation threw little George into a difficult emotional triangle. He desperately wanted to respect his father, as do most young boys. Little George certainly needed his daddy's disciplinary hand. Mrs. Jones spoiled the boy rotten. Yet Mrs. Jones's obvious contempt for her husband's drinking etched a strong impression on her young son's psychological opinion toward his daddy. Mimicking his mama, George Glenn developed a disdain toward his daddy at a dangerously young age. The boy simply found it difficult to respect his father or to take his orders seriously.

"You know, George really can't tell you too much about his daddy," observed Helen. "He was so pampered by Mama and the rest of us, he thought Daddy coming in drunk was terrible. Daddy was rough-talking anyway, so Glenn got to where he thought, 'Well, my Daddy is real bad.'" Of course, at his young age, George didn't have any way to know that his mother sometimes over-reacted to events. "Mrs. Jones was a scary woman," informed W. T. Scroggins. "If her and the kids was at home at night by theirself and something bumped in the house, she would swear somebody was out there. She wouldn't stay by herself even to let me and Helen go to the grocery. She would go with us or we would have to call somebody to stay with her while we would go, even if we wouldn't be gone fifteen minutes. When George W. would get to hollering and yelling, it would scare her and she would grab the kids and run off. Well, the kids got it in their head their daddy was mean. I think he was having more fun than he was mean."

The older man's increasing drinking did nothing to thwart his son's growing contempt. Mr. Jones's sometimes abusive and rough-handed actions only fed fuel to the fire of little George's scorn. "Every now and then, when he got a little drinking," recollected George Glenn years later, "you know, to let off some of the steam, we [George and sister Doris] would have to sing for him. It didn't make much difference what time of night it was, on the weekend or whenever. When he come in drunk he'd say, 'Get up and sing me some songs.' We didn't want to sing. We wanted to get back in bed fast as we could so we'd say, 'If we sang this one and that one, would you let us get back to bed?' He'd say, 'Uh-huh' and so we sang."

"He [George W.] would make George sit up and play that guitar even when he didn't want to," recalled Herman Jones, George's older brother. "Actually, it's not right to look at it just one way," Herman added, excusing his daddy's actions. "[The late-night singing] helped George a lot, 'cause he played more and got more practice."

But Herman's wife, Ivalene, was not so quick to overlook Mr. Jones's unorthodox method of coaching his son. "Mr. Jones liked to hear Glenn sing," she agreed. "And I guess he made a singer out of that boy," she added with an affirmative nod. "But I got so mad at that old man, I could have killed him the way he done that kid. He made that kid sing all the time.

"When Herman was gone to the Navy I went and stayed with Mrs. Jones," continued Ivalene. "Where I lived we didn't get around anybody for two or three days, and we didn't have phones out there. So I come to Beaumont and stayed with them. I fixed George a pallet down in my room. The old man had him in there playing that guitar, and he'd play that guitar, and George would be just so wore out and would want to put that guitar down, and the old man would take that belt and whap him one. He'd make him play it. So when George would finally get to where he could slip out, he'd crawl down that hall and crawl in my room. When I locked my door, the old man never come to my door. He never knocked on my door or nothing. George knew that. If he got in my room he was safe. He'd want to get away from his daddy. So he'd come in there, and I'd fix him a pallet on my floor, and he would sleep in there with me and my two babies."

George deeply resented those late-night singing lessons. The young boy certainly needed the discipline of learning to sing on demand, but he didn't benefit from the manner in which his daddy handed out the indoctrination. So it was that George learned to resent his daddy's authority. "What made it all so bad was that George can remember him only when he was bad drinking," reflected Helen. "Glenn didn't know about the life before that when we was all at home before George was born and when he was little, before Daddy started drinking so bad."

George could recall only the tall, towering figure that would stand over him during the quietness of the black nights demanding that he sing, sing until he thought his legs would give out. George remembered begging to stop. But invariably George Washington wanted to hear more. A passerby of the Jones's apartment on one of those all-night marathons probably thought the sight strange: a skinny, cotton-haired boy wrapped in the illumination of a single lamp, standing in front of a seemingly dozing hulk of a figure collapsed in a rocking chair. Against the stillness of the evening the boy's voice could be heard by neighbors several houses away. And every time the melodious voice petered out, the roar of a booming voice could be heard in response. "Stand up and sing, George. Stand up and sing."

6

Old-Fashioned Singing

USIC WAS IN George Jones's genes, so much so that when asked why he started singing, George usually responded very matter-of-factly, "I just did."

For a George Washington Jones clan member, natural musical propensities were a birthright. It would have been more surprising if little George had been born without the ability to carry a tune. Both his mother and his daddy had descended from bloodlines that had produced strong musical personalities. When George attained recognition as a country music singer his family members thought of him simply as carrying on the family tradition but for a larger audience.

Clara was the stronger musician of George's parents. "My mother played organ and piano in church," explained George Glenn. "Course, I don't remember that part. She did it before I was born. The other kids told me about it." By the time George came along, maternal responsibilities had necessitated Clara's total devotion. She no longer had the time for such musical frivolities.

Even when she went to church in those later years she refused to go in for fear that her many little ones would disturb the congregation. She stayed out in the car with her younguns and listened to the preacher through open windows. But she still loved to sing an old gospel hymn and sent little Glenn to slumberland many a night with the humming of a tune that she had learned while growing up.

"We had singin's," recalled Josie Marcontell, Clara's younger sister. "We sang songs like 'Over in the Gloryland,' 'The Old Rugged Cross,' and 'Amazing Grace.' Not the whole family [would sing]. Papa and Mama didn't join us. [It was] just us girls. I remember that Clara sure could play that organ. She played by ear."

"George's mama could sing real good," observed Katy Hooks, a Big Thicket neighbor. "All those Pattersons could sing. [George Glenn] was also kin to the Breckins up there. His grandmother Patterson was a Breckin up there in White Oak. All of them could sing real good." One division of the Pattersons even got together and formed a singing quartet. Family members claim the quartet garnered quite a reputation as a Big Thicket gospel group. Be it understood that music was so much a part of the Breckin clan that one of Clara's brothers was known to have said, "If I had a kid that couldn't sing, I would have to get rid of him. And believe me, I ain't lying."

George Washington's musical training was not as structured since they were not churchgoing people. Nonetheless, the musical inclinations were strong. "My daddy played guitar a lot," recalled George Glenn. "He helped out at square dances every now and then. He played the harmonica."

One way or another, music permeated little George Glenn's youth. Whether he was tagging behind his older sisters while they picked blackberries in the late summer or sitting in the house while his mother ironed, attending church or standing outside the local tavern, music infiltrated the air. "I can't remember not having music," recalled Helen. George's mama had the initial impact. Those cold, dark winter days while the rest of the children were at school and her husband was working were greatly enriched because she sang. Her melodious voice added color and life to an otherwise bleak and dreary surrounding. Family members can recall the baby's total enchantment with his mama's singing, his cooing and gurgling when she directed her singing exclusively to him. Not surprising that the baby picked up singing quickly. "Glenn could carry a tune by the time he was a year old," recalled Katy. "Clara taught Glenn a song called 'Billy Boy,' and he was singing that song when he was a year. The words went 'Billy Boy, Billy Boy, can your wife make a cherry pie? Yes, siree, she can make a cherry pie. But she's a little bitty young thing and can't leave home.' "

As he grew older, Glenn began joining the family sings. "We would all sing," reminisced Helen. "Daddy would have us all sitting around against the wall, and every night we would sing maybe until we all went to bed. We sang mostly religious songs. Mama had a good tenor voice, and Daddy had a good voice, and so they sung real good together. 'Red River Valley' would be the first song him and Mama would sing. Then we all just sung. Sometimes Daddy would play the French harp."

As years passed and the older children began leaving home, and the friction increased between Clara and George Washington, the singings became increasingly dominated by Glenn and Doris, one of the younger twins. "For some reason, me and Doris sang all the time," recalled George. "Daddy got aware of it and started making us sing more." Then even Doris dropped out, leaving little George as the only family member to carry on the family tradition.

The Big Thicket of the 1940s was barren of children's structured extracurricular activities as are commonplace in current times. There was no football or basketball team. Children did not stay late at school to attend Boy Scout meetings or even the Future Farmers of America activities. Such clubs did not exist. The children as well as the adults had little opportunity for pleasurable pastimes. They were too caught up in the daily survival struggle. Music was about their only form of entertainment. It was an inexpensive form of recreation and was available in various formats. On Saturday night families flocked to the local tavern for an evening of dancing, clapping, and foot-stomping. They went to church the next morning more eager to join in on the singing than to listen to what was usually a sermon peppered with fire and brimstone.

Few Big Thicketers played musical instruments. Only those born with a musical gift were so ordained since the community boasted no formally educated music teacher. And those who were blessed to play were regarded something akin to the community jesters. They provided what little entertainment the local folks were able to enjoy. Because of their musical abilities, the Jones family was well known throughout the Thicket area. "The Jones family was the only musical family I can think of in the area," recalled Tom Wood, a childhood friend of George's who still lives in Saratoga. Their musical talents made them valued folks in those parts. The children sang in church, Mr. Jones entertained at the weekend jamborees with both his quick dancing feet and his nimble fingers on the guitar strings, and there was many a discussion of the days when Mrs. Jones had played the church organ.

Any one of them may have possessed the necessary raw talent to become a noted entertainer. But none until little George had the leisure time to commit to the art. His mother, whom several regarded as having immense talent, devoted all her time and energy to her family in lieu of musical pursuits. The older children were obliged to pitch in and help out with the chores. Little George was afforded the great luxury of having to do little other than sing and play his guitar. "They never had a chance to do anything with it [musical talent]," recalled George. "You know, back in those days, they had to work hard. Daddy had too big of a family to feed, I imagine, for anyone like that to try to make it. They would have never thought of making any money at it."

Little George's advantage was that he didn't have to make money at it to continue his practicing. Otherwise, he would not have been able to spend countless hours sitting in the woods singing and, after he got his first guitar, learning his chords.

At the same time the other children did not display such devotion to a singular interest. In that sense little George was regarded as something of an enigma. "Other kids could party or whatever," recalled Herman, "but when the Grand Ole Opry came on, George was going to be there listening to it. He wouldn't miss the Opry for nothing." "If he wasn't on that couch picking on his guitar or something like that, you could find George up at Beaumont walking the streets with his guitar and playing," Helen concurred. "He was different from other kids. He didn't get out and run and play like most kids. I've seen him just sit by himself all day long, against a big tree with his guitar. Just like he was off in another world."

Little George, unlike his older brother and sisters, was a dreamer. While they had been forced to deal with the harsh realities of life at an early age, he remained the perpetual child. Protected by a hovering mother and a cocoon of musical sounds dancing in his head, George passed his young days in an imaginary world of make-believe, where his music was reality and the day-to-day struggles became nothing more than an occasional annoyance. "I just wanted to go out in the woods and hide and play the guitar," recalled George. "That's all I wanted to do. That was more important to me than anything else in the world."

Music was little George's escape from a life that otherwise was not all that pleasant. As the years passed and he was expected to assume an increasingly responsible role, his devotion to music accelerated until everything, including school, was pushed out of his mind. Music was all that the child thought about or wanted to think about. Circumstances allowed him the indulgence. "You've got to have a deep-down drive for it," theorized George. "You've got to love it to stick to it. It's just not something you say—'I'm going to go to Nashville and make it big.' That's not for the love of it. That's for the love of the dollar. If you sing for the love of it, you don't care if you get paid. I didn't care if I got paid [back in those early days]. And I wouldn't mind giving up every dime I could ever make if I knew I could play and just tell me I could be on that stage and sing. It's that important to me."

By the time George was ten he was already pretty much ensconced in the mystical world of musical magic. The child seemed intrigued with the very sound of his own voice. A natural progression was that he start singing publicly, which he did when his family moved from Saratoga to Kountze in 1941. During the few months that the Jones family lived in Kountze, a small community of about 1,000 people located midway between Saratoga and Beaumont, little George became a devout churchgoer, even though he showed little interest in the minister's hell-fire sermons. "I went to Sunday school all the time," reminisced George. "I got to be real close friends with the preacher and his wife, Sister Annie. We'd do specials, what they called specials, like sing a song in church every now and then."

Byrle and Annie Stephens founded their church, The Kountze Full Gospel Tabernacle, just a few months before the Jones family arrived. They were a husband and wife team; he the strapping, gruff old-time preacher, she the gentle, understanding wife who tended to the small congregation's emotional and spiritual wounds. They both sang, and singing was very much a part of their spiritual services, whether it was on Sunday morning in their wood-framed, paned-windowed structure or out on the town sidewalks where they commonly took their services on Saturday or Sunday afternoons.

On certain Saturdays they hosted a children's service at their church. The Saturday meeting lacked the rigidness of the regular Sunday morning services. "We had a service at about one o'clock for an hour, and then we let them play. We gave the children a turn at the grab bag. They'd put their hand in a bag and pull out a piece of candy or a piece of chewing gum," recalled Sister Annie, a tall, sturdy, plain woman in her sixties. Since the youth services attracted children whose parents did not attend Sunday morning, the couple were hopeful that God's word could be taken into each and every home at least through the mouths of the community's babes. The church prayer meetings were held each and every Wednesday night, regardless of the number attending, which Annie admitted was sometimes none. "We had anywhere from nobody to about 75 attend our services," she reflected. "We didn't pay no mind to the number."

After the Jones family got settled in their house over the hill from where the one-room church structure stood, little George became a devotee of Brother Byrle and Sister Annie. "The Joneses were real good people except for the daddy's drinking," recalled Annie. "But Doris and Glenn were the most faithful." But even Annie knew that little George's engrossment with the church's activities was because he was allowed to sing. "George liked to go down there so much because they'd let him sit at the ole piano and beat on it," reflected Helen. "Finally they got him into singing a little."

Gradually the Brother Byrle and Sister Annie evangelical team became Byrle, Annie, and little George. "Before George came along I sang alto and Byrle sang the lead," said Annie. "Then, when George started, I sang alto and George sang the lead. My husband just did the preaching." Little George went everywhere with them and was instrumental in persuading Preacher Byrle to expand his ministry to include neighboring communities. "Brother had a '38 automobile, but he couldn't drive it," explained Annie. "George encouraged him [Byrle] to go ahead and drive. George said, 'Oh, come on, Brother Byrle, come on, you can do it.' Byrle got out there and ran into the side of a building. But that got him started driving." After that, the Brother Byrle and Sister Annie evangelistic efforts branched out to the outlying communities that had previously not been privy to their message. And, of course, George Glenn went along. W. T. Scroggins suspected that the reason George spent so much time with the Stephenses was that he liked to travel so much. The Stephenses were a way for him to stretch his wings and fly to yet a larger circle of listeners. "First we'd go to Woodville, and we got there about ten," continued Annie. "We had an hour service, and then we drove to Jasper and got there sometime about a quarter 'til eleven. By the time we set up, it was 11:30. We had a service there, and then we drove down to Kirbyville. Most of the time we went ahead and had a service in Kirbyville, but they just didn't seem to gather there as much. Then, sometimes, if we felt like it, we had a street meeting in Silsbee. But if we didn't feel quite up to it, we'd omit that."

The street meetings, whether held in Kirbyville or in Woodville, were basically the same. Holding a hand-held mike, the suited Brother Byrle launched into a sermon peppered with biblical quotes and personal observations. After about thirty minutes of gestured comments Preacher Byrle asked for a moment of prayer, and then little George and Annie led the flock in several minutes of old-time religious standards. "We had what we called in those days a gathering place that people [in each community] would go to," explained Annie. "In Kountze, [for example] it was the H & H. That was the largest store up there. It was a grocery store. It was during a time before they had air conditioners in these stores. They just had ceiling fans, and people would stand on the outside of the stores to keep cooler. Up until World War II people didn't have any money. It was very meager getting by during the Depression years. So when they had money to spend they flocked to town every Saturday. So we had good attendance, real good attendance for our street meetings. We built up attendance 'cause we had certain times we'd be [at each town] every Saturday. We had this regular schedule we went on, and people learned it, and there would be a lot of people there waiting."

Even after his family moved to Beaumont George continued his association with the Stephenses, catching a bus and riding into Kountze to join them in their weekend preaching tours. The child was a popular addition to their crusade efforts, and Annie recalled that little George kept both her and her husband entertained during their long, hot, and dusty drives from one town to another. George was such a hit that eventually the preacher and his wife took the child along to one of their regional religious meetings. Several hundred people attended. "The first time that George had his first big audience was at one of our camp meetings," recalled Annie. "He cracked down and started singing, and he done real good. They gave him a love offering."

Ironically, in spite of little George's singing devotion, Sister Annie did not consider the child's talent anything special in those early days. "He was just another kid to me," admitted Annie, while sitting in a large wooden chair that she still oftentimes uses as a prayer chair. "And we had so many of them up there in that church," she reflected, glancing into the living room where a photo of her dead husband sat on a mantel. "I didn't know what to look for. I didn't think of the potential of the child then, or I would have learned him how to play the guitar much, much earlier."

7

We Love to Sing about Jesus

EORGE GLENN became infatuated with the guitar even before he was large enough to hold one. "Our cousin that lived there close to us in Saratoga was a Patterson," reflected Helen Scroggins, "and she had a guitar. I seemed to remember George sitting on her front porch when he wasn't nothing but four or five years old. He would have to sit with it across his lap because it was so big. I can still visualize him sitting there on that front porch with that on him and him trying to play."

But he didn't learn to play until some five years later, not that he didn't try. While other children used broomsticks to pretend to be riding a horse, little George positioned them like a guitar, making believe he was strumming imaginary strings. Nothing could hold George's attention like the sound of a guitar being played. He begged for one of his own, but his family could not afford such an extravagance during the Depression years. Since guitars were such a valued item, little George didn't have much better luck playing borrowed guitars. "When the Joneses first started coming

61

there to church," recalled Annie Stephens, "Glenn didn't have an instrument to play on. I just had bought my guitar, and I took real good care of it, and it didn't have any scratches. I didn't let children hold it, whether it was him or whoever. But he was really hyperactive, and I didn't let him have my guitar. So he didn't learn how to play until his daddy bought him one. They had already moved, and I think Glenn was about eleven by then."

The Joneses had been settled in Beaumont for several months when Mr. Jones took his young son downtown to make the guitar purchase. We can imagine that he had saved some small part of each of his paychecks until he had accumulated enough. "The biggest prize I ever got for singing for my daddy was him letting me go downtown to Beaumont with him," reminisced George. "Then one time he got me a guitar. I was so happy. The Sunday school teacher showed me three or four chords, real country type, making chords. But I was picking my notes out before she even showed me the chords. I just had an ear for it."

"Glenn caught the bus and came up to Kountze and wanted me to tune it up and show him his chords," Annie recollected of that summer of 1942. "We spent pretty well the day of me training him and showing him how to hold it with his fingers. Then I wrote out the chords for him, and then he didn't come back for about a couple of weeks. The next time he came back he was showing me what he had learned besides what I had showed him. That kid was all ready by the time he came back. He taught himself the rest of it. I gave him the first lesson of the basic chords, which was B, C, and F. And he was doing real good that day. But by the time he had come back, he was already playing and singing with his guitar."

What had been an infatuation was now an obsession. George clasped his little guitar to his heart, both literally and figuratively, as though it were a new appendage. "I didn't want to do anything else," recalled George. "You could have whopped me, beat me to death. Nothing was going to make me quit loving that guitar. That's all I wanted to do."

Which is what he did, to the exclusion of everything else. He practically stopped going to school. On any given school day, more often than not, little George could be found walking the streets of Beaumont strumming his guitar or out in some deserted alley, practicing. "Listen, I barely made it through," admitted George. "School wasn't worth a durn. I never did pass out of seventh grade. I passed out of sixth into seventh and stayed in the seventh two years and that was it. I just couldn't think of nothing but that guitar and music." East Texas rural children rarely completed their education in those days. George's oldest sister, Helen, was the only Jones child actually to finish her schooling. But most children dropped out to work the fields or to help out their folks at home. Little George was unique in that he quit to play a guitar. As always, his mother allowed him the indulgence for it was she who finally acquiesced and let him quit.

According to family members, little George had already developed quite a lazy streak. George is suspected to have dropped out of school, in part, because of his sluggish, easygoing manner. His behavior in those ensuing years seems only to have confirmed their conviction about his adolescent behavior. "He didn't do nothing but loaf," asserted Helen. "He played for a little while at Neva's [a Beaumont nightspot], and it seems like I remember him playing at another place on Sourlake Highway called Hayseed. But he'd go a long time and wouldn't do nothing. If they asked him to sing somewhere, he'd go sing and play. But for about three years there after he got out of school he was just singing at one place or another. Anything he could do concerning music, he'd love it. He'd go do it. Otherwise, he didn't do nothing."

In the old Big Thicket world the day a child quit his schooling was the day he became self-sufficient and self-supportive. George did neither. He continued to live with his mom through his mid-teens, and he brought in very little money. From time to time he shined shoes. He picked up a few odds-and-ends jobs; he even took a regular job at one point as a driver for a funeral home. But he didn't stick with any work for more than a few months. When he needed a little extra money the young boy increasingly turned to his ability to sing and play the guitar as a source of revenue. "Glenn got a can and went down to town and sat that can down on the street, and he would stand there and play that guitar," recalled

Josie, George's aunt. "That meant for them to throw money in that can. Some of the family got embarrassed over it. But after he made what he did they was tickled for him then."

If he had been given a choice, George would have liked for those carefree, do-nothing days to have lasted forever. He would spend much of his adult life pining for their return. But life changes, seasons come and go, and one day George found himself entrapped in the body of a young man. Even his mother couldn't stymie his physical maturation, although she did much to help preserve his emotional immaturity. But eventually the day arrived when George had to give up many of his childish ways or suffer the consequences. Mostly, he suffered the consequences.

Perhaps George's transition from choir-singing church boy to honky-tonk warbler was inevitable. After all, he did have to make some money. There was little else he could do to earn his keep. Singing in church brought money in for the Lord but little for himself. As he passed from puberty into his mid-teens, George increasingly parlayed his God-given talent into a money-making tool. Not that he ever sang for the love of the dollar. Rather, singing was the quickest and easiest way for him to make a buck. It was the path of least resistance, a road down which George seemed destined to travel most of his life.

Until George was fifteen years of age he went to church nearly every chance he got. It particularly pleased Clara, who thought that none would go to hell after death as long as he was faithful to his church while still alive. Church was also one of the few places outside their home that the Joneses allowed their children to go. They were strict, especially George Washington, and neither wanted their children acting in a way out of line with the Jones family's strict fundamentalist Christian code. They felt that, while at the Lord's house, their children would be required to act in the same well-behaved manner as they were expected to adopt while at home. George Washington, however, left little to chance.

"Mr. and Mrs. Jones had confidence in my husband and I, so if we wanted their kids to go with us somewhere, they didn't mind trusting us with them because they knew we were going to see after them," explained Annie Stephens. "They knew we wasn't going to let them go because we were strict with our child. We had a little boy. But Mr. Jones was real strict. He wanted to know what his kids were doing. One time we had a young people's service down there, and we dismissed them kids a few minutes before church time so they could get out and take a little exercise and play a bit.

"So somebody come up out there with a bicycle out in the front of the church. The highway people had dug a pond, bigger than this room [an eighteen-by-twenty-foot room], which was about two and a half feet deep. Those kids were out there playing [with the bicycle], and Ruth asked Glenn to push her down the hill. He pushed her right down that hill and guided her right into that hole of water. You can imagine the commotion a bunch of kids made. That was fun to them. So Ruth come wading out of that water right into that church nearly freezing. She was wet from her head to her toes. Her mama and daddy was at home, but they heard all the screams and all that laughing. You have to understand that when they sent those kids to church they meant for them to go to church. They didn't mean for them to play. So here Mr. Jones came, mad as a hornet. He come in there and said to me, 'Mrs. Byrle, where is Ruth, Doris, Glenn?' I said, 'Glenn is out here, and Doris and Ruth, they're here somewhere.' I was trying to get out of telling him the truth because he had a pole about that long in his hand," she continued, holding her hands about two feet apart. "He was going to really work them over. I didn't want him to whip them. So I told him, Mr. Jones, 'We dismissed them from young people's service to come out here and take a little exercise before church, and Ruth fell in that hole of water out there.' He said, 'I knew there was something up.' That man headed out and rounded up all those kids, and I mean whenever he did, they didn't move. Ruth had already gotten to their house, but he came in too soon for her to get the wet clothes off, and he made her sit by the heater until she dried. He would not let her go and pull those wet clothes off. I don't know whether he did it for punishment or if he did it for some other reason like letting her wet clothes dry on her so she wouldn't catch cold. He was real strict."

Little George's playful nature frequently placed him at odds with his daddy. "Glenn wasn't mean," observed Sister Annie. "He just had something going all the time. He liked to have his fun."

But much of the time George Washington did not appreciate his son's sense of humor. And by the mid-1940s the older man's personality had been soured by his excessive drinking. Clara tried to avoid him. She frequently went visiting in those days. The older children had either already left home or were working. Little George escaped to church.

George Glenn tried to escape growing up for as long as he could. Church, under the auspices of Brother Byrle and Sister Annie, was a playground, a land in which all he had to do was sing. But at fifteen, a phase of his childhood abruptly ended. George Washington told him that, if he wasn't going to school, he must then get a job. An uneducated East Texas boy had few work choices. So, like his brother and sisters before him, George Glenn became a common laborer, relying on the sweat of his brow to earn a living. Annie Stephens recalled that the idea of little Glenn's having to do physical work depressed her. "Byrle told me he had seen Glenn out doodling slabs one day," recalled Annie. "I just couldn't stand that boy out trying to do hard labor. He was such a little feller. The next time I saw Glenn I told him he should start singing."

George Glenn was quick to take the advice. "The next thing I know, he started singing with [local singers] Eddie and Pearl," continued Annie. George Glenn was sixteen when he teamed with the regionally popular husband and wife nightclub act. Initially he played guitar for them, then later the couple gave George a featured slot in their show. The young man was quickly a hit with the saloon crowd. "We didn't like to see Glenn play in places like that," Sister Annie reflected, "but where else are you going to start from? I don't know of any place that he could have started from other than playing them beer joints. His mother didn't like it. She came down and talked with us. My husband told her, 'Well, it's better than the boy doodling slabs and having to get out there and push that lumber on those carts like that all the time.'"

But, while doling out their advice, the Stephenses had not bargained for one particular turn of events. "We were quite pleased with him," reflected Annie. "But we didn't see him much after he started singing with Eddie and Pearl. Maybe during that time was when Glenn began to drift away," Annie added with a faraway gaze in her eyes.

Ironically, Annie Stephens did not understand that the conservative, fundamentalist brand of religion that she and her husband taught left George Glenn little choice but to defect. Clara Jones thought that those who entered a saloon were sinners. Family members claim she never so much as stepped foot into one. What was a young man to do who made his living in such places? "After he first started playing in those honky-tonks George made the remark one time that he didn't feel right singing in a church anymore while singing in a place like that," reminisced W. T. Scroggins. "He said he couldn't play in a church after playing in a beer joint. He enjoyed singing those Christian songs, but you're not going to get him to sing a dancing song around here at home if somebody else is singing a Christian song. That's one thing he respects. If he knows it, he ain't going to do it."

George's abandonment of his religion was unfortunate, especially because of his nature. For when all was said and done, George's personality was as fluid as water. He was extremely sensitive to his environment and to those with whom he spent his time. As a child who regularly attended church, he was emotionally and spiritually ensconced in the safe, secure world of his religion. The walls of his fundamentalist faith protected him from being touched by life's seedier side. While he had those walls upon which to lean, George Jones was safe. It was only after he stepped out beyond that emotional fortification that he began to experience personal pandemonium. George was as whimsical as he was undisciplined, and once he had opened Pandora's box lid a little, he wouldn't keep from swinging it totally open to see what else there might be in the murky, ill-defined, mercurial world of the honky-tonk life.

As a youngster, little George was remembered as a good boy, discounting his occasional pranks. "He didn't give his mother any trouble, mind you," recalled Helen Scroggins. "I don't guess he ever gave his mama any worries like that." "He liked to pick and tease or get a big laugh going," concurred Annie. "But I didn't see anything towards violence or to harm anyone. He would help you when he could. He was not a bad child." He lived by his religion's rules and was even thought to have been saved. "It's hard to tell about a little kid and how their status is other than their faithfulness to come to church and their activities," reflected Annie. "But I know at one time I saw my whole Sunday school class, when he

was among them, confess. It was a revival, and every one of them
went down to the altar and confessed Christ as their Savior. How
long Glenn held on to that, I don't know. I took it that Glenn was
saved 'cause it wasn't so much what he would say, but it was the
life he lived."

But times changed, and while in his mid-teens George found
himself living outside the boundaries of what he had been taught
was a good Christian life. Not that he was doing anything bad. But
his religion sanctioned few grey areas in which to live, only blacks
and whites. Either he lived according to the teachings or he didn't.
"Let's say I believe strongly," George once explained. "But I'm
doing things I shouldn't do." So George Jones quit going to church
and started attending honky-tonk bars.

Singing in the saloons was an enormous boost for George's
youthful ego. From the start, the crowds loved him. "I heard them
crowds gave George more money than they did Eddie and Pearl,"
said W. T. Scroggins. And by those day's standards, the money was
good—$17.50 a week, just for picking his guitar and singing.
From the vantage point of a sixteen-year-old, there was every
reason to continue his honky-tonk career and little reason to
return to the church. And since there was no intermingling of the
two, George's life course was set. The saloon circuit became his
life's work, and the king of country music, Hank Williams, became
his god.

"I had two heroes," George once admitted. "There was God, and
the only other one was Hank Williams." Williams was one hell of
a contrast to God. "Hank was the first [country music] outlaw,"
country music observer Peter Guralnick wrote in his book, *Lost
Highways*. "He was the only one. Perhaps as extraordinary as his
musical influence [Williams wrote 'Hey, Good Lookin'',' 'Cold, Cold
Heart,' 'I'm So Lonesome, I Could Cry,' and 'I Can't Help It if I'm
Still in Love with You'], the image of Hank Williams has dominated the mythology of contemporary country music. Driven,
desperate, as haunted as the doomed blues singer, Robert Johnson,
Williams has come to symbolize both the lure and the nightmare
of the honky-tonk world—live fast, love hard, and die young." As
Guralnick so aptly pointed out later in his book, perhaps the greatest constant in the legacy left by Williams was his insistence on
individuality. But whatever his appeal, young George Jones fell

under the Williams spell as strong and hard as anyone. And with as much fervor as the younger George had sought biblical salvation, he craved to receive a blessing from Williams. He didn't have to wait long.

"It was about 1947 or 1948," recalled George, referring to when he went in to play his guitar on Beaumont radio station KTRM. "Hank had 'Wedding Bells' on [the music charts. Actually, 'Wedding Bells' wasn't released until 1949]. I had a chance to play on a radio station, and he came by for publicity to advertise his song. He knew the program director, Nevel Powell; at that time he was a very close friend of Hank's. Hank talked him into coming by, and there was the three of us on this radio show doing 'Wedding Bells.' I was playing lead guitar at the time, starting off in the business, and he stood right across from me singing it, and I ain't never hit a note just staring at him."

After the radio station encounter with Williams, young Jones tried hard to live his life and sing his songs in the great Hank Williams mode. "George thought that Hank was it," remembered Helen Scroggins. "He could sing like him, and when he was a disc jockey there on KTRM he would sing one of Hank's songs. One of the other fellows would come in and say over the air, 'You all thought you was listening to Hank Williams then? I want you all to know that was George Jones.' He tried to sing just like Hank Williams when he started out singing. Hank was always his idol. The best songs George sang was those sad songs like Hank Williams sang."

But George's imitation of Hank was much more involved than simple mimicry of his singing style. "I've sometimes been athinkin' that George wanted so much to be like Hank Williams that he wanted to die young like him," added W. T. Scroggins, after a moment's reflection. At sixteen, George set out on a new path. He did so with all the intensity and eagerness with which he had pursued God's will. The new road was to be much more turbulent than the lazy, relaxed days of his youth, but nothing could stop George then. He was young, energetic, and enthusiastic. "He had a future of money, love, and dreams, which he was spending like they was going out of style," (from the song "The Pilgrim, Chapter 33" by Kris Kristofferson).

CHAPTER

8

Not What I Had in Mind

EANWHILE George's home life, what was left of it, had fallen on hard times. "Those last two years George was at home, his mama and daddy stayed crossways half the time," claimed W. T. Scroggins. "That kind of mixed George up." "Clara stayed on the road, but George [Washington] did, too," recalled Ivalene Jones. "The old man would stay with us some, and he would stay with Lois and around like that and then with some of his friends."

Disharmony loomed over the Jones family household like a rain cloud. A fierce commitment to provide a stable home for their children had kept George Washington and Clara together in the earlier years of their troubled marriage. But in 1947 the offspring had all left, except for young George. Neither Mr. nor Mrs. Jones was inclined to tolerate the other for more than a day or so at a stretch. Instead of taking short jaunts to the woods with a child under each arm as she had done in earlier years, Clara started the practice of packing a bag and staying away for several weeks, even months. "When all her children left home she lived with some

71

of them all the time," recalled Josie, Clara's sister, with a heavy sigh. "She couldn't stay with him on account of his drinking." Nor was Clara about to stay alone on those nights when George Washington stayed out all night because he either was passed out or had been thrown into the local jailhouse. "He [George Washington] would get drunk, but the [officers] learned about his family," continued Josie. "They wouldn't make him pay a fine. They would shut him up and leave him 'til he got sober. Then they would turn him out. They knowed he had to work. They were just that good, and them officers liked the family. They would come tell Clara where he was at. He would get out and go back to work." Invariably George Washington would come home to an empty house, however. Clara would have been long gone, still too spooked by solitude to remain alone.

So at sixteen, just at an age when he most needed the emotional support of a mother and dad, George lacked a home life. He became a wanderer, staying where he could, always in need of a place to rest his head for a night or two. Sometimes George would go stay with Brother Byrle and Sister Annie; at other times he camped out at one of his sister's houses. Eventually he sojourned with working compatriots. "The kid would catch a bus and leave," recollected Annie Stephens. "He would come up there and stay with his aunt [Mrs. Elizabeth Creal] a few days and then stay with us a few days until things cooled off back home, and he would go back. That was if his mother didn't catch the bus and come up hunting him. She knew where he was."

"Ruth lived at Beaumont, and George went there and spent the night with her if he was close to her house," recollected Helen Scroggins. "He was just like that, you know. If somebody was the handiest and if he was playing, he stayed."

"Lois and her husband went and separated, and she got a room up there in Beaumont to live in, her and her baby," recalled Ivalene Jones. "George would come in and sleep with Lois in her room. She had a cot put in there for him. He just lived around like that. He stayed with us some. One time Glenn went off when he was about fifteen or sixteen up around Victoria. He was selling pictures. He went from house to house and selled certificates for one dollar or 50 cents. He went up with a crew up around Victoria, and that was a long ways for us then. Seemed like that was way away from home. I liked to have worried myself to death about him until we finally got a letter from him. He was doing all right but with people he really didn't even know. But he was taking care of himself." After George started singing with Eddie and Pearl he lived with them from time to time. But regardless of where he stayed, no place could supplant a real home.

George did not deal well with his abrupt autonomy. "George was pretty young when he got pulled away from Mama," observed Helen Scroggins. "He wasn't nothing but a kid, and Mama had overprotected him. He just got throwed out there in a different kind of world with country music." Occasionally George found himself in situations he did not know how to handle. "He got cut up while he was in Houston this one night," recalled W. T. "He was too young to be in there. He was fooling them on his age, 'cause he was running with a bunch that was older than he was. I don't know how he got cut up, but he got on the stage in Houston and they cut him. He's got a scar on his back. Lefty Frizzell was singing there, and he was supposed to have stole a lot of money from Neva. Anyhow, that's what got George into trouble that night."

George may have been playing the role of an older fellow. But those who were close to him knew George was still plagued by the emotional insecurities of a child. "He had a fear of being alone," recalled Helen. "And he had a fear of any kind of trouble. I don't know why he was that way. I guess 'cause he stayed by hisself too much when he was a kid coming up, just in his own little world." "He wasn't about to live by hisself," added W. T. "He didn't even like to be in the same room by hisself. You know, years later, when I'd go over and have to stay with him when he would get on one of those sprees, they'd call and want me to go over and sober him up where he could make a show. I'd have to stay where he could hear me 'cause he couldn't stand to be alone."

When George was seventeen and singing with Eddie and Pearl in Beaumont's Playground, his daddy retired from the shipyards. George Washington and Clara went to Vidor to live next door to Clara's sister, Elizabeth Creal. After his parents moved George really was out on his own. He had a regular singing slot with Eddie and Pearl at Playground; so, for work reasons, he needed to stay in Beaumont. Besides, by then George had grown weary of his parents' constant bickering. He was young and restless and wanted to put all that unhappiness behind him. But family members recall he was terribly lonely. "His home was busted, and I think that throwed George for a pretty good loop," observed W. T. "Not long afterwards he met up with that family of Bonvillians," recalled Helen. "They met while he was over there at the Playground."

George's family thought that from the outset the Bonvillians paid an inordinate amount of attention to George. "They started coming over to see him all the time while he was playing at the Playground with Eddie and Pearl," recalled Helen Scroggins. "They had a girl named Dorothy, and she really liked George. But Mrs. Bonvillian liked George better than Dorothy did. They bought George a beautiful guitar and done everything trying to get that girl and George together. They let him drive their big ole fancy car, and that's how really George married her. They tried to push all that. He didn't really love her. He told me if it hadn't been for the old woman and the old man, he would have never married her. He married her because he was getting what he really wanted."

Of course, life rarely turns out as human beings plan. But young George had reasons for thinking that a life with the Bonvillians would be advantageous. By Big Thicket standards, the Bonvillians were a well-to-do couple. He was a local banker. And Mr. Bonvillian displayed a strong interest in young George's singing. Both of the older Bonvillians were supportive. It was understandable that George began to rely on them as he might have otherwise depended on his parents. Their young daughter and George were naturally thrown together and started courting. Marriage was part of the natural order of events.

Byrle and Annie Stephens were in Port Arthur conducting revival meetings when George's call came. Annie recalled that neither she nor her husband had seen George in quite some time but that George spoke as though he had seen them the day before. "He wanted to get married real bad," Annie recalled. "We kind of felt like George sure was young. I don't know whether or not Byrle had a chance to talk with Glenn before the wedding or not. I kinda have a doubt of it. It was kind of too late. Glenn had already made up his mind."

Like George's brother and sisters, Annie had her misgivings about the marriage, especially after she met the Bonvillians. "It was the in-laws pushing that wedding a little bit," Annie recalled, pinching her lips as though not to say too much. "Glenn was playing that guitar so beautiful, and he was getting a little bit of fame going around. And then Glenn was awful tired of that carrying-on at his house."

The wedding took place even though George was only eighteen. It was a small, intimate affair that included George, Dorothy, Mr. and Mrs. Bonvillian, Mr. and Mrs. Jones, and the Stephenses. The couple and their respective parents drove down to Port Arthur for the services. "George wanted the wedding right away, and we couldn't leave because of that revival," explained Annie. "So they all came down here. After George called I told the maid at our motel that we were going to have a wedding that afternoon. I said, 'I'd like for the room to be real nice,' She put the polishing on and all that. We had a pretty good size motel room, like a house. The house maid had everything perfect for the wedding. It was a real cute wedding. George got married in a little checked suit. The bride looked pretty, but George was plum handsome."

For a couple of months after the ceremony George's life proceeded pretty much as it had been before. After settling in with the Bonvillians he resumed singing with Eddie and Pearl. The Bonvillians continued to show their support. "Whenever he first got into that family the father would go out and help set up the equipment for George and his band to play," Herman Jones recalled. George felt happier than he had for some time because at long last he had a family to go home to. But his contentment was short-lived.

The young couple was still getting acquainted when Dorothy announced that she was pregnant. Suddenly, George's tranquil times were over. He was not much more than a kid himself and certainly not ready to assume the financial responsibility of a young wife and child. But his immaturity did not change the facts of life, and for a little while young George did try to do what he thought was right. "Mr. Bonvillian got George to painting,"

reflected Herman. "He decided, well, George don't need to sing
and play anymore because he's not going to make it." "All I could
play was on the weekends and in the taverns," George explained.
"It was hard with my wife being pregnant. I couldn't make it. I
worked for her dad and worked as a house painter. Mostly,
though, I didn't paint that many houses. We did commercial jobs,
you know, like hospitals." Then, after a short pause, George added,
"I didn't stay with it long."

George soon discovered that he could not bear living a life that
did not include performing and singing. He had neither the
aptitude nor the desire to be a laborer. "George wanted to go back
to the guitar, and the Bonvillians told him, 'George, you're not
going to get nowhere,' " recalled Herman. "They tried to interfere
with his talent."

Other factors strained the already fragile marriage. Dorothy
was no more adept at managing a marriage than George. She, too,
was still a child. And to hear George's family tell it, the Bonvillians treated her as the child she was rather than the adult she
needed to be. "They were living with the Bonvillians, and one
morning George was running late to go to work," mused Helen
Scroggins. "He said, 'Honey, would you go out there and feed my
rabbits afterwhile 'cause I'm going to have to go on? I'm running
late for work.' He said he might as well have dropped a bomb in
that room. He said the old man jumped on him and told him, 'Don't
you never ask my daughter to feed them filthy rabbits.' George
said, 'You would have thought I had really asked her to do
something bad.' "

Weary of the bickering, and determined to continue his singing,
George decided to move out of the Bonvillian home. He had
learned that each household has only one master. So George told
his young wife that they were going to move into their own
apartment (where he could have the final word as a Big Thicket
man should). "He told her, 'If you don't move into an apartment,
we are not going to live together. We're not staying in the house
with your mama and daddy,' " continued Helen. "He just didn't
believe in living in that house with them, and he did have the
knowledge that two people would get along better if they are by
themselves. Over there at the Bonvillians', he didn't have no say-so

about nothing. They told him what to do and where to go and when to go to bed. He didn't like that."

Dorothy was of a different frame of mind. She relied on her parents' interference. "When he got her out looking for an apartment, a bunch of us was standing there in the middle of the apartment looking at it," reminisced Helen. "Me and Lois and T. H. [Lois's husband] were there. Dorothy said, 'George, I haven't never had to cook, and I'm not going to start now. My mama and daddy have always waited on me, and I'm not going to cook, and she said that she wasn't going to do this and that. She was pregnant then. But I knew they weren't going to live together. He moved her into an apartment for a while, but it didn't last long. That's when she quit him."

Dorothy's coddling parents made it convenient for her to abandon the marriage. When she called her mama, complaining of her life with George, Mrs. Bonvillian was quick to suggest that she come home. "They'd be doing good, and then George'd have to play somewhere with Eddie and Pearl, and when he'd come home she'd be gone," Ivalene recalled. "She'd have left a note and had her mama come pick her up and take her back home. It was just like that. They probably would have made it better than what they did if her parents would have left them alone. But they didn't," concluded Ivalene, adding, "George was OK then. He wasn't drinking."

Eventually Dorothy refused to return to the apartment she shared with George. And George rebuffed her requests to come live at her parents' house. If she had not been pregnant, their parting would probably have evolved without any further conflict or anxiety. They would have simply put their marriage behind them and gotten on with their respective lives. But their forthcoming child presented problems. The Bonvillians demanded that George financially support his young wife and child, regardless of whether or not they remained married. "I think they charged him $35 a week," recalled W. T. Scroggins, "and $35 was a lot of money then. He had to pay her every week besides pay her doctor's bill. It was hard for him to get jobs, and he couldn't pay it."

The Bonvillians lacked sympathy for the young husband, who they thought was irresponsible for not taking a regular, steady-paying job. When they didn't receive their money they called the law. "Every time that poor boy was just a few days over they had him throwed in jail," explained Helen. "Every time you turned around he was in there. I don't guess he'd ever been locked up before in his life for nothing until they locked him up for alimony. He'd shy away from any kind of trouble, even the fussing in the family. If anybody had a quarrel, he'd be gone. He never seemed the same after being put into the jail like he was then. I think it hurt him real bad."

The situation became so preposterous that finally a county judge recommended to George that he join the United States Marines. "The judge told him the Marines was the only place he had to go," continued W. T. "He didn't tell George he ought to go. He told him, 'You can go, get in the service, and let them pay, or else.' " Weary of living half his life in jail and the other half trying to scratch up a singing job, George took the only route that seemed feasible. He joined the United States Marines.

9

Play It Cool, Man

EORGE'S FAMILY heard little from him during his two-year stint in the Marines. "My mother used to have to call the Commandant of the Marine Corps and find out if her son was all right," George recalls. "She'd say, 'I haven't got a letter from him, and he don't even call me up from there. Make him write.' I never was much of a writer, except for signing my name where I shouldn't sign it."

George had other matters on his mind, like carousing, drinking, and picking up young, wild, and loose women. His had been a protected, sheltered, and confined upbringing. The armed services introduced George to a new world. While making the rounds of the honky-tonk bars with Eddie and Pearl, George had witnessed the darker side of Texas life, but he had not been a participant. He had been Mrs. Jones's little boy and all knew she would disapprove. But out from under her auspices, George yielded to temptation. At last, he was a man, at least in the view of the service. And George did his best to act accordingly.

"When I was ten and eleven, maybe younger, I used to pick up cigarette butts off the ground and smoke them," George once admitted. By the time George returned to Beaumont on leave of absence from the Marines he was buying his own. Drinking was the brew of the devil, according to Clara Jones, and little George had thought his daddy terrible for consuming the evil spirits. Yet in the early fifties while in the service George soon came to realize that a *real* man drank. "I didn't know George to drink until after he come back from the service," recalled Helen. In Beaumont nice girls were supposed to withhold their sexual favors until after marriage, yet while in the service, George discovered that the world was full of young women more than eager to grant special privileges to a youthful and amusing singer such as him.

"I think her name was Virginia," reminisced Ivalene, about George's second and last visit back to Beaumont before being released from the Marines. "George brought her with him on a leave of absence. She had a new car, and George had to show that new car off to all his friends, making them think it was his. I think she done acrobatics, but I don't rightly recall for sure. George took her to Lois's and said she was his new wife. We later heard that George had annulled their marriage, but after he got out he said he never married her at all. George knew he wasn't gonna stay at Lois's if he told them he wasn't married," Ivalene concluded with a chuckle.

George did not limit his shenanigans to the pursuit of fast women. Ivalene recalled that he had also grown fond of driving with a heavy foot. "We [Ivalene and Herman] went over to Rainbow Bridge Cabin in Port Arthur with him and her," she related. "It was one of the scariest days of my life. George had started drinking a little beer by then. He wasn't drinking a whole lot but a little. We had to come over from Beaumont down this old road. The freeway wasn't in then. He drove like heck. I said, 'My God, if I ever get back home, I won't never get in the car with him no more.' I know he was making ninety miles an hour. I told him, 'George, if you don't break that speed before you get to the top [of the hill], you're gonna break down the other side.' He said, 'You're probably right about that.' He slowed down, but I was scared."

George was certainly learning to appreciate traveling down the fast lane. But at the same time Ivalene recalled that George expressed a certain disdain for life's fast travelers, as though his own transgressions were somehow not as tainted as those committed by others. "What was so funny was that he stood there crabbing about Virginia," continued Ivalene. "He had sent her to a little old place over there to get some beer, and he said to me, 'You know what? That damn woman is old enough to be my mama.' He was always talking and cutting up. I said, 'What, George?' He said, 'That damn woman is old enough to be my mama, and she's got so much damn makeup on 'til you can't tell whether she's got skin or if she's artificial.' I never will forget that. I said, 'Oh, George, she ain't no older than you are.' He said, 'I bet if you get all that makeup off her face, you'd see.'"

Not all of George's stay in the United States Marines was passed in such a carefree manner. George has little recollection of his service days, probably because, after he was out, he wished to forget the ordeal. Novelist Leon Uris observed in *Battle Cry* the unpleasantries of serving in the Marines in the early 1950s. "The corporal launched another tirade," described Uris of one typical basic training episode. "He cursed for ten minutes, seldom repeating an obscenity. He expanded on the group's future status in life. Isolation from the outside world . . . loss of all traces of individuality . . . no candy . . . no gum . . . no newspapers . . . no radios . . . no magazines . . . speak only when spoken to . . . salute . . . address as sir and obey all men within the confines of boot camp above the rank of private."

Wake-up calls for George were at 4:30 in the morning, and privileges were few. Suddenly life back in the Big Thicket didn't seem so tough after all. George had been a child when he entered the Marines. The fact that he survived his stay was testimony that he became a survivor.

By most standards George the Marine was lucky. He avoided what young soldiers most dread—active duty. If he had volunteered for service a year earlier, he would most likely have been shipped to Korea, where a war was raging between the Democratic People's Republic of Korea (North Korea) and the Republic of Korea (South Korea). An estimated 5 million persons lost their lives in that war, including several hundred thousand American soldiers. But on April 11, 1951, just a few months before George started his basic training, President Harry Truman stopped the battling by relieving General Douglas MacArthur as United Nations commander and as commander of the U. S. forces in the Far East. MacArthur had urged a bombing of Chinese bases, and if he had been left to his own devices, the nation surely would have been plunged into a larger war effort. But as it was, George, along with countless other young men, never saw any fighting. George passed his entire time in the Marines serving peacefully in San Jose, California. His two-year stint passed by uneventfully, at least as far as the war was concerned.

The early fifties were to be remembered as a self-contented, complacent, smug era. In *The Glory and the Dream,* William Manchester describes the youth of the early fifties as "prepared to embrace—and if need be, to defend—the status quo; they would obey the law, pay taxes, fulfill their military obligations, and vote, though thereafter politics would be none of their concern. They would conform to the dictates of society in their dress, speech, worship, choice of friends, length of hair, and above all, in their thought."

As is usually the case, the era's popular music reflected the national temper. Country music was no exception. "Country music in the 1940s was becoming increasingly pop-oriented and slick, and while old-time artists like Roy Acuff and Molly O'Day were at their peak, the bulk of the public's attention—especially in terms of record sales—went to the big band sound of Bob Wills and His Texas Playboys; the smooth, orchestra-backed sound of Gene Autry; the plaintive, pop-tinged vocals of Eddy Arnold; or the honky-tonk sounds of Al Dexter and Ernest Tubb," reflected writer George T. Simon. Certainly, their music was good, but the performers were not venturesome or particularly innovative. They clung to musical forms already tried and proven and were content to sing more of the same. Country music lacked a full-blown stylist. Hank Williams changed all that.

"Then along came Hank Williams, who went firmly and bull-headedly against the grain, proudly singing his own songs in an old-fashioned, high, tight, hillbilly voice. Slurring with bluesy intonation, breaking with feeling, yodeling with good cheer, Williams's approach encapsulated the joys and sorrows of country life with his technically limited but spectacularly moving voice," added Simon.

Because of the growing popularity of Hank Williams, George's life would never be the same.

Hank had captured George's imagination years before he went to the service. George had long been an admirer of the Williams singing style, but their coincidental meeting at the Beaumont radio station had made a strong and lasting impression on the young boy. "He was my hero," admitted George. George dreamed of being just like the rebellious, moody, restless young Williams. Although Williams had been born and raised in Georgia, the two men had similar upbringings and temperaments. George felt that he, more than anyone, understood Williams. Why he died at such an early age, however, was not understood. That death made an undeniable impression on the twenty-one-year-old Jones.

Circumstances under which Williams died are still clouded, but nonetheless history has claimed that Hank was found in the back seat of his automobile on January 1, 1953, in Oak Hill, West Virginia. He died at the height of his popularity and success. In 1951 he had captured the public's attention with "Cold, Cold Heart," "Howlin' at the Moon," and "Hey, Good Lookin'." The year prior to his death had produced "Honky-Tonk Blues," "Jambalaya," and the prophetic "I'll Never Get Out of this World Alive," the biggest hit of his career.

At the time of his death George was nearly three thousand miles away, in San Jose, California. But as most people can remember exactly what they were doing when told of tragic news, George possesses total recall of how he heard. The news had been announced for several hours when George had returned to his barrack from a holiday liberty. "It was three or four in the morning," recalled George. "A buddy of mine sleeping in the next bunk picked up a paper and said, 'George, a buddy of yours died.' I said, 'What?' Then he showed me the paper, and I read the headlines that Hank Williams was dead. I liked to have died [too]. He had had seventy-something number one hits in five years. He was only twenty-nine years old and only five years in the business. Nobody has or ever will do what he did. He was put here for a reason.

"I think he died of heartbreak," philosophized George. "He died of worshipping the wrong love. As he told Minnie Pearl a few weeks before he died, 'That's just it, Minnie,' he says, 'it just ain't no light. There is no life.' But there was. He just saw the wrong light. He saw the light bulb burn out. [Like the old-time gospel song,] 'I Saw the Light, I Saw the Light,' Hank saw the light about those things, those loves. [He saw] too strong. Life itself will make you a dopehead, a drunkard. He was a real involved person. That's why he stayed so dumb of the facts [of life]. He got so involved in something like his music, like I feel I have, that he was happy all the time, blind to the other things in life. You don't have time to be bothered. There's a song going round in there all the time."

But on January 1, 1953, the songs no longer whirled in the head of Hank Williams. The great vocal stylist and musical maverick was dead, leaving a vacuum of major proportion within the country music field. Hank's songs continued to sell. "Kaw-liga," "Your Cheatin' Heart," "Take These Chains from My Heart," and "Weary Blues from Waitin'" sold in abundance during the year following his untimely death. But by the end of 1953, Williams's record label stopped releasing his songs. A void, dark and majestic, hovered within the industry's ranks. Ironically, twenty-two-year-old George Jones had served his time with Uncle Sam and was back in Texas about the same historical moment that the public began hankering for a Hank Williams replacement.

CHAPTER

10

Don't Stop the Music

O ONE EVER denied George Jones's talent. All along his young life's way were those impressed by his ability to sing.

Archer Fullingim, the cantankerous, liberal, bachelor editor of the Kountze newspaper was outspoken about George's singing, even back when George was just a local singer. "It must have been about 1951; George was nobody then," recalled Fullingim. "He wanted me to sponsor him [for a concert] in the high school. So I called up the school and got the permission for him to sing there. Then I put in the paper he would be there. Nobody hardly came, but I was there. He sang the songs of Jimmy Rogers, Lefty Frizzell, and Hank Williams. I was the first person that sponsored him a concert.

"I liked him because he was singing his own sadness," Archer reflected on his earlier insight. "He was singing his own love; he was singing his own sorrow. He was singing right out of his own emotions, good or bad, and still does it. The others sang a song that

85

somebody wrote for them. But George and Merle Haggard are real hillbilly singers. They sing their own emotions."

A couple of years later, after George had returned from the service, Gordon Baxter reflected upon his first chance hearing of George. "There was a big dragon lady that ran the club here in Beaumont called Neva," Gordon said. "She was a big redheaded mama and her name was Neva Starnes. She and her husband were always on the fringes of getting some kind of label going. She had set up a recording studio near her honky-tonk. It was a very crude arrangement with just one room for the artist to play in, and one room had a big old magnacorder. Neva's fourteen-year-old son was the chief engineer and recording artist. There wasn't any such thing as a mixer or anything like that. I had some hopes then of recording myself. So I was over there one day to record when up steps this little kid with his eyes too close together and his brush haircut.

"He picks up his guitar, and the mike was hanging off the boom, and he began to sing," continued Gordon. "I'm not sure what song it was. But I remember feeling all the hair stand up on my arms and chills run up and down my shoulder blades when he started to sing. I thought, 'My God, what a voice.' He had this complete range and was accompanying himself on the guitar and playing surprisingly well and was just absolutely into the song. He was even coming up on his toes. You could have set fire to the place and he wouldn't even have known it."

But talent by itself does not guarantee a successful singing career. Regardless of his talent, George's chances of rising above his obscure club performances and becoming a major entertainer were slim. He was poor. Talk of becoming a Grand Ole Opry star was laughable among his family members. Not because they didn't think he had the talent but because such things didn't happen to poor people like them. "When he was just a little kid he'd talk about singing on the Grand Ole Opry one day, and I'd just chuckle," remembered Ivalene Jones.

Little George had few hometown supporters. Archer Fullingim was the exception. "People 'round here thought he was part of the poor white trash," reminisced Archer. "He didn't have any formal training to get out and get himself a legitimate job. They just saw him as some boy who lazed around, pluckin' his guitar. He didn't get much interest."

Neither did George's prospects improve immediately after returning from the United States Marines. He was one of several hundred trying to earn a few bucks by singing and picking in East Texas honky-tonks. Singers like George didn't make any real money, just whatever an audience might throw into a collection pot while they were singing. Most of George's peers just gave up, several of whom seemed more likely candidates for stardom than did George. After a while, living off nickels, dimes, and quarters was more than most could deal with. "George was like all those other singers," observed Gordon Baxter. "Nobody knew him, and nobody gave a damn. He was an unknown. He didn't even have a very impressive manner about him when you first met him. He was kind of shy and laid back and didn't have anything to say. When I was watching him sing I remember thinking that, with all his talents, this kid really ought to go somewhere, but he's got all the chances of a snowball in hell. He's got no personality to speak of, he's too shy, and he's unimpressive-looking. I thought then that he'd just be a nightclub singer forever with this tremendous golden voice."

If George had lived at another place and time during the history of country music, Gordon's prediction may well have come to pass. But the late 1950s and early 1960s offered unique musical opportunities for those willing to grasp them. A new developing musical audience was beginning to emerge. The economy was booming; times were good. The American people were better off financially than ever before. Part of their funds went to buy records, thus creating, for a short period of time, musical demands that outstripped the supply.

Small, independent record labels sprung up across the Southeast like dandelions on a spring morning. The music industry was open and allowed free access to whomever pushed the right doors. In Memphis, Sam Phillips was offering a deal by which anyone could come in and for $4 walk out with an acetate disc of his own personal recordings. In 1953 a young truck driver by the name of Elvis Aaron Presley came in and recorded "My Happiness" and "That's When Your Heartaches Begin" as a present for his mother.

A year later Sam called Elvis back in for a commercial recording because of Elvis's unique voice. Later in the same decade Sam recorded Jerry Lee Lewis, Johnny Cash, and Carl Perkins on that same little label.

The atmosphere in Texas was much the same. "It was happening all around us," recalled Gordon. "Everybody knew that, with a little luck and enough brains, it could happen here in Beaumont. Jim Reeves had come out of Carthage, and Elvis was coming down to the 'Louisiana Hayride.' Little labels were popping up everywhere."

A successful Beaumont businessman, Pappy Daily, and a nightclub owner, Jack Starnes, wanted their own slice of the musical pie phenomenon. Consequently, they started up a little record company called Starday, the name originating from the merging of their two last names. Start-up costs of a record label then were minimal. Facilities were crude and primitive. "My first record was cut in a living room of a house in Beaumont," George would later tell a reporter. "Then I advanced to a bigger city, but another living room, in Houston. Those were mostly the things I recorded on Starday. In fact, everything I recorded on Starday was in a living room. We had four or five musicians and egg crates on the wall. There was no such things as production. We'd go in with the band; we'd go over the song. I'd look over and tell the steel player to take a break or kick it off, and I'd get the fiddle to play the turnaround in the middle. I'd just let them know if we were going to tag it or not. We'd just go through it. We didn't take the pains of making several takes. They'd say, 'Well, my God, this is costing us money.' So we'd just get it down as good as we could. If we went a little flat or sharp in a place or two, they'd say, 'The public ain't gonna notice that, so put it out.' "

Success for an upstart record label then was dependent on the talent it offered and whether or not the owners could convince country music disc jockeys to play their records. Once played, the record's future was determined by audience response. If there was none, the record's life fizzled. The deejays tossed it into the garbage can. But if a record was well received among its listeners, a deejay responded by playing it again. The record label owner would then relay the record's popularity to another deejay and so on. If the record was popular in a variety of towns and villages across the United States, the song became a hit. Loretta Lynn pitched her early records herself. George was not as daring; but Pappy Daily was.

Pappy was listening to an array of young singers in 1953, the year he first heard George. He didn't think much of most of them. Then he heard George. But Pappy was quick to point out that George was no overnight success story. "George had just got out of the Marines, and Jack Starnes brought him over here to my place," quipped Pappy. "Then he was the world's greatest imitator. When he sang he sounded like Roy Acuff or Hank Williams or Lefty Frizzell."

But Pappy recognized the talent and signed him up. "I gave him a chance," continued Pappy. "When we first started out we couldn't sell his records. It was hard to do. I kept trying to get his record heard and kept trying to get it played on the radio stations so that people would know about him." They also experimented. They tried a little rock and roll sound. "I got started when rock and roll was beginning to be big," George related years later in a *Country Music Magazine* interview. "They didn't have that many stations that played country music. Country music hadn't got all that big yet, so I thought I'd try a rock song. So I wrote one of the stupidest things I ever wrote. I wrote and recorded two things. One side was called 'Rocket,' and the other side was called 'Dad Gummit, How Come It.' I recorded under [the names of] Thumper Jones and then later under Glenn Patterson."

Nothing happened. So they went back to recording country music. "There Ain't No Money in This Deal" petered. Then, in 1955, George recorded, "Why, Why, Why." It hit. But George's follow-up efforts fizzled. Much of the reason may have been that George was still mimicking others. "A Texan who stuck with striking fidelity to the sound of Hank Williams early in his career was George Jones, whose early Starday records reflect an amazing resemblance to Williams's sound of just a few years earlier," observed *The Illustrated History of Country Music.*

Pappy Daily recalled, "One day I said to George, 'George, can you sound like George?' And he says, 'Yes, sir.' I said, 'Well, sing like George Jones, 'cause people don't want somebody that sounds like Roy Acuff or Lefty Frizzell or anybody else. You have to have a voice that belongs to you and sing like yourself or else you're not going to get any recognition at all.' So he started trying to sing like George Jones. But it took us two or three years before we ever got him kicked off."

Musically, George began to grow, gaining enough confidence along the way to interpret a song the way he felt it rather than echoing the sounds of others. He began to realize that by singing his own way he could attract more attention than by copying the style of another. The self-confidence instilled by Pappy Daily turned him around. "I've had lots of people say that I made George Jones," reflected the feisty old man in 1983. "I says no. I didn't make him. I just gave him a chance. He had what people wanted, and he went on from there. I figure he would have made it if somebody had stayed with him long enough. Some people might have given up on him, but I didn't. 'Course, I went along with other people as much as I did George, and they didn't make it. I figure if you've got it, you make it, and if you don't, you don't make it. But a singer has got to have the opportunity and the exposure. That's what I gave George."

11

Take the Devil Out of Me

OUNG MEN will be young men, and George was no exception. "He was pretty wild back in those days," recalled Buddy Killen, now president and chief executive officer of Tree International, Nashville's largest country music publishing company. "I was single during those years and working on the road as a musician with him. He would get drunk and carry on and have a good ole time. We partied a lot. We'd get together, go out, and swarm all over the place."

But regardless of what he did on the road or even out in the nightspots of Beaumont and Houston, George needed the love and security of a good wife and family. He was too traditional in his outlook to have it any other way. George wasn't home from the service a year before he was hitched again, this time to a young East Texas girl who was working as a carhop at a Houston drive-in. Her name was Shirley Corley, and she recalls that she married for much the same reason that George wanted to marry. She was young, alone, and wanted to feel loved.

Shirley Corley was eighteen and fresh out of high school when she met George in the late summer of 1954. She had grown up in Tenaha, Texas, a small community comprised of some 2,000 residents that lay sixty miles southwest of Shreveport, Louisiana, or approximately 120 miles north of Beaumont as the crow flies. "We was just as poor as could be," she disclosed. Her natural father's family had money, she claims, but her daddy, Bryan Corley, died in a railroad accident when she was only one year of age. When her mama remarried she picked herself a poor man. "My stepdaddy never left the farm," Shirley continued. "We were pea pickers. I had one aunt who had a bunch of cattle on my grandparents' farm, and she sold half of those cattle and gave me the money. I got $750, and I finished high school on that. I bought my lunches, clothes, everything.

"When I finished high school I went to Houston to work for the telephone company," the attractive blonde reminisced. "My best girlfriend's brother was hiring gobs of girls." She had intended her stay in Houston to be only for the summer. That fall she had plans of returning to Tenaha and marrying her hometown sweetheart. "I was brought up to think that getting married was the thing to do," she recalled. "Back then I didn't think about having a career so that I could be on my own." But her well-laid plans and dreams went awry. She and her boyfriend broke off the relationship, and Shirley found herself in the worst of predicaments for a small-town girl living in the early 1950s. She was unmarried and, worse, unbetrothed.

She took a job as a carhop at a Princess Drive-In in Houston, coincidentally not far from where George was singing at a little dive on Navigation Street. Shirley recalled meeting George after only a few days on the job. "Then he kept coming by to see me," she remembered. Their courtship was short-lived only because after a few dates George asked for her hand in marriage. Shirley claims she knew little more about George than that he was a singer making $10 a week and that he drank from time to time. "I grew up Southern Baptist," she continued. "So I knew better than to marry him. I knew I shouldn't marry him because he drank, and I knew I really didn't want to marry somebody who drank. I didn't drink, and I knew better than to be drawn into that." But she recalled that her loneliness and her old-fashioned belief that a good woman could make a man happy dissipated her doubts. "He got my sympathy," she mused. "He told me nobody had ever really loved him. I thought he could change if I made him a good home."

Shirley notified no one of her impending marriage. "I didn't tell anybody 'cause I really didn't think he'd go through with it," confessed Shirley, who was then still suffering the aftereffects of the dissolved engagement to her hometown sweetheart. "My girlfriend came, but that's all," she whispered as though embarrassed to talk about her small and austere wedding. But marry they did in the fall of 1954. And as it turned out, their relationship was about as emotionally spartan as their ceremony. Each wanted what the other could not give. "I was too indulged with country music to really love like you're supposed to love," George admitted years later. Yet he wanted a loving, supportive, caring wife. At the same time Shirley wanted to be loved and appreciated by her new husband. She certainly wasn't prepared for the reality of George's constant absences from home and his philandering with other women. But both were accustomed to hard and trying times. So for a while they both shrugged off their marital disappointments and went on with their day-to-day existences.

In Shirley's view, their marriage started off on the wrong foot. Shortly after tying the knot with George, he informed her that they had to leave Houston and move to Beaumont. He wasn't making enough to pay the rent, and he figured living was cheaper back in Beaumont, where they could hole up with various members of his family. The move depressed Shirley. As a child, she had frequently visited relatives who had lived in Beaumont. She had never liked the town. "I used to say there was one place I wouldn't live and that was Beaumont," she recollected. "I hated it. I still don't like it." But their lack of funds gave them little choice. Besides, Shirley had another human being to consider. By January she was in a family way.

They lived first with one member of George's family and then with another. Or it should probably be said that Shirley did. George was usually gone, getting work where he could on the road. "I had cut three or four mediocre tunes, but the money I made allowed me to get work playing my guitar," George later reminisced. Sometimes Shirley went with him. But after she gave birth to their first son, Jeffrey, in the fall of 1955, she was confined to staying at home, which by then' had become a small apartment adjacent to her aunt's house in Beaumont.

Shirley most likely would have quit traveling with George on the road anyway, however. George's wild and raucous honky-tonk bar existence didn't appeal to her. For Shirley had been cast from a different mold from George. She possessed a quiet and genteel nature. Her features were refined and delicate. She found most of George's friends and associates to be gruff, crude, and offensive. And she passed many an hour trying to persuade George to leave his honky-tonk life behind and try for the big time. "I thought he was the best," she reflected years later. "I pushed him. I did everything I could to help him. I think he could have been as great as Elvis or Frank Sinatra. I tried to get him to be on TV, but he said he just wanted to be a country music singer. I never understood George. If I had had that kind of talent, I would have tried to go to the top with it."

The birth of a son in 1955 brought a little happiness to their otherwise bleak existence. But even the arrival of the new child had a dark side to it. The additional burden of another mouth to feed worried George. He began to spend even more time away from home, on the road. "I needed the money," he admitted. Then, in the winter of the same year, George recorded "Why, Baby, Why?," a spiffy little tune about the hurts caused by a spouse's cheating. It proved to be George's breakthrough record. "Why, Baby, Why?" stalked up the *Billboard* country music charts and didn't stop until it hit the number four spot. George was on his way.

The success of that one song provided George the chance to travel to Shreveport, Louisiana, and audition for the "Louisiana Hayride," a live radio show that was second only to the Grand Ole Opry in both popularity and stature. "I became a 'Hayride' regular, and the company was mighty good," George later told a reporter. "Elvis Presley, Johnny Cash, Johnny Horton, and Jimmy 'C.' Newman were all there."

While George's success eased their financial worries somewhat, it also sparked further friction between him and Shirley. She became insistent that he upgrade his act. After meeting Elvis at the 'Hayride,' Shirley described him as "dirty." "After that I didn't care for Elvis," Shirley recalled. She became convinced that George's associates were having an undesirable influence on him. "Shirley used to get mad and wouldn't go to see George play 'cause he'd dance all over that stage," George's oldest sister, Helen, recalled. "He really showed his feelings. She told him if he didn't quit doing that and embarrassing her to death, she wasn't going no more. She stayed on him for years with that. She told Pappy [Daily] herself. She said it embarrassed her. I never could understand why that would embarrass her. He was happy then, and he didn't drink that much, but after he quit that, having to be so still and trying to be so precise with everything on the stage, that's what started him drinking so much. I guess he had to have something to calm him down and keep him still 'cause he would just dance all over that stage before." "It was a way of him showing his emotions," added W. T. Scroggins. "Then he couldn't get it all out and he had to hold all that in. He had to have something to keep him calmed down and to be able to get out there and face the public."

Actually George was deeply hurt by his wife's criticisms. His fragile ego needed her endorsement, above all others. And when he didn't get her approval he suffered. Never in his life had he anticipated such success and the demands that naturally followed along. "I'm just a singer," George said repeatedly. And when others began to treat him like something more than just a honky-tonk singer he felt uneasy and insecure. He instinctively sought out the affection of "his loved ones" for strength. When rejection, rather than acceptance, greeted him at his heart's door, his self-confidence withered along with all his resolve. Drinking and carousing became an easy escape hatch.

But Shirley had her own inner struggles. She was weary of her husband's way of life—his long absences and loose ways. "George wanted the good life," Shirley admitted bitterly. "But another part of him wanted the dirty life of going to those beer joints." "I don't know how Shirley put up with what George was doing for as long as she did," Shirley's second husband, J. C. Arnold, Sr., would later observe. "George'd mess around on her. He'd go out and pick up the ugliest and scrawniest, shapeless, crudest tramps in town. And we got some pretty bad ones," reflected J. C., who had lived most of his adult life near Beaumont. "He'd do that right here in town where everybody knew him. Everybody knew about it except Shirley. Nobody would tell her."

But she suspected. And her suspicions caused her to grow resentful and caustic toward George. In the early years of their marriage Shirley had hoped that the creation of a family might mend George's wayward habits. "I knew he did what he wanted, I guess because he was young," she once reflected. "And I almost left him a couple of times before I got pregnant. But George would always soft-talk me into overlooking what he had done. Then, too, I had been raised with the teaching that, if you make your bed, you lie in it. I figured, well, I screwed up. I'll have to try and make the best of it."

Then Jeffrey arrived and, in 1958, their second son, Bryan, came along. The birth of each child gave Shirley new hope for a happier marriage. And for a short period of time following each of his two sons' deliveries George repented and mended his ways. "When both children were born he tried to straighten up," continued Shirley. "The first one or two years after Bryan was born was the best. [Otherwise] he'd go for two or three months [without drinking and carousing], then stay on a binge for a week."

In retrospect Shirley suspects that she should have left George when she realized that he was not going to change. But at the time she had her children to consider. "George did provide for her," inserted J. C. Arnold. "I think that's what held her to George for so long." Besides, she had nowhere else to go. "So, I just closed myself up," she explained. "I mostly just held it [the resentment and loneliness] in."

Perhaps it was too much to expect George to have been more sensitive to his wife's growing isolation and aloofness. After all, George had never dreamed of being the center of such attention. He discovered a world of make-believe where young women threw themselves at his feet, where crowds swooned at his singing, and where life seemed to be one long, continuous, never-ending party. He had had no reason to think that he could have ever lived such a life. Therefore, he had no reason to think it was ever going to end. Rules, he thought, governed others. His own existence seemed once removed from the lives of mortals. Only later, when it was too late, did he realize that he was an earthling like everyone else and that his life was governed by the same universal laws that affect all mankind. But in the late 1950s, while still a young man full of unspent energy, George had few reasons to reflect on words of wisdom.

CHAPTER
12
Nothing Can Stop Me

Y THE LATE 1950s George had begun a career roll that would continue throughout most of his life, although there were to be a few sputters and stammers along the way. After the success of "Why, Baby, Why?" George didn't have another hit until 1956, "What Am I Worth?" Then he struck another dry period. But in 1957 he began to pick up momentum. After leaving Pappy Daily's small Starday label, George signed with the larger and more prestigious Mercury Record label, headed by Art Talmadge. But Pappy remained his producer. For the first time, George and Pappy started cranking out authentic George Jones music. "Don't Stop the Music" broke in the top twenty during the summer of 1957. "Too Much Water" hit about two months later.

By 1958 George was riding a snowball tumbling down the side of a hill. It had little direction and was picking up unwanted debris from its downward drive, but with each roll, his snowballing career was building speed. In 1958 he had three hits—"Color of the Blues," "Treasure of Love," and "If I Don't Love You." The next year marked four hits and included his first number one song, "White Lightning," a tune written by a fellow Texan, J. P. Richardson, better known as "the Big Bopper." His other tunes that year—"Who Shot Sam?," "Big Harlan Taylor," and "Money to Burn" did not reach the chart heights of "White Lightning," but they kept the momentum going.

More hits followed in 1960. "The Window Up Above," a poignant song of unrequited love, stayed on the country music charts for an impressive thirty-four weeks. "Tender Years" hit the number one slot in 1961. Then, in 1962, George started churning out top forty hits like a Xerox machine. He had seven hits in 1962 (including "She Thinks I Still Care"), three in 1963, six in 1964 (including "The Race Is On"), six in 1965, and three in 1966. Finally, after twenty years of professional singing and ten on the road, George Jones had made his mark on the country music world.

But, oh, what a price he paid. "I worked like a dog," George said. He was on the road 90 percent of the time, driving from one honky-tonk bar to another. "Before those luxury buses, we'd spend four days a week just getting from date to date," described George. "Bookings weren't as numerous as today, and we'd have to drive five hundred miles overnight sometimes, packed six in a car. There was no room to stretch out, and if you wanted to sleep, you had to lay your head on someone's shoulder. As soon as you got to sleep, one of the guys would wake you up for your turn to drive."

And once he got to where he was going, life wasn't much better. Dressing rooms were the exception rather than the rule. Audiences were oftentimes rowdy, raucous, and even threatening. Occasionally George performed on a stage barricaded with chicken wire. At best, the honky-tonk rooms were smoke-filled, crowded, and loud. George loved to sing, but he sometimes wondered if anyone was listening. At other times he felt like a prize cow, paraded around for others to examine. "In the taverns," noted George, "the owner would sit you in a window when you weren't singing and playing for the dancing, so everyone passing by could see you."

The pace was treacherous. Breaks and vacations were rare. George took the work as it was offered, even if it meant rarely going home to be with his family and to rest. "I needed the money,"

George rationalized. "I had a wife and two kids." In fact, George was on a roll and was afraid to pause for fear that it might all disappear. He was a Big Thicket man, born and raised in an environment where forces unseen and unpredictable determined a person's fate. George never thought to pace himself. He just did what he was told to do. But as his career flourished and one year gave way to another, he grew weary. Eventually he succumbed to road life's temptations. "For three years I drank only Cokes," George reflected, "but the people you were around were always drinking and blowing alcoholic breath in your face. It really got on my nerves. It got to where I felt like I had to have a drink, and soon I was sneaking off to the rest room or the car to have a fast beer. That graduated to hard liquor.

"After you get started like that you're on your way. After you were finished playing, everyone wanted to have a party, and you'd stay up all night. I'd end up fatigued and hoarse the next day. I'd take a drink to get started, and after one or two I didn't want to stop. When you play taverns ten or fifteen years, like I did, it draws everything out of you. The people became overbearing and I'd respond accordingly."

George's plight was not unusual in the country music industry. "A lot of the singers would put away a fifth or two of Jack Daniels a day back then," noted Melba Montgomery, a country music singer who later sang duets with George. "George wasn't the only one." The road life and the conditions under which the singers lived tested even the strongest characters. For country music was not yet a well-paying profession. Country music accounted for only about 5 percent of the nation's music market. An artist would typically struggle by year after year, earning just enough to get to his next job. Then, if he was lucky and was one of the few to sing a string of hits, he might make enough to purchase a modest house. "In those early days artists didn't make the money they make today," recollected Buddy Killen. "In the 1950s, if you were red hot, you might go out and make $750 a night. Now, a country artist, if he's red hot, can probably make $75,000 a night. In many respects the country music industry was a babes-in-the-woods operation back then. We were not sophisticated. It just wasn't like it is today. We didn't have the audience that we have today to accept

us. We were internationally virtually unknown. Nobody knew anything about Hollywood. Roy Acuff did some movies and stuff like
that because of Roy being so hot, but I'm sure he did it for
practically nothing. We didn't know in those days how to handle
the things like we know today."

In the fifties and sixties country music singers sang primarily
for the love of the music and to be around the other artists. Except
for a handful of stars like Eddy Arnold or Elvis Presley, country
artists had little hope of getting rich.

Most of the country artists were like George, financially naive
and professionally unworldly. "It was a much slower pace then,"
reflected Melba. "Everybody was real friendly. A lot of times five
or six different artists would be on the same show, and everybody'd stay at the same hotel or motel. Everybody would eat
breakfast together. Then they'd usually line up and follow each
other going to the next show. That don't happen anymore. Now it's
very impersonal. Now it's almost a cold feeling in a lot of packaged
shows. A lot of big artists with a band is trying to see who can
outdo who on the show. It wasn't that way years ago. I remember
a bunch of us on a tour one time down through Georgia and the
Carolinas: Me and George and Buck Owens and several others,
probably eight or nine acts traveling together. Back then George
would come out in the middle of Buck Owens' show and do
something, or one of them would come out in the middle of
George's. It was just everybody having a big time and enjoying
themselves. It was really a fun thing back then."

The artist's goals were simple: to get a number one hit and to
work as many road dates as possible. Little else mattered or was
even considered. "I don't remember talking to anyone then that
had anything else they were striving for," continued Melba. There
were a lot of county fairs, a lot of state fairs, a lot of clubs. Some of
them clubs weren't near the size of the clubs they have now. Like
there was the Old Chestnut Inn in St. Louis, Missouri. It wasn't
something you'd take your grandmother in, but every artist
worked it."

But going from fair date to honky-tonk date took a treacherous
toll on the country music artists. They pretty much lived from day
to day with little regard for the future. George was no exception.

"I've always thought that George's potential was unlimited," Buddy Killen reflected. "George Jones could have and still could do anything he wants. I've never known another singer who has the phenomenal respect as a singer by his peers as George Jones has. But I'm not sure George Jones ever wanted to be a big star. In all the conversations I ever had with him, I don't think I ever heard him tell me how big a star he was going to be someday. He just wanted to do his thing."

George wanted to sing, have a good time, earn enough money to get by, and give his little family a decent life. He never thought of having more. So he trudged along, never planning or saving for the future. His indifference toward his career was obvious; he didn't even have a manager. Nor did ne want one. Pappy was like a daddy to him. That meant more to George than having any big-time manager. "I was George's advisor," observed Pappy Daily. "George was more like a son to me than anything else. I treated him just like I would have my own boy. If he did things I didn't like, I'd raise hell about it. No, I never was a manager. They might call it manager but, contractually, no, I never took a dime of George's money."

While blinded by the glow of his own success, George was probably the least able to see what was best for him. "It's a matter of the artist using good sound judgment in determining out of those wonderful offers that he's getting whether he wants to do them or not," explained Buddy Killen. "Greed can cause him to try to do it all. He wants all the money that's available to him, and he doesn't want to turn anything down. So he goes out there and takes everything. That way the artist is going to wear down. 'Cause to keep going, he's going to take pills and drink or do whatever he needs to do to overcome that tired feeling that he eventually gets from being on the road day in and day out, every day of the week, every month. Then the artist should say, 'I don't want to go anymore.' So if George or any other artist is working too much, it's because he doesn't say to somebody else, 'I don't want to do that: give me a week off, give me a day off, or whatever.' "

In 1961 George left Mercury and signed with United Artists. "Mercury's interest had switched to rock 'n' roll," George told a *Music City News* reporter. "When my Mercury deal expired I was offered a fabulous deal by United Artists. So many folks were telling me I [shouldn't change labels] that I became depressed, but luck was with me." Actually George went to United Artists because of Art Talmadge, a prominent record executive who had been with Mercury and then had left to join United Artists. Later George was to follow Talmadge again when he left United Artists to form his own record label, Musicor.

George's shift to U.A. proved to be one of the best moves of his career. For it was while he was there that he recorded some of his best material, including "She Thinks I Still Care" and "The Race Is On." While he was at United Artists George added another dimension to his career. On a hunch, George decided to record with a then unknown singer by the name of Melba Montgomery. Together they sang some of the most memorable duets in country music history. "The first time I met George he probably wouldn't remember," drawled the tall, spindly singer with a chuckle at old memories as she sat in her comfortable, suburban Nashville home that she shares with her husband, Jack Solomon, and two children. "I was working with Roy Acuff at the time on the Grand Ole Opry house, and the artists would go over to Tootsie's Orchid Lounge across the street afterwards. The first time I saw George was in Tootsie's back room. He was so ripped, he wouldn't have remembered anything. It was so funny. He said something real cute to me, but he wouldn't remember today.

"The next time I met him was when Pappy Daily had signed me to United Artists Records," she continued. "I had had two records out on a small label called the Nugget Label, and George had heard them, and he told Pappy, 'I want you to sign that girl to U.A. I want to do a duet with her.' I was living in Nashville with Roy and Mildred Acuff, but George was still living in Texas. So he and Pappy had come into town and were staying at the Capitol Park Inn. I went over and shook hands with Pappy and George in the hotel room, and George says, 'Have you got us a duet song?' I said, 'I've got one I wrote. I don't know if you'll like it or not.' He said, 'Well, sing it to me.' I was so nervous because George at that time was the number one male artist. But I sang them 'We Must Have Been Out of Our Minds.' I was scared to death. I sat down on the end of the bed with my guitar and started singing. George just kind of fell in singing it with me. That's how we cut it. I did the lead, and he did the harmony with me. We got through, and George said, 'It's a hit.' So we went to the studio, I guess, the next day."

United Artists released the song in the spring of 1963 and George was proven right. "We Must Have Been Out of Our Minds" became a best-selling song and went on to become a classic country music duet. George and Melba continued to record together until 1967, when George became involved with Tammy Wynette. During their professional courtship Melba and George charted seven hits and would even occasionally perform together during live concerts. Having come from similar backgrounds ("George and I were pretty much raised alike," Melba reflected, "except I guess George may have been raised a little more poor than I had."), they also became good friends. "I enjoyed just sitting down maybe backstage or in a dressing room and talking a lot with George," Melba recalled. "We'd get to talking about how we was raised and the times we had when we was kids and everything. George just really seemed to enjoy that 'cause those are things that a lot of people, especially someone that hasn't lived that way or wasn't raised that way, wouldn't know about. He really enjoyed going back to his childhood days and growing up and things that happened to him years back. I'm sure he didn't get much of a chance out on the road all the time to just relax, sit, and really talk to someone."

George enjoyed those chats with Melba; he was wishing he had more time to sit around and "jaw." By then, the road life, the parties, the drinking and bar-hopping had begun to take their toll. "I was tired of waking up sick and having people talk about me," George would later reflect. "The headaches and hangovers were pure hell. I needed help. There comes a time in everybody's life when they need help."

Unfortunately, George came to his newfound realizations a bit too late. He had burned a lot of bridges; he had ignored his family too long. George had lived his twenties as though there was no tomorrow. His thirties were to be an era of retribution for his careless ways and unresolved inner conflicts. Between 1964 and 1969 George began to face that he had a wife who no longer cared about him and that he barely knew his own children. Then, in 1967, his daddy nearly died. Not until that crisis in his life did George realize how important his daddy had been to him. Only after being slapped in the face with these new understandings did George come to accept that, while he had garnered success, money, and a long string of good times, he was as emotionally empty at thirty-five as he had been the day he had gone off to join the Marines nearly fifteen years earlier.

13
I Woke Up from Dreaming

BY THE TIME Shirley and George celebrated their tenth wedding anniversary they were strangers living in the same house. Affection from one for the other was rarely displayed. One knew little of what the other was thinking or feeling; neither did one give the other any indication that he or she cared. "I remember one evening me and W. T. were over there at their house," recalled Helen Scroggins, "and George come in, and she hadn't seen him in weeks. He walked over to her and tried to kiss her, and she wouldn't let him kiss her. She turned her head. I seen her do that lots of times." Shirley defended her indifference toward George by stating, "George would be gone for six months, then come in and never so much as say hello. The kinfolks would be here, and he'd be more interested in talking to them. He wouldn't speak to me."

George was proud and preoccupied. Shirley was wounded and resentful. Instead of calling a truce and asking forgiveness of each other for their past sins, they became embittered. Each wanted to hurt the other. Both were more concerned with their own individual pain than with that of their spouse. Shirley began looking else-where for love and George took to the bottle.

When they had first started out together they had longed for the day when financial hardship was no longer the paramount con-cern of their lives. It was one of the reasons George had been so willing to work so hard and the reason Shirley had accepted the lonely stretches of isolation. But they were to discover that financial security did not bring happiness because no other aspect of their marriage had been nurtured or cared for. Consequently, their marriage drifted along for years after they stopped caring for one another.

George and Shirley's financial existence became easier in 1970. "Then we bought a little house there in Vidor [suburb of Beau-mont]," recalled Shirley. "Bryan was a little baby. That was the best time of our lives together." It was also the beginning of the end. For after that calm, when George returned to his philander-ing ways, Shirley came to the conclusion that he would never change. Then she forever severed her emotional ties with George. "After that I just wished he would make the money and send it home and him stay wherever he was at," she gloomily admitted.

If she had left him then, perhaps so much of the ugliness and the hurt that each inflicted on the other during those ensuing years would not have occurred. But she stayed, resentfully embedded in what she considered to be her hell-on-earth trap. Her own unhap-piness begot others' unhappiness. She even began to resent others' happiness, especially George's. And she became determined to find a little of her own, whatever the cost.

Her affection for George's friend and business associate, J. C. Arnold, began gradually, like the formation of an icicle. At first there was a mutual attraction. She was lonely. He was widowed. They lived in the same small town, and they saw each other frequently. Not by choice, at least not in the beginning, but because George rented a building from J. C., which housed the "George Jones Chuck Wagon" restaurant.

"That is when J. C. began to get into Shirley's panties," pro-claimed Gordon Baxter. "It was when the family was drawn together in the common business of the restaurant. George was on the road all the time and, well, things happen."

Ironically, the ultraconservative, small-town members found little fault with Shirley when the word got around about the two. "I don't know how Shirley put up with what George was doing for as long as she did," reflected one townsman. Not even George's family members could pass judgment on Shirley. "Shirley had a lot of room to feel hard toward George," related W. T. Scroggins. "She was always getting a phone call from some woman or a letter telling her what day [the other woman] had been with George. Then one called Shirley one time and said she was pregnant with George's kid. You just shuffle it all around. That's kind of hard for a woman to swallow." Helen concurred. "I knew George was doing the same thing," she reflected. "You can't run one down when the other is just as bad."

Shirley's interest in J. C. may have also been sparked by George's apparent fondness for Melba Montgomery. Shirley had accepted his sleeping around as best as any woman could, as long as the other women remained anonymous. But when she became convinced that George was developing a real affection toward Melba, she could no longer contain her resentment.

"I heard about how they carried on together," touted Shirley, referring to the rumors that would float in from the road. But Melba vehemently denied any wrongdoing. "Shirley's problem wasn't me," Melba proclaimed. "There wasn't anything going on like that between George and me. Shirley's problems were them roadies." Nonetheless, Shirley only knew that she wasn't receiving the affection she needed from George.

What happened next between George and Shirley was the subject of many rumors and allegations whispered behind the closed doors of Beaumont. One story alleged that George not only found Shirley and J. C. together but that George actually shot at J. C. But one thing was for sure—something dreadful happened between George and Shirley in 1964. That year marked their marital demise. Neither was very kind to the other after that point.

"Dr. Smith [the local doctor] said it was a fact that George did shoot on them," said Helen Scroggins. J. C. Arnold denies any such happening. "I've never been shot in my life," he proclaimed. He further denied having an affair with Shirley. "She's never done anything wrong in her life."

George and Shirley tried to carry on as though nothing had happened. But after that night, George was never the same. His drunken sprees turned dark and unruly. "It looked like after that when he come home he got mad as soon as he got home," observed W. T. Scroggins. "There was several years there I didn't have no trouble with George. He would come in drunk, but he didn't get really mad. Then, all of a sudden, he wouldn't come in unless he was drunk. I'd have to catch him and sober him up to send him back. It got to be a routine."

Nor would George talk about what happened with anyone. He seemed ashamed and embarrassed. The closest he came to opening up was with W. T. Scroggins a few weeks after the incident. W. T. had gone to find George to sober him up. W. T. recalled that on this night George was particularly resistant to going home. "I want to tell you the reason that I ain't going to go to the house," W. T. recalled George as saying. "You needn't start on me 'cause I'm not going to go up to that house and be a husband. I'll sleep by myself. When I find out if any woman is in the bed with another man, that just turns me off. I don't have any use for her."

But in his usual quiet and determined manner, W. T. helped his young brother-in-law up from his stupor and guided George to the house. "Shirley was gone to town, and he went in and took a bath and cleaned up," W. T. recalled. "I messed around for a while. I didn't pay too much attention to George 'cause he was drunk. He had a fifth setting between his legs. But from then on, nearly every time George was coming home, Shirley would get a call that he was drunk. A lot of times she would call me and want me and Helen to come over there."

So George kept his anger pent up, and it festered in him like the heat in the core of a nuclear plant, ready to slip out through the slightest crack. He was emotionally torn and confused. The singer wanted to go home, but his manly pride would not let him enter the doorway without causing a scene. Sometimes he threw a table. At other times he crashed dishes. "The first thing he tore up was the brand-new sewing machine he had just bought Shirley," remembered Helen. "I got to where I wouldn't leave anything out," noted Shirley. "He'd tear up everything. I got to where I was scared of George." One time he even slapped her. "The only time she ever told me that George was physical with her was when George was playing a gig somewhere," said J. C. Arnold, whom Shirley later married. "I think he was at Magnolia Gardens in Houston. He was up on the stage singing, and when he got down he was writing autographs. He came to the car, and Shirley was signing autographs. There was this one guy that George thought was flirting with her, which he probably was. But George slapped her that day. That's the only time she told me that George physically hit her. The rest of the time when he wanted to get mad or something he would come in and tear up the house."

Actually, George shouldn't have been so surprised if Shirley had had an affair in the aftermath of all the rumors she had heard about him. But from where George had come, the rules for women were very different from those guiding the men. Heads of households were to govern their women. "The prevalent social crime in the Thicket is wife-beating," mused Gordon Baxter. "An old saying that you will hear in the Thicket is never to hit a woman except with the flat of your hand. Furthermore, women are to take their punishment in silence and in perfect obedience to their husbands. What's expected of the women is that [their husband's misconduct] is not mentioned. They're not supposed to take any kind of action."

Changing mores and codes were passing George by. Better economic times were enabling young women to be educated and subsequently to question the subservient role they had traditionally played. Because of instant communication by way of television and radio, Shirley was not ignorant of a new mode of thinking. She, too, wanted happiness. "George needed to find somebody like his mother Clara," George's childhood baby-sitter, Katy Hooks, wisely observed. "But women nowadays just don't put up with what they once did. They don't have to."

Clara's only hope, as was most of the women of her ancestry, was to wait for her husband's eventual redemption. Then and only then were the Big Thicket women rewarded for their long suffering and patience. For Big Thicket custom placed the burden of leading their men to the holy altar squarely and heavily upon the women's shoulders. By example, the women were to lead their wayward husbands. And they clung to their righteousness like a dehydrated cowboy to a water pouch. For without their belief they had no hope. Their faith gave them strength and courage in the shadow of overwhelming grievances and trials. "Someday each of the women hoped that her man would quit drinking and quit screwing around and come to church and die in the arms of Jesus," explained Gordon.

Shirley was not as long-suffering as Clara. Justifiably, she wanted her rewards before old age left her with nothing but sad memories. "I tried to get him help," offered Shirley, who continued to stay with George in spite of his tantrums. "But it didn't work out. One time when I was wanting a divorce he checked himself into a neurological hospital, and when a friend went to visit George they found him hiding in the bushes. He told the friend he couldn't take it. I finally decided George had some basic emotional problems. A doctor said he had the biggest Napoleon complex he had ever seen."

In 1967, they purchased a small ranch outside Beaumont, as though a change of scenery might wipe out disruptive memories. George entertained himself with the purchase of farm animals, horses, and equipment. They also bought a little getaway place in Florida. But George's anger and drinking remained. Shirley kept talking divorce. In 1968 George agreed. "Let me tell you why George decided he wanted a divorce," insisted Shirley. "He left Beaumont. He was in Nashville with Bill Starnes [Jack Starnes' son]. They were going to start a new recording company. I'd been trying for two or three years to get a divorce, and George would always end up talking me out of it. I screwed around and never got the divorce. I just gave up. I said I would stay home and mind my own business. Then he came home one day and decided he wanted a divorce because he was fixing to start a recording company and all that stuff in Nashville. He didn't want me to be able to get any of it. I think somebody talked him into that."

Actually George's reasons for wanting a divorce from Shirley were far more complicated and numerous than just wanting to hold on to assets. By then he had met Tammy Wynette. His feelings toward Shirley had been dead for years. And Tammy stirred in him emotions he had thought impossible. "I was always in love with Tammy," George would later admit. At first he had been attracted to Tammy's voice on the radio. But after meeting Tammy, his feelings had turned into something else again. Tammy was energetic, gentle, and eager to please, while Shirley seemed lackluster in comparison.

"Shirley is really a fine woman," observed Gordon Baxter. "Everybody agrees to that. But George had to go on down the road and didn't want to bring her. I'm sure that George always had the feeling that he had one kind of existence here in Vidor with Shirley and the kids, and he was playing the local clubs, and his records were doing pretty good locally. Then he wanted to go to Nashville. But he knew Nashville was going to be so intense, and it was going to be the big time and was going to spoil whatever small-time family he had. This happens a lot. I think he knew she wasn't going to be good enough when she got to Nashville. These are the things you know deep down in your heart that you ain't never going to tell anybody, that when he got there he was going to be picking up a lot of really high-class stuff and that if he ever was going to get another wife, she was going to be a whole lot classier than Shirley. He sure didn't want the kids hanging around. This is like a snake shedding its skin a size larger. You just leave it there in the last yard you were in and go on down the road to the next place where you're going to be a bigger snake—still a snake but a different size. You just instinctively know this from having seen it happen a lot to other people. When a guy really does become a super-something there is the fracture of the original family with damn few exceptions. So old George might not have thought it all the way through, but it's just a fact ol' Shirley wouldn't have fit in with his new life in Nashville."

When the split finally came after fourteen years of marriage George tried to be fair with Shirley. She kept their modest house in Vidor plus two adjoining lots on either side. George retained possession of the Florida house. He also gave her $100,000 in cash over the last two years for the support of Bryan and Jeffrey. George sold the ranch house for a reported $45,000 and reinvested that money in a tour bus. "All the money we had when I got that divorce in savings or anything was $5,000," Shirley added.

She may have been cash poor at the time of the divorce, but she was certainly asset well-to-do, because, as part of the settlement, she was assigned the royalties for the songs George had written up to that time. "The reason I wanted that was because I thought if anything happened to him right away before I collected the child support, I could have probably collected some money off those old songs," Shirley reasoned.

In retrospect, she has concluded she deserved the royalty payments as much as George would have. "I helped him work on all of them," Shirley claimed with a touch of haughtiness. "And George didn't write a lot of those songs he took credit for. He didn't write 'Ragged But Right.' Darrell Edwards probably sold it to him. Darrell Edwards wrote most of those songs. He killed himself. Now, don't misunderstand me. George reworked lots of those songs. He'd change the music or arrange them. He changed them some, but he got half of the rights. He wrote 'Window Up Above' because we had just bought our first little house here in Vidor. He sat in the house and wrote that song on a tape recorder, and he sang it over and over. He wrote 'Why, Baby, Why?' I helped him write that one. I helped him write a lot. That's really why I took half of those songs."

So they parted, George and Shirley, going their own ways. George migrated to Nashville, and Shirley stayed in Vidor, the place she had sworn as a little girl she would never live. And as their individual lives moved forward through the funnel of time, they rarely glanced backward to what they had had. "I told him he could come here anytime he wanted," Shirley added, as though an afterthought. "But he never set foot in this house after the divorce. I thought he might at least have wanted to come back to see the boys. But you know George; he thinks about what he's doing at the moment and little else."

CHAPTER
14
World's Worst Loser

S IF FATE hadn't thrown George a severe enough pitch in 1964, it threw him an even swifter and more hard-hitting toss in 1965. His daddy nearly died from a stroke, and even though he survived, his doctors gave him less than six months to live.

Upon hearing about his daddy's impending death, George was invaded by guilt like worms permeating an apple. There was little he could do to prevent his daddy's demise. Regardless, he felt guilty. Vapors of guilt hovered when George thought of all the fun he had been having, much to the exclusion of the family, the people who meant everything to him. He felt guilty about his success, his marriage, his money, even his singing. But he could no more express his guilt in a healthy way than he had expressed rage toward his wife. Weakly and conveniently, he once again turned to the bottle.

According to Rick Blackburn, vice-president of CBS Records in Nashville, guilt is a standard accruement of a country music singer's personality. "There's something that runs true to entertainers and performers, particularly if an entertainer comes out of a low-income, almost borderline-on-poverty background," Rick explained. "As their success comes and their financial means is elevated, it's almost like a guilt trip for them. I've seen it happen to a lot of artists. It's like they feel they don't deserve it. There's a guilt trip that sets in because usually the friends back home, or certainly the family, have not been able to enjoy the kind of fame and success that comes with power and money."

Understandably, the Big Thicket had been structured in such a way so that its members could emotionally and mentally accept never-ending poverty. Few Big Thicketers were prosperous. Success and wealth were practically unheard-of achievements. Thus Big Thicketers were content to live humbly, drawing their satisfactions from planes much more elusive and mystical than material fulfillments. "The great Big Thicket claim is that I've done it for the love of it," explained Diane Baxter. "Lord knows that money is not important to them. To work for money just doesn't fit in with who they are. Maybe the concept originated in their need to have control and to know that they could not be bought. They like to think they are above all that."

"I don't write my books for money," further explained Gordon, author of several books about the Big Thicket. "I write for love. I believe that, if I'm good enough, then the money comes in. But as a Big Thicketer, I wouldn't just go out and sing for money or write for money. I'd be doing it because I'm a performer, because the stories are in me, the songs are in me, and they have to come out. You see, royalty doesn't do things because they have to have the money to do it. That behavior is beneath them.

"According to Big Thicket standards, being a professional musician is such an enviable place that it's treated like a form of priesthood. No priest ever went into religion for money. Just because it's a safe, secure profession all the rest of your life is not the reason a kid would go to a seminary. He goes to the seminary because he's been deeply smitten by the love of God and call of God. For the same reason, country music musicians have got to put in this long, wearisome apprenticeship in miserable dives where there's little money circulating, sort of to prove that the reason that they are staying with it during those years is 'cause they love it. The reason George went to Neva's and hung on that stage, hoping that somebody was going to ask him to come up onstage and sit in with them, was because he loved the music."

Even before his daddy's illness George was demonstrating an inability to handle financial success. He sometimes spent money foolishly, as if he were trying to rid himself of part of it. "He would blow money before he made it," reminisced Shirley, "He'd buy buses and cars. He traded cars sixteen times in one year. He sold $50,000 worth of quarter horses for $10,000. That's where a lot of George's money went."

But his daddy's illness brought to a head the financial guilt. It made him realize that his daddy would never enjoy the same kind of financial bliss. George's guilt was compounded because he had for so long actually wished his daddy ill. At the time he had had the hateful thoughts, George had been convinced he was justified in fostering the resentment toward his daddy. After all, hadn't his daddy inflicted grief and suffering galore on his mama? How many times had she run out the back door, disgusted and even somewhat frightened by her husband's drunken ranting and raving? This was the man who had intimidated him as a child into standing for hour after hour singing one song after another until he had thought his legs would fold and he would wet his britches. But now that his daddy was facing death, George felt only shame and disgust that he could have had such thoughts.

In his own guilt-infected way, George sought to make restitution with his daddy. He figured he could do that by destroying a little of his financial kingdom. He wanted to prove to himself and his family that he didn't need any of those things after all. George surely would have been better off reconciling his inner conflicts, accepting that wealth can be had without compromising integrity or his values. But the dictates of the Big Thicket had been deeply instilled. George's recourse was to eradicate rather than to resolve.

"George was hurt 'cause no amount of money could help his daddy a bit in the world," continued Helen. "So George wanted to destroy part of what he had. He wanted to get hisself back down to the level of his daddy."

His harbored guilt thundered forth the morning after he was told about his daddy's impending death. George Jones wasn't able to handle either the pain or the guilt. "The night before I had went to the hospital to get George," recollected W. T. Scroggins. "He sat right there at my table and cussed his daddy with the old man down there nearly dying. But the next morning George was drunk. He had tore down every fence, run through the car shed, tore all the fences down. All of his horses got out. George run through the barn and everything else. The ranch hands called me and told me that I was going to have to come out there and do something about him. They said, 'He's going to kill hisself.' I got in my truck and went out there, and that Cadillac wasn't as broad as this table. He'd knocked off all the fenders, the doors, and everything. The horses were everywhere. He found out I was acoming, and he run in there to the house and got on the couch and turned his face to the couch. I walked in there, and I said something to him, and he just snored. He had on his cowboy boots and his feet were hanging off, so I slipped a foot up on his leg and just flipped him a somersault on the floor. I told him, 'Boy, I ought to stomp you right here in the floor.'

"I thought he was drunk," confessed W. T. "I had gone to see about it and do something with him. I carried him out on the porch and showed him what he'd done. He was just as sober as I was. I told him, 'Boy, you ought to be ashamed. You ought to be whooped just like a mule.' I said, 'I'm having enough trouble trying to help your daddy and all, and you're out here tearing everything up.'

"He walked just as straight and told all them boys what to do and told them to call the carpenter and have him fix all that fence and call the wrecker and have them get that car, and he wasn't a bit more drunk than I was. I said, 'George, just tell me what you done it for.' He said, 'I just done it, is all I know. I just done it.' I said, 'Well, you had to have a reason to do it. Who done something to you?' He said, 'Nobody done nothing to me.' I just went on, but I guess that one collision that he done cost him $10,000 before it was all settled."

George's guilt did not cease after his morning tirade. But after that massive explosion his outbursts were of a more tranquil nature. "W. T. and me had George in that old pickup truck of ours going to visit Daddy some days later," recounted Helen. "An old pickup is all we had. I was joking with George. I said, 'George, you're just laughing 'cause the old truck is making so much racket.

It may be old and raggedy, but it'll get us there.' Oh, my God, I could have been throwing bombs at him. He just started crying. He said, 'I ain't better than anybody. Everybody tries to think I'm better than they are. Even Mama and Daddy thinks I'm better than they are. I ain't better than nobody. I ain't as good as they are.' George don't want you to think that he's better than anybody. That breaks his heart if he thinks you do."

George Washington went on to live nearly another two years. It was time enough for him to make amends with his son, the world, and prepare to meet his Savior, Jesus Christ. Without a word spoken, George Washington made peace with Clara, quit drinking and cussing, and even returned to church. He followed Big Thicket law to the letter. In return, his soul was assured of eternal peace. No one questioned or marveled at his miraculous turnaround. For the law was written. Disobedience was unthinkable.

George Glenn did his part at making amends with his daddy in those last days. Again, the law was written. "George was startin' to make a little money there in 1965," recalled Helen. "And George built Mama and Daddy a little house. Daddy was so tickled about that house. Most of his life, Daddy knew that, if he didn't make enough money to pay the apartment rent, he had to get out. Then George built them that house. Daddy didn't drink much from then on 'cause he had a home. He kept that place tip-top."

George Washington died peacefully on September 7, 1967. "Daddy was aworkin' on his car, and the next day he died," recalled Helen. From all accounts, he died happy, perhaps the happiest he had been since the death of his dear Ethel nearly forty-two years earlier. His own impending death had at last put Ethel's death in proper perspective.

Amazingly enough, George's career did not miss a beat in spite of his emotional turmoil in the mid- and late 1960s. To the contrary, he continued to have numerous hits, including "When the Grass Grows Over Me" in 1967 and "I'll Share My World with You" in 1968. He had changed record labels in 1964, again following record executive Art Talmadge, who left United Artists to form Musicor. "Musicor offered me a great deal," George later told a reporter. "I couldn't resist."

Eventually, however, George grew weary of his Musicor association. There were several reasons for George's disenchantment. First of all, he was bone tired. His fifteen years on the road had worn both his stamina and nerves thin. His personal problems had exhausted him further. Neither did he any longer have the motivation of a young eager singer starting out. He was successful. He had little left to prove. Because of his daddy's illness, he had also come to realize that his family life was more important to him than his profession.

But George's primary disillusionment with Talmadge, Daily, and Musicor was his belief that they no longer were concerned with the quality of his records. He complained tartly. "I was bitter over the way they treated me," said George. "My sessions were never mixed, and Pappy Daily was not a producer or an A & R man. All he did was sit in the studio and keep time with his stopwatch. He would handle the paperwork. Me and the musicians, and I worked with some of the best then, would get the songs, go over them, work out the arrangements on the spot, and then record. We cut at the old [Owen] Bradley's studio. There were good engineers on the sessions, but no one supervised the mixing. That is a big regret of mine. Those were the prime years, and those sessions sounded much better than they do on record.

"When we finished the sessions, Mr. Daily would say, 'Put it on tape as best as you can, gentlemen. Send me a seven-and-a-half-inch reel and send another to Musicor.' No one ever went over my tapes to get the right voice or instrument levels. Often the music drowned me out and I sounded like one of the background singers."

George's concerns were real. Several of the recordings were inferior to his earlier work. But he retained his popularity even though his record sales were reflecting a career plateau for him.

All in all, George Jones was a fairly disillusioned fellow toward the end of that decade. He had lost his daddy and forfeited a wife. His career was in a lull. George headed to Nashville because he figured there was nothing left for him in Texas. Besides, George was a sucker for believing that the grass is greener on the other side. Nashville's lights were shining for George. And an attractive blonde by the name of Tammy Wynette had caught both his eye and his ear.

15

Your Angel Steps Out of Heaven

IRGINIA WYNETTE PUGH, later to be known by millions as Tammy Wynette, was a war baby, destined to make a few rumblings of her own. She was born on May 5, 1942, eleven years before her future husband, George Jones. Five months before her birth, almost to the day, the Japanese had bombed Pearl Harbor and the United States had been drawn into a world war that had already been raging on other parts of the globe for nearly three years. The times were troubling, but under the guidance of President Franklin D. Roosevelt, the American people felt strong.

Tammy was to be as reflective of the times into which she was born as George was of his. The United States in 1942 seemed hardly the same nation as when George had been born in 1931. She was as aggressive and assertive as George was passive and humble. Tammy was determined to take life's bull by the horns. George moved aside in the face of adversity and confusion. She was filled with hopes and dreams. George had none. He lived life one day at a time.

"Virginia" was a ball of fire from the day she popped in. She was the product of a long line of hearty, robust, English-Irishmen who had settled in Itawamba County, Mississippi. They had been strong-willed and hard-working souls who had cleared a six-hundred-acre farm by the sweat of their brows. Her maternal granddaddy had even built the wood frame farmhouse that stood in the midst of the property. They were proud country folk, who had made their way through the darkest and worst of times without asking for handouts or pity.

Her fate was to grow up without a father. When she was born, Hollis Pugh was already dying of a brain tumor. He died when she was nine months old. She had no memory of him, of course, but he did leave her a legacy. "I was told all my life of how great my father was in music and I was told all my life that he wanted me in music if I wanted to," Tammy recalled. "That always stuck in the back of my mind." Sometimes, when she thought about what he must have been like, she gazed at his guitar, mandolin, accordian, and bass fiddle, or listened to one of the records he had recorded on his own. It was her intense desire to please the father she had never known. "When I'd go someplace and sing," Tammy later mused, "I knew that he would have wanted me to have done that, even if my mother or somebody else was against it."

She soon realized that she had a musical gift, and at the age of ten, began taking piano lessons. The lessons continued until the piano teacher told Mrs. Pugh that the lessons were a waste of time and money. "He told my mama that I'd listen to what he played and then go home and play the way I wanted to play it," Tammy remembered. "I learned just to read enough to know what key something was played in, and if I wanted to sing it there, okay. Or if it was too high, I lowered it to something else. I played songs the way I thought I heard it. I played strictly by ear." The Pughs were religious folk and devoted Southern Baptists, who regularly attended the small Providence Baptist church near their home. It was a small congregation, with only thirty or thirty-five people in attendance, but Virginia enjoyed going regardless of the small numbers.

"I played for Sunday school every Sunday from the time I was ten years old until I left home at about seventeen," she reminisced.

"I sang solos, trios, and duets. We'd go around to various churches singing for their services. I'd sing with our group on Sunday night and Wednesday nights. We had curtains in the back that divided off the areas for Sunday school classes. It was just one big room. I also went to the Oak Grove Church of God because my daddy's people were [from the] Church of God. I enjoyed going there more than Providence because they let members bring guitars, drums, and stuff like that so we could really sing and make lots more noise." Certainly if Virginia's father had lived, he would have been proud of his daughter.

Perhaps it was Virginia Pugh's passion for making a lot of noise that led her into the musical fold of Hank Williams, who was making quite a sensation in the mid-1950s with his rather unorthodox brand of country music, a style of music that challenged the stodgy and staid nature of traditional music. "I can remember going to bed so many nights listening to his music," recollected Tammy. "After working in the fields, I'd go to bed and I'd have a small Mickey Mouse record player that I'd set in a straight chair right beside my bed and I'd put on Hank Williams albums that have the yellow center and there was one song on there, I'd play over and over, 'No One Will Ever Know.' That was always my favorite song. I'd lie on my stomach sleeping, and I'd take my finger and scratch the needle back to the beginning and I'd play it over and over 'til I went to sleep. I just idolized Hank Williams. He was always my hero. He was just it."

But Hank Williams's music reflected a very different kind of life from what Virginia Wynette Pugh knew while growing up. Her mother remarried in 1946, while Virginia was only four, and moved to Memphis to live with her new husband. The little girl stayed on in Mississippi to be raised by her maternal grandparents. She became part of the Southern rural community where hard work and discipline were the golden rules. "Everybody had to work hard," she recalled, almost forty years later. "It was unbelievably hard. We'd get up at four A.M. and cook supper before we'd go to the fields, and we'd leave for the fields at 5:30 A.M.—no later—and we'd be in the fields by 6 o'clock. We didn't stop 'til noon. Sometimes, we'd find a wild watermelon growing in the field and we'd stop long enough to bust that watermelon and eat it with our hands. We'd go on until 12 or 12:30 and we'd stop and eat our potted meat that we'd have stuffed in a little bag and we'd carry ice water and wrap newspaper around it to keep the ice from melting, to keep it cold. We'd eat that and start right back. We'd take maybe thirty minutes off and work until the sun went down. Lord, we'd sit out there and pray for it to rain or for a big cloud to cover the sun so it'd be a little cooler.

"Everybody lived pretty much the same," Tammy continued. "My family wasn't richer or poorer than anybody else. Everybody had the same amount of money, the same things. Everybody did the same thing. Hard work was expected for everybody to do. I was lucky because being the only child and the only grandchild, I got to reap more. Most of the families had ten or twelve children. They had so little at Christmastime. I never had a bad Christmas. I can't remember ever just getting a pair of shoes or something like that. We always had a great Christmas because I was the only one to buy for. But otherwise, we all lived pretty much the same."

Pleasures for a young, southern rural girl growing up in the fifties were sparse. Mamas wanted their daughters to be "nice girls" above all else, even at the cost of stifling adventuresome spirits. "We worked every day in the field from sun up to sun down and then have only half a day off on Saturdays," recalled Tammy. "We'd go to town and then Mama [her grandmother] wouldn't let us do anything. She wouldn't let us hang out on the corner because that's where all the bad girls hung out. She wouldn't let me sit in the car with anybody. So we'd go to the drugstore and stay a little while and have a cherry Coke and that's it. I was sick to death of it all. By seventeen, the most important thing on my mind was leaving home, getting away from home and being my own boss. All of my close girlfriends felt the same way. We wanted to get away from our mamas and dads, get away from the farms and be totally different. We were all told what to do by our parents. There was no talking back, there was no second guessing them on what to do, we just did not say 'I don't want to' or 'I can't.' You did what they said do and you never questioned it. I think we all felt that when we got away from home, it would be totally different, that we could be our own bosses and we could do just what we wanted to do."

But the women's liberation movement was yet another decade away. Young women in the rural south did not up and leave home on their own, unless they were willing to run the risk of acquiring a tainted reputation. Freedom was another word for getting married.

"I thought if I left home and got married, I'd have a whole different life," reminisced Tammy. "Boy, getting married was it, that was the only way to get a house and get away from everything we didn't like. At seventeen, I wasn't ambitious. I didn't know anything I wanted to do. About all the women did around there was work in a garment factory of some kind or shoe factory or work for the lunchroom or some kind of Head Start or work on the farm. That's about all there was to do there. Being a factory worker was the highest you could get. I don't care what kind of education you've got. There was no need in getting any because there's nothing else to do except farm, work in a garment factory or shoe factory. I knew I loved to sing, but I didn't think about people getting paid to sing. Until the day my granddaddy died, he didn't understand how I could make money singing. He never understood that."

At seventeen, Virginia had had only one thing on her mind—getting married. "I thought I'd live in a little house of my own, have kids and have a husband who worked eight or nine hours and would come home and I'd have dinner ready when he came home. That's exactly what I thought. I didn't think I'd have to work too or that I might end up starving nearly to death or that he might not work or that I would live in a shack. I just thought that when I left home and got married, somebody would take me to a little house and say 'this is yours' and that was it."

For Virginia Wynette Pugh, finding a husband was an easy accomplishment. She was popular, a member of the Trenton High School band. The dark-haired Virginia was already a well-developed young woman, tall enough to play basketball, yet feminine enough to be a homecoming queen. Being in the small town limelight, she quickly caught the eye of many young suitors. But Virginia chose an older boy, Euple Byrd, a good-looking, virile young chap who was just home from the Marines. When he initially proposed marriage, Virginia was a little reluctant. But after a battle of wills with her mother, young seventeen-year-old Virginia decided she was ready to be her own boss. Shrouded in a thick cloud of false pride and youthful arrogance, Virginia marched out the door of her family home in late 1959, convinced she was going to prove to her family that she would triumph over all.

Of course, nothing worked out as she had planned. She had two children within three years. Gwendolyn Lee was born April 15, 1961, and then on August 2, 1962, Jacquelyn Fay arrived. Her new husband was frequently out of work. Often, they didn't have enough to eat. They lived in a succession of delapidated shacks. By the time she was 21, she was pregnant with a third child. "I definitely felt that life had not done for me what it could have done," recalled Tammy. "I don't know what I thought I deserved but it was certainly more than what I had at 21 with a third child on the way."

With her marriage on the rocks, Virginia and her two daughters went to live with her grandmother in Birmingham, Alabama. She had already attended a beautician's school during the early days of her marriage, so she drew on that schooling to earn a beautician's certificate which enabled her to work in a Birmingham beauty salon.

Still, she hoped for a better life. "When Tina's and Jackie's father left and I went to Birmingham to live with my grandmother, I talked about how much I loved singing," reminisced Tammy. Mama [her paternal grandmother] would always say, 'You sing better than the girls I hear on the radio, so why don't you do it, you can do it.' Mama's pushing really motivated me to go and try. All my life if I was told something was impossible for me to do, I tried so hard to prove it could be done."

Even though she was pregnant, Virginia auditioned and succeeded in clinching a singing spot on a local Birmingham morning TV show, "The Country Boy Eddie Show." "I was pregnant at the time and they'd only film me from the waist up," recalled Tammy. "They didn't like that. I liked to have never gotten the job because I was pregnant. But working on that show was when I really started thinking that I could sing professionally. That really gave me the bug because we traveled some. It was only in the state of

Alabama, traveling with 'Country Boy Eddie,' going out and opening up shopping centers and things like that, but I got a taste of what it could be like to do that for a living."

After the birth of her third child, Denise, in late 1965, Virginia set her sights on going to Nashville, where she knew she had to be in order to break into country music. "When I was told I could not go to Nashville, that I was stupid, that I was a Mississippi farm girl who didn't know the city ways and who wouldn't even know how to take care of myself, I was bound and determined to show somebody that I could. Me and the kids almost starved to death those first few months there. But I wanted so hard to prove to the people at home, my family and friends in Mississippi that you could do something else other than have to be a farmer or a factory worker. It was almost an obsession to get away from that way of life. I just had to do something else. I just knew there had to be a better way of life."

So, in 1966, Virginia quit her beautician's job, which she had kept while singing on the TV show, packed up her three small children and few belongings, and headed for Nashville. Years later, she would say that it was ignorance and stupidity that enabled her to go. "I didn't know any better," she later reflected. "I just hung in there when I didn't know any better."

16
A Good Year for Roses

HEN VIRGINIA Wynette Pugh Byrd, soon to be Tammy Wynette, strutted into Nashville in 1966, the country music industry was in the midst of tumultuous change. Power was in the process of being transferred from one generation of leaders to another. Country music was on the verge of appealing to an increasingly wider audience and was about to break out of its traditional mold. Many in Nashville saw the potential. Predictably, the old guard was resistant. "Country music will be destroyed," they feared. But amid the construction sounds of a new $270-million Opryland complex and the jingling of the cash registers, their protests were quickly muted.

Grand Ole Opry founder George D. Hay had defined country music back in the 1920s by laying down the law "Keep it simple, boys." It was music indigenous to the rural South. The songs were poignant tales of tragedies based on stern, Calvinist morals. Early recordings featured the fiddle and guitar as lead instruments over a rhythmic foundation provided by guitar or banjo. Other instruments occasionally used included dulcimer, harmonica, and mandolin. Vocals were done either by a single voice or in high close harmony.

Country music was somewhat popularized during and following World Was II due to the migration of farmers and rural people into the industrialized towns and cities. Naturally, the music came under new influences. But the purist breeding remained a strong ingredient. Then, in the 1950s and 1960s, country music's appeal widened, due mostly to the swiveling hips of a poor, young, Mississippi boy named Elvis Presley. And the gap between country music and the mainstream of popular music narrowed. Still, there had been a resiliant force in Nashville that had resisted the change. As a result, the power of the purists was being wrenched away from them.

The new Opryhouse and adjoining complex perhaps symbolized the changes most of all. Construction on the park began in 1970 and wasn't completed until 1974. The multimillion-dollar auditorium, with its lush seats, elaborate sound and lighting systems, and technically advanced TV studios, was in stark contrast to the Opry's former home, the delapidated Ryman Auditorium. "I knew something had to be done," reflected WSM's president, Irving Waugh. "The Ryman didn't have air conditioning, and people kept passing out during the summer months because of the heat." Street bums commonly slept on its steps, and occasionally someone wondered if the entire structure was on the verge of crumbling.

Chet Atkins, the famous guitarist and head of operations for RCA Records in Nashville during the late 1950s until the early 1980s, has been credited with bringing about much of the change in Nashville's musical style. "Atkins set out to broaden the scope of country music," according to *The Illustrated History of Country Music*, "adding a fuller, lusher sound—which was, of course, to become part of the Nashville sound—to country recordings in the hopes of making them broadly palatable. His method had a twofold purpose and result. He succeeded in expanding the production values of country music—mainly through the use of strings, horns, and background voices—thereby broadening the potential and actual audience for the music and his work with pop entertainers like Perry Como and Al Hirt convinced New York and Los

Angeles record men that Nashville musicianship had something of value to offer noncountry performers."

Another warlord stood on the horizon, however. His name was Billy Sherrill. He didn't appear on the Nashville scene until the early 1960s, but his impact would be felt strongly and envied for the next quarter of a century. He was the son of Alabama evangelists, and he had played piano during their meetings while growing up. He arrived in Nashville by way of Memphis, where he had apprenticed with Sam Phillips, one of the originators of rockabilly. "Phillips was one of the pioneer crossover producers," *The Illustrated History of Country Music* stated, "and much of his attitude and many of his techniques impressed Sherrill. Moving to Epic Records [a division of CBS], Sherrill produced a wide range of music from the bluegrass of Jim and Jesse to the black gospel of the Staples Singers. In 1966 he produced David Houston's recording of 'Almost Persuaded,' a song he had written with Glen Sutton (who would later marry and manage Lynn Anderson) and found himself with the No. 1 song of the year. With this Sherrill began an enviable string of hit singles and albums, and within a year he was recognized as one of the most successful and innovative producers in Nashville." Sherrill would eventually produce Charlie Rich, Tanya Tucker, Johnny Paycheck, Barbara Fairchild, Janie Fricke, Lacy J. Dalton, among others. But back in 1966 he just happened to be searching for a female artist. They were, after all, something of a rarity in the country music ranks. Much of Sherrill's genius was his ability to recognize musical trends long before his cohorts.

Country music had traditionally ignored female singers just as the typical country music listener had snubbed the feminine perspective. Kitty Wells began to change that when she broke into the country music charts in the 1950s with tunes like "It Wasn't God Who Made Honky-Tonk Angels," "Paying for That Back Street Affair," "Searching," "Mommy for a Day," and "Amigo's Guitar." In the 1960s Kitty pried open the door a little further with her recordings of "Heartbreak, U.S.A.," "Unloved, Unwanted," "Password," and "You Don't Hear." Loretta Lynn later observed, "I remember how excited I got back in 1953, the first time I heard Kitty Wells sing 'It Wasn't God Who Made Honky-Tonk Angels.'

See, Kitty was presenting the woman's point of view, which was different from the man's."

Patsy Cline came along in the late 1950s and early 1960s with her versions of "Walkin' after Midnight," "I Fall to Pieces," "Crazy," and "She's Got You." Unfortunately, her career was cut short by a fatal plane crash in 1963. But the real breakthrough for women did not come until the late 1960s and early 1970s. Even then, a blessed handful had broken through the barriers. But the female listener was there, and she wanted her feelings expressed. She didn't identify with the bra-burning feminists marching across the nation's college campuses. She still believed in the traditional female role. Loretta Lynn began touching that untapped market throughout the 1960s with "Wine, Women, and Song," "You Ain't Woman Enough," "What Kind of a Girl Do You Think I Am?," "Fist City," then, in 1970, "Coal Miner's Daughter."

Now entered Virginia Byrd, like a character walking into the scene of a very complex play. She was unaware of all of the changes in the music industry, and she hardly cared. She only knew that she wanted a chance to be a singer like a hundred others who had gone to Nashville before her and like the thousands who would follow afterward. The majority would fail, eventually leaving Nashville in despair and lost hope. Virginia would succeed, partly because she had an extraordinary voice, partly because of her determination, but mostly because timing was on her side.

Virginia Byrd met Billy Sherrill after having been cast aside by five other record executives. The last one had referred her to Sherrill. And by the time she walked into Sherrill's office, Virginia was near desperation. She was already living on money borrowed from generous relatives, a source that was quickly running dry while she had the responsibility of feeding three children. "I was still determined to show my family I could do it," she explained. "I wanted to do it so bad. I knew that if I stayed long enough and worked hard enough and tried enough, that I could do it. I knew I could do what the other girls were doing if I had a chance to do it." Sherrill decided to give her that chance. He began by changing her name to Tammy Wynette. "Virginia Pugh Byrd was not the name of a country music star," observed Sherrill. The second step was to find Tammy a hit song.

Sherrill was unique in Nashville at that time because he sought hit singles. The then prevailing attitude was that an established singer would sell a limited but steady number of albums solely on the basis of his personality and fan appeal. But Sherrill was after a bigger audience and knew that the current approach was ill suited for the fickle but more lucrative pop market.

For Tammy, Sherrill selected "Apartment No. 9." It stayed on the national country music charts for nine weeks and tipped in on the forty-third position, a respectable showing for a new artist's first record. Then, in 1967, Sherrill had Tammy record "Your Good Girl's Gonna Go Bad." It soared to number three. That song was followed by an astounding six straight number one hits—"I Don't Wanna Play House," "Take Me to Your World," "D-I-V-O-R-C-E," "Stand By Your Man," "Singin' My Song," and "The Ways to Love a Man." Consequently, Tammy was named Female Vocalist of the Year by the Country Music Association in both 1970 and 1971 and was duly dubbed "The First Lady of Country Music." Tammy had hit Nashville like a storm, and she owed her success to the talents of Billy Sherrill. She sang whatever he selected. She didn't know enough about the business to do much else. "I had no idea then of how a singer could sound like three people," Tammy once reminisced. "Then, after I had done my first recording, Billy Sherrill told me I had to stay and overdub. I had no idea what overdub was but I knew that meant something to do with a record, so I stayed. Then he told me to listen to my voice and sing along with it. I knew what he was talking about then and I understood how singers had done it. But then I had no idea what overdub was. I just knew I was supposed to do it."

Tammy's calculated appeal, at least according to writer Patrick Carr, was that of a woman content with being a suffering, dominated, middle-class housewife. "Such an appeal is nothing new to country music," he stated. "It has been traditional in the music for twenty years. The songs that sold millions for Tammy showed little or no consciousness of the sexual revolution; divorce was something to be dreaded and avoided at all costs—for the children's sake. You stood by your man, even if you had to endure the archaic southern double standard of morality, and having a good man was much more important than any vague notion of self-fulfillment."

Naturally, Tammy quickly developed an intense respect for Sherrill, one of the few men in her life she would hold in such high esteem. "Billy is always right," she asserted. "He's a genius. If he came in and told me to record 'Yankee Doodle,' I'd do it. As a producer, he is without equal. He has an uncanny ear for good material, his own and other people's." There is no question that Sherrill produced hits. He had one of the longest string of hits with a variety of singers in country music history, much to the chagrin of some, who still were convinced that his use of elaborate studio work, which included strings, backup vocals, and even self-harmonization, somehow debased country music. Sherrill would always disagree. "Nobody can ever put down Hank Williams and Hank Snow and Ernest Tubb," Sherrill once reportedly said. "But to say we can't broaden the appeal is ludicrous, ridiculous. I don't think we'll lose our identity. I think our identity will grow with people who can do something with a wider range of lyrics, melodies, and instruments. It doesn't necessarily have to be two guitars and a banjo. I don't think you're losing anything; I think you're gaining something."

Ironically, Sherrill would eventually produce George Jones, one of the reigning country music traditionalists. In the beginning George would resist Sherrill's introduction of strings and backup vocalists on his records. "I went along with him [Sherrill] against my better judgment," George once told writer Nick Tosches. "I didn't wanna do it, but I let them put strings on my sessions just out of curiosity, more or less, just to see what they might do." Eventually George kept quiet, for it is difficult to argue with success, especially the kind George was to have with Billy Sherrill.

CHAPTER
17

Those Were the Good Old Times

TRANGE AS IT MAY SEEM, George Jones and Tammy Wynette were in love with one another before they were introduced. "I was always in love with Tammy," George observed one time. "In fact, I was in love with her before I even met her. I loved her singing." Concurrently, Tammy had fallen in love with George while a young girl growing up in Mississippi. "Tammy loved George Jones, the singer," Joan Dew, co-author of *Stand By Your Man*, noted. "She idolized him. He was the epitome of the great country music singer. What would anybody do if they had a chance to have an affair with their idol? I'm real doubtful about whether she loved George Jones the man."

Their first meeting occurred in 1966, but nothing happened between them until some two years later. George was still married to Shirley, and Tammy was about to remarry, this time to songwriter Don Chapel. Ironically, it was Chapel who introduced Tammy to George. "I had written 'When the Grass Grows over Me,' " recalled Chapel, who at the time had just been signed to

135

Musicor as an artist/writer. "The song became one of George's biggest hits. I took Tammy to one of his recording sessions and introduced her to him."

The Tammy and Don Chapel union was a comfortable relationship, one instigated by need and loneliness more than passion. "When Don asked me to marry him, I knew I wasn't madly in love," admitted Tammy in her book, *Stand By Your Man*. "But I honestly thought it was more important that we were friends. We both had so much in common—both divorced with three children, both trying to make it in the music business—that I thought we could be happy together."

But Tammy was not to have the same luck with love that she was to have with her career. Her expectations of men were far more illusionary and sentimental than her career goals and therefore, less attainable. She had been blessed with a voice, a very good one. Because of her determination, and with the aid of lucky timing, she had been given an opportunity to record. And she had taken advantage of every opportunity along the way. So it was not unrealistic for her to think she might make it as a singer. She had long since proven she had the fortitude. But what she wanted in a man was extraordinary. Tammy wanted a prince, one in armor who would charge in on his white horse and whisk her away to paradise. Unfortunately, Tammy was doomed to be disappointed. As might be expected, her marriage to Chapel was short-lived. Her second marriage wilted just like the first one had.

Following their initial meeting in 1966, George and Tammy saw each other sporadically. Both have claimed their meetings were strictly professional and friendly during the next two years. But the stage was being set for their romance. In 1968, George got divorced from Shirley. It was only a matter of time before they were to admit their fascination with one another.

"I tried to date her, but nothing doing," George recalled. "She had remarried and was living in Nashville with her three children. [But] Tammy was unhappy. Her husband was mean to the kids. One night [in 1968] when I was over to their house he was yelling at the kids. They were running around the house crying. Tammy asked him to stop and he started calling her names. That got all over me! I hauled out and said, 'Just don't talk to Tammy like that. It ain't nice. I don't appreciate it even if this is your home.'

"You could've heard a pin drop!" George continued. "Don looked at me and said, 'George, you better mind your own business. What's this to you?' I replied, 'It is my business. I love her. I love Tammy.' Tammy was just as surprised as her husband, as surprised as me. We had never dated a single time and had never really even been alone. Then I said, 'And she loves me too, don't you, Tammy?' And she said loudly, 'Yes, yes, I do!' And we just grabbed the kids and got out of there."

In a way, they were good for one another then. George had been despondent since his own divorce and desperately needed the love of a woman. Tammy seemed ideal. He loved her singing, and nothing gave him greater pleasure than to sit around and sing with someone he cared about. Of course, Tammy thought her prince had finally arrived. "I didn't know where George was taking me and I didn't care," relived Tammy in her autobiography. "I would have gone anywhere with him. My heart was so full of love for this man I'd worshipped since childhood that I felt as though it would burst in my chest. He had rescued me from a husband I didn't love just like the knight on the white charger saved the captive princess in fairy tales that I'd read as a little girl. The fact that his 'white charger' was a burgundy Cadillac and that he wore cowboy boots instead of shining armor didn't make the impact any less romantic. I wanted to bask in the safety of his arms forever, and I would have done anything he asked."

In 1983, five years after publication of her book, Tammy reflected further. "I never went back [to Don Chapel] and I never regretted it," she said during a pensive moment in her seaside house in Jupiter, Florida. "George and I were to have some rough times but I never regretted leaving with him that night. It was just fantastic. George got me out of a way of life that was unreal. I couldn't even write how hard it really was. It was rough with Don Chapel. Anything Jones could have done wouldn't have upset me compared to what I had been through with Chapel. I had all these big ideas that George was drinking just because he was lonely. I knew he drank when I met him. I knew he had a problem. But nobody could have told me that I couldn't be happy because of

what I had gone through with Don. Jones was to be mild compared
to the unhappiness I had gone through."

Their romance made quite a splash in Nashville. Everybody
kept count of the gifts George gave her—the new white Continen-
tal Mark IV, the four-carat diamond ring. People buzzed about the
fact they weren't married. Illicit sex between two famous stars created such tantalizing tales. Tammy was having the time of her life.
"Tammy can live in a complete fantasy world," mused Joan Dew.
"She loves clandestine meetings, the old kind of Victorian images
of sneaking off to meet somebody." Their affair seemed to be the
kind that folks usually read about only in books. But George's and
Tammy's romantic frolicking was real. Don Chapel seemed to be
the only one who was forgotten and lost in the shuffle. He was
emotionally devastated by Tammy's departure. "I thought we had
a good relationship," he sputtered years later. "She had no reason
to leave at all."

Oddly enough, George and Tammy didn't marry for nearly
another year. There were the legal entanglements of getting her
divorce from Chapel, of course. But even after all that was
resolved, George hesitated. "If a man is sexually attracted to her,
it makes her feel attractive," reflected Joan Dew. "But Tammy
wants to marry the guy when she's had an affair. She's kind of like
Elizabeth Taylor in that way. Tammy wants total commitment.
When she loves a man, she wants marriage and she wants more.
She wants 100-percent total commitment from that person. She
had to get pregnant before marriage came up [between her and
George]. As it turned out, she lost that baby. [Tammy miscarried.]
But he was stalling on marriage. But I do think George loved
Tammy as much as a guy like George is capable of loving
somebody." But Tammy finally won her man. On February 16,
1969, she became Mrs. George Jones.

What God had joined in marriage, George and Tammy wanted
to celebrate in song. "George was very much in love with Tammy,"
recalled Billy Sherrill. "She was on CBS, and he wanted to do
duets with her and couldn't unless he signed with CBS. His love
for her was the reason [he signed with CBS]. It wasn't any great
thing about me. He just wanted to get with Tammy. I'm glad he
did."

Since Tammy was already signed to the larger, more prestigious, label, it was only natural for George to be the one to change. He was already dissatisfied with the way he was being recorded at Musicor. In addition, his hits had tapered off somewhat. In 1969 he had three—"I'll Share My World with You," "If Not for You," and "She's Mine/No Blues Is Good News." "Where Grass Won't Grow," "Tell Me My Lying Eyes Are Wrong," and "A Good Year for the Roses" did well for him in 1970. But by 1972 George's popularity was waning. Only "Right Won't Touch a Hand" had broken through into the top ten on the country music charts. George was convinced his career needed a boost.

In 1972, George asked to be released from his Musicor contract. He was now practically chomping at the bit to record with Tammy. But negotiations stalled when the Musicor executives requested George's artist royalty rights for those songs he had recorded on Musicor. He had had sixteen top ten hits during his six-year tenure at Musicor. Whoever ended up with the royalties stood to make a good deal of additional money with the rerelease of George's old hits. At the time, George claimed that Pappy Daily and the record label ended up with the royalties. "I had to sign all rights for my royalties over to Daily and the label," George claimed. "These are the tapes RCA bought and reengineered and remixed. I don't see a penny from those reissued albums." But Pappy claims he didn't get any money out of the deal even though he should have. "George didn't give them to me," asserted Pappy Daily. "That's a lie, a damn lie. I didn't get a penny of it. My deal was with the record company. They paid me so much a record. So when George gave Art Talmadge $100,000 and gave up all the artist royalties, the record company wouldn't pay me anymore because they had all of George's artist royalties. My contract provided that I would get this percent of the money that they paid to George Jones. So, that [arrangement] eliminated me, according to them. But it didn't. I had the contract with the recording company. I could have gone to court and sued them. But I was seventy-some-odd years old and didn't think I wanted to wrestle with that."

Understandably, George was bitter about the parting with Musicor. But it was his alienation from Pappy Daily that saddened him. They kept in contact after their split, but their relationship was never to be the same. Associates of the two claimed Pappy felt betrayed by George. But in 1983 Pappy reflected no ill will toward his former protegé. "I still love George," said Pappy. "And I still think he's the greatest country music singer of all times." Meanwhile, George would only smile at the mention of Pappy's name. "I think George, at times, misses Pappy," Melba Montgomery once observed. " 'Cause I feel like George really loved that old man. But Tammy wanted him to come over to Billy Sherrill." The change was the first real indication of just how dependent on Tammy George would become.

Professionally, the move to CBS was to be one of the best of George's life. The music industry's largest record label provided him a larger platform from which to perform his music. George received marketing and promotional support that he had not known existed. But in the beginning George was apprehensive. He was teased about Tammy's getting him a record deal. And he didn't know whether or not he would like Billy Sherrill, who had a reputation for being difficult at times. "I don't even remember the first time I met George," recalled Billy. "I saw him sporadically with Tammy from time to time before the signing. We just met to say hi a few times. Then, when he signed with Epic Records, we were standing there looking at each other. Both of us were kind of nervous, wondering if we could get along in a studio together. Then later, after about ten minutes into our session, after he found out I wasn't an ogre, we had a good time. We've had good times ever since."

George was pleased to discover that, while Sherrill may not be totally predictable outside a recording session, he was strictly professional while working, probably one of the most proficient and masterful producers in Nashville. George began to understand why so many people considered Sherrill a musical genius. "Billy works hours before, during, and after my sessions to get everything right," George once said. "I was really lucky."

Trust became the key ingredient in their working relationship. "I don't know if anybody else could really have had the rapport with George that Billy does," analyzed Sue Binford, then a publicist for CBS Records. "I don't know if George would trust anybody else. The big thing for an artist is trust. Any artist has to believe in the record company and the producer. If they don't, they just go through the motions of singing, but you don't get the enthusiasm and feeling. Billy Sherrill is an integral part of ʻGeorge Jones's music. I think that Billy understands what the George Jones sound should be, almost like a formula he works from."

Billy Sherrill was quick to point out, however, that he does not reign supreme when in the studio with George. "My relationship is fifty-fifty with George," Billy explained. "If he loves the song, we'll do it whether I like it or not. It's worked out pretty good that way. But I treat producing like it was a business. I'm in this to make hit records. There are no stars in this office. I'm in this business because it's fun and I'm not going to do anything that's not fun. When the artist leaves this office I have no idea where they are or what they're doing. In here they are a person. Out there they are a star."

That arrangement suited George just fine; he had never considered himself a star anyway. But it was the trust in Billy that prompted George to go along with Billy's elaborate production techniques. Together, they started producing a long string of hits that would not only be popular but admired and respected outside of country music circles. With Sherrill's guidance George developed into a stylist, a singer who could not only sell records but who was able to establish trends and set standards by which all others would compare their own work. It was Billy who pushed George into singing with new clarity and depth. "I started doing probably smoother-type music with him," reflected Billy Sherrill. "He changed within the boundaries of the song. Jones used to never record anything with over two chords in it. I think if you do something a little more complicated, it sounds like the style changes, but it's really not. Some songs require singing and some songs don't. You can take a song like some of his old stuff, like ʻWhy, Baby, Why?,' and that don't require any singing. But you take something like ʻHe Stopped Loving Her Today,' and that requires singing. You can't just mouth through it and expect it to be good."

Epic Records released George's first single, "We Can Make It," in February 1972. It went to the sixth position on the charts. The second release, "Loving You Could Never Be Better," piloted up to the second slot. They weren't the two-million sellers that Tammy had with "D-I-V-O-R-C-E," but they got the attention of those who knew and respected classic country music. "['Loving You Could Never Be Better'] clearly marks the beginning of a series of recordings that would firmly establish George Jones as the decade's purest singer of country music songs," noted Diana Johnson and Kyle Young in their George Jones profile for Country Music Foundation's *The Greatest Country Music Recordings of All Time.* "Haunting strains of a steel guitar are beautifully interwoven around George's clear, understated vocal performance."

In the same year (1972), Billy united George and Tammy in music. Their recordings were an instant success, not only because of their incredible harmony, but because the songs so aptly mirrored their personal lives. In 1972 they sang "Ceremony" and "Old-Fashioned Singing." The next year they harmonized on "Let's Build a World Together" amid reports that they were struggling to maintain their marriage. Then, in 1973, right after they had split and then reunited, "We're Gonna Hold On" zoomed up to become a number one duet hit. Fans seemed inclined to purchase the record just to hear again how George and Tammy were trying to make their marriage work yet another time.

Their popularity as a duet soared. Eventually, they stopped touring as individuals completely. They became the highest-paid duet in country music history up until that time, reportedly commanding more than $1 million a year. They quite literally became Mr. and Mrs. Country Music. And the fans reacted to their spats, partings, reunions, and confrontations as if Tammy's and George's troubles were their very own. Their private life and their music became so intertwined that those around the couple often wondered if George and Tammy knew where their private life stopped and their public life began.

CHAPTER
18
We Go Together

HE FANS THOUGHT George Jones's and Tammy Wynette's marriage had been made in honkytonk heaven. They sang so beautifully together, who would have thought otherwise? But away from the glare of the stage lights, when they settled down alone with one another, they were like strangers, separated by a wall created by their disparate psychological cravings.

They needed so much from one another that neither had much to contribute. They were two takers; neither was a giver. Helen Scroggins once observed that George and Tammy were too much alike to get along. Actually, they were like two children, each seeking the acceptance and approval that they had not received from their parents. Tammy, a successful entertainer, still felt rejected by her mother. George, even as a grown man, still hid from his mother when he was drinking. So they each turned to the other to find fulfillment, never realizing that contentment had to come from within, not from without.

Reluctance to accept reality was the primary reason that they stayed together as long as they did. Tammy was searching for the ideal man, perhaps the daddy she had never known. She needed to believe that the right man could make her dream of living in the white cottage come true. When George eventually turned out to be less than ideal and her cottage less than pristine, she grew bored and impatient with the relationship. At first, she blamed her dissatisfaction on where they lived, which accounts for the reason they moved so many times during their marriage. But regardless of how many times they moved or how grand their new abode, nothing seemed to match her make-believe world, resplendent with visions of fairy princesses and white knights. In the end, she blamed George for her disappointment. It was easier to find fault with him than to reexamine her view of men and marriage.

George craved a woman's total acceptance, like that his mother had displayed when he had been a boy. George sought the same from Tammy. He needed to be emotionally caressed with the gentle, reassuring manner of a doting mother. As singer James Taylor would later observe, George needed emotional walls upon which to lean. Alone, George was neither strong nor sturdy.

George and Tammy changed residences one-and-a-half times for every year of their marriage. These upheavals suited Tammy, as she thoroughly enjoyed redecorating extravaganzas. "Tammy could redecorate a house in three days," recalled Joan Dew, co-author of Tammy's autobiography. "I've been with her on these redecorating jaunts. She would go to John F. Lawhon, a big warehouse kind of place and she would walk in the place and she would say, 'I want this and this and I'll pay cash if you can deliver them this afternoon.' Then she'd have the painters come over and it would be done in three or four days."

When they first started living together, they moved into George's house in Nashville. Then, deciding that his place was too small, they moved to her much larger place on Old Hickory Lake. According to Tammy, George redecorated that place himself "from top to bottom," choosing wallpaper, paint, furniture, and the like. But George and Tammy, one of the most popular and publicized couples in town, found that the house wasn't big enough for the groups of people who were always dropping by. Songwriters, Music Row executives, and associates popped in on them at the drop of a hat. So a few months later, in March of 1969, they decided to try living at George's house in Lakeland, Florida—one that he had purchased while still married to Shirley. "It was a rambling ranch-style house with a swimming pool in the back-yard," described Tammy in her book. Before moving in, George and Tammy redecorated the house and added two bedrooms.

They had barely settled into the Lakeland house when one day, George took Tammy on a surprise excursion. He showed her a 100-year-old, six-bedroom, colonial home located about 12 miles out of Lakeland that he wanted to purchase and renovate. One of George's lifelong ambitions was to have a home such as he showed her that summer of 1970. It wasn't just the house that attracted him. He loved the forty-three acres that surrounded it. For George's dream was to come off the road, except to make a few major, important show dates and to have his own stage. He was bone weary of touring and decided to build his own showplace, where he could sing and perform without going any further than his own backyard.

"The park was something he had wanted to do for years and years," recalled Tammy. "It was a way of bringing music to our home, bringing our friends to our home. When the groups would come down to work, it was almost like they were coming to the house."

The land George showed Tammy was ideal for his plan. A few hundred yards from the colonial house was a natural bowl where George envisioned a performing area complete with stage and benches. The acreage was heavily vegetated. Giant old moss-laden trees clothed the grounds in shadows. And while the house was in bad shape, he envisioned it, that day, as it would be—majestic and serene.

George wanted his project completed in time for the arrival of the new baby. For by now Tammy had learned she was pregnant. So George went to work like a wild man, lining up workmen, surveyors, plumbers, landscapers, electricians, and the like. "It really occupied George because he's the type person who loves to be doing something. He has to be occupied doing something constantly, all the time," reflected Tammy. "If he's idle, he gets bored very, very quickly. He worked like a slave on that park. He did so much of the work himself and it was such satisfaction for him to see it go up and for him to know that, 'Hey, I did this. I helped do this with my own two hands and this is going to be something we can be proud of years from now.' He was so happy trying so hard not to drink, drinking mostly beer and wine at that time, trying to stay off hard liquor for about a year and a half." He became totally preoccupied with the project and seemed almost irritable when he had to go back on the road for previously arranged show dates.

But finally the project, which George christened "Old Plantation Music Park," was completed in the late fall of 1970, just five weeks after his thirty-ninth birthday and two weeks after the birth of his daughter, Tamala Georgette. "George loved that place," recalled Herman Jones, George's older brother. "He said he was gonna stay there. He rode us around over that place one time and he told us, 'This is what I have always dreamed about having.' That was the time he went for two years without drinking. They had a playground, places to put mobile homes, and they had electric cars to take crippled people down there to the plantation where he played, and they had golf carts."

In 1970 the park was somewhat of an ingenious and innovative idea, constructed long before Conway Twitty built Twitty City in Nashville or Loretta Lynn had Hurricane Mills. George's idea was to provide a place where country people could come and bring their children for a day of listening to country music. Few such facilities existed. Country music could usually be heard only in saloons and honky-tonks. Based on his own experience, George knew such places had been the downfall of many a good-hearted man. So no alcohol was allowed on the "Old Plantation Music Park" grounds. Special playground equipment was constructed so that children could play while their parents took in the performances. Hundreds of picnic tables were constructed so that visitors could either bring their own picnic tidbits or buy food at on-the-grounds food stands.

But what made the project ideal to George was that all of this was no farther than a few footsteps from his house. He liked the idea of providing a place where country men, like himself, could stroll, relax, and spend some time with their families. When the project was finally finished George was practically overwhelmed with happiness and a sense of achievement.

The roofed arena held up to 11,000 people. The grounds could hold several thousand more. On the opening day the park was filled to capacity. George had guessed correctly that there was many a good man out there who wanted to do right if given a chance. Shows were scheduled every other weekend and included every country music artist from Waylon Jennings to Connie Smith and Barbara Mandrell. After a year of successful shows George and Tammy began to breathe a sigh of relief. George had taken an enormous financial gamble. He had more than $250,000 invested in the park by the time they finished. But when the place started breaking even George just turned around and kept investing. He expanded his antique car collection, which already included a 1929 Model A Ford, a German Styre, a 1936 Chevy, a 1940 Lincoln Zephyr, and a 1923 Cadillac. But regardless of what other cars he purchased, none was more popular with the visitors than his customized Pontiac Bonneville convertible. It was a one of a kind with more than four thousand silver dollars embedded in the dashboard, in the door panels, and around the seats. Authentic pistols served as door handles, Texas steer horns were the hood emblem, and a leather saddle served as the console between the two front seats.

"Those were the happiest days of my life," George said in retrospect. Tammy was miserable, however, recalled Joan Dew. "I think George was perfectly happy down there with all his little cars, fishing, and friends," Dew reflected. "Tammy was bored. I think she really got bored with him very quick down there. Actually, George is a little fuddy-duddy. He's like a little old lady. He's not exciting. He sits around and watches TV all day and goes fishing. George is only exciting onstage. He's not funny; he doesn't have a good sense of humor. He's smart but not intellectually witty. Apparently, he's a lousy lover. I haven't heard of an alcoholic who wasn't. [Sex] was very, very important to Tammy. And I think by then she was bored."

Tammy claimed she had other reasons for wanting to leave. "When he'd get to drinking and leave, I didn't know what to do," Tammy later explained. "If there were shows coming in, I didn't know what to tell the people if Jones wasn't there to do the work. I just really didn't know what to do because I depended on him for everything on shows. I loved it down there. But when I knew that things were really getting rough for us and we were going to have to make some decisions and had to either try to get along with our lives or either I had to get a divorce, one or the other, I felt Nashville was the best place for me to go back to because I had more people there that I could depend on—Shorty Lavender and Hubert Long, Billy Sherrill, people who I was close to, people that could help me. I guess I just never understood some of George's moods and I wanted to get to where I could get some advice and support."

Apparently, by the late fall of 1972, Tammy could tolerate the situation no more. They pulled up stakes once again and moved back to Tammy's house on Old Hickory Lake in Hendersonville, leaving behind George's dream and a huge chunk of his self-contentment and pride. As if to appease his bruised ego, she suggested they purchase a 340-acre farm in Springfield, Tennessee, about thirty miles outside of Nashville after selling the plantation park. Again, Tammy and George began redecorating with a furor. They brought in another host of painters, plumbers, and wallpaper hangers to redo the working farm's colonial house. But their life, after leaving the plantation, was never to be the same.

And that didn't keep them from moving yet again. Deciding that they were living too far out of Nashville in her Old Hickory Lake house, they purchased a French Regency house atop a southwest Nashville hill. From there, they could get to Music Row in a matter of fifteen minutes. But after spending a winter there, they decided that battling the ice- and snow-covered hills was not worth the mountaintop view. In the spring of 1974 they hopped houses again. This was to be their last jump. For by the time they moved into the sprawling 17,600-square-foot Franklin Road house, complete with sixteen bedrooms and fifteen bathrooms, their marriage was over. Neither the Olympic-size swimming pool nor the tennis court was able to rekindle their now burnt-out passion for one another.

Tammy was quick to announce to the world that their breakup

was caused by George's excessive drinking. The explanation seemed so tightly packaged, so efficient and final. Yet, when examined under a microscope, the explanation did not hold up. First of all, she had known about his drinking from the beginning. In fact, he had been drinking heavily the very night that he had swept her off her feet and carried her out of Don Chapel's door. Should she then have been surprised later when he repeated the same scene, those times being no different except that they were not conducive to her getting what she wanted?

"I would have thought Tammy was more sincere than what she was," retorted Helen Scroggins. "I'd have never thought she would have let little things like him going off and getting drunk break them up. 'Cause, like George said, he drank when he married her. That was too flimsy of an excuse. He told me the first time he saw me after they broke up that she was wanting a hit [song] real bad. He said he was in a hotel in Houston and that several nights before he left, before he got drunk, that all she had done was cry all night long, begging him to help her make a hit record. He'd been laying off for nearly eight months then. He said he kept telling her she would finally make a hit on her own, that has to have time. 'You'll make a hit,' he said to her. Then he said he just got tired of it one night and he just went off and got drunk. Then, when he called back to come home, she wouldn't let him come home."

"Tammy wanted to walk away," asserted Joan Dew. "But she wanted George to be the villian and, of course, she gave him ample room to do so."

If they had been a typical couple of the country music community, their breakup would not have caused such a stir. But their split was more than the dissolution of a marriage. It was the demise of an institution, the end of Mr. and Mrs. Country Music. Anyone who had once been married had understood the meaning of their duet hit "We're Gonna Hold On." Fans had identified with their romance and marriage so strongly that they were now forced to suffer the couple's heartache and pain in breaking up. Finally, in the fall of 1974, George and Tammy sang their last hit while still man and wife. The song was entitled "We Loved It Away."

CHAPTER
19

A Picture of Me without You

AT FORTY-THREE YEARS of age, George felt like he had lost everything. Only two years earlier he had had everything he had always wanted—a great home, a loving wife, a little baby girl, and, of course, his music. He had begun again to hum one of his favorite tunes, "Ragged But Right." "I knew I'd settle down and build a little love nest right here in my hometown, so now I've got a family, one that I'm proud of," George sang to himself. "I know that I'll be happy 'cause they're the ones I love. Well, a big electric fan to keep me cool when I sleep, a little baby boy to play around daddy's feet. I'm a rambler, I'm a gambler, and I lead ev'ry life, 'cause I tell you folks, I'm ragged but I'm right."

"I was athinking I was happy and was going to always be happy," George revealed after his breakup with Tammy. But in a twinkling of an eye it was gone, all of it—his home, his park, his wife, and his baby daughter. "I was wrong," George reflected, referring to his excessive drinking, his violent escapades, and destructive temper. "And I hate myself worse than anything for

151

what I did. [If I had it to do over again,] sure, I'd do it different. I wouldn't step on as many people as I have. A lot of them, unintentionally, but a lot not giving a damn, you might say, or not realizing how bad the damage I was really doing [was]. But I've never cheated, I've never beat nobody out of a dime. That's one thing I couldn't do.

"But I don't think I was given all the fair chance," he continued, referring to that December night when Tammy refused to let him back into the house. "I don't think you kick someone out of the house when they haven't drinked, when [I've] done everything in the world to satisfy [my] halo as a boss. [Either things went Tammy's] way or they don't go no other way. I don't think [it was fair that I hadn't] drinked even a beer and I just went the last step of doing anything [she wanted me] to do, that she would keep me up all night over stupid things [that would] irritate and aggravate me, knowing my nature that it would drive me to drinking. So without any sleep one morning, I fought it. But I went ahead and did it. One day and one night. I went to the Holiday Inn in Franklin, checked in 'cause I didn't want to go home and let my kids see me. Next morning I called several times all day long. She called me the dirtiest names you could ever think of, and 'You will not come home,' she said. I should have realized right then, hell, she worked like hell to get rid of me. I felt like a letter that's been declined on every step. Now I'm not putting her down," emphasized George. "I very much respect her. She has a lot of love in her heart, but she loses it too quick. Subjects change and she changes. I guess we all do it."

Tammy changed when she finally stopped pretending that their marriage was something it wasn't. The bubble burst the day Clara Patterson died. Neither Tammy nor George had a reason to pretend anymore.

Clara had been a diabetic for years, but she had paid no attention to the warnings of family and doctors to check her sugar intake. W. T. Scroggins recalled, "We'd hear her get up in the middle of the night sneaking sweets."

In late 1970, Clara suffered three heart attacks in quick succession. "She had a heart attack and they did surgery on her," explained Helen. "They put a pacer in. They had to go through the hard way. Mama never had surgery in her life, and so they couldn't go through the easy way of putting a pacer because she had too big of an opening going through her heart. I said all the time the shock of surgery would kill her. But there was a year and over that we had to keep somebody hired to help. It was a fight 'cause she didn't know what she was doing half the time."

George came to visit when he could. "He sat with his mama," Helen pointed out. Then, in April of 1972, Clara became gravely ill. George dropped everything to be with her.

"We were sued for missing dates because his mom was dying," Tammy pointed out. "We left a Canadian tour to go back to Texas to be with his mom. But she lingered on a lot longer than the doctors had expected." Clara's condition upset George, but family members were proud of how he handled the situation.

"George was playing records for her," Helen continued. "She looked over at George, and Mama said, 'You all stay here. Helen will talk with you. I'm sorry, I can't talk. I've got to lay down.' George said, 'If Mama had been in her right mind, she would have never said that to me.' I put her to bed, and it seems like that done something to George that his mama didn't know that was really him. I think it tore him up bad."

But finally, George and Tammy had to leave. "We had to go on to England," continued Tammy. "We were in England and had just gotten to the hotel and laid down to get some sleep from the jet lag and the phone rang. They called to tell us George's mama had just died. So we had to turn right around, and four hours later caught a flight back to Houston and drove to Beaumont and then on home. We cancelled the tour in England."

Tammy recalled that nothing was ever the same after Clara's death. "I loved her and thought she was a wonderful lady," reflected Tammy years later. "She was always very helpful to me and very supportive of me. She stayed with me when George would go off someplace and wouldn't come back. She'd stay with me and tell him, 'Glenn, don't do what your father did to me. Don't make her pack up a paper bag and run through the woods in the middle of the night with a bunch of kids. Don't make her do that, that's what your daddy made me do.' She was always very supportive of me," continued Tammy. "I'm thankful that she never saw us divorced because I think it would have broken her heart completely 'cause she really wanted us to stay together. It affected Jones because he loved his mother deeply and he didn't want to disappoint his mama. He would hide things from his mama to keep her from knowing things he did because he truly loved her very much. When she died, he handled it very well. He didn't start drinking more or anything like that. But our marriage was already deteriorating. And after she died, he probably didn't try as hard and I probably didn't try as hard. I really did try a lot for his mom, especially when she was with us. I tried very hard for her to know that I loved him and he loved me and that we had a good marriage because it was very important to her. I think we both quit trying so much when she died."

While Tammy accepted the fate of her doomed marriage, George kept hanging on to the illusion. With his mama now gone, he needed Tammy's emotional support more than ever.

George was not able to accept his failed marriage without inflicting pain onto himself. He blamed himself and started drinking with a vengeance.

For months after their separation George pondered about what had gone wrong, and, finding no answers, he continued to drink heavily. George had the impression that the world was changing around him and he wasn't changing with it. Even the country music business had evolved into something he no longer recognized or felt comfortable working in.

By the middle 1970s country music had become big business. Whereas ten years earlier artists customarily made a few hundred dollars a night, now they were making several thousand. George and Tammy had certainly benefited from country music's new popularity. They had earned millions, commanding as much as $20,000 for one appearance. But as a result of the increased money-making potential, George was seeing a new kind of artist enter his field: kids who didn't necessarily feel any great passion for their music but who, instead, viewed country music as a way to be famous, get rich, and be a star. "This middle-of-the-road crap, this southern pop music for the dollar bill don't hook it," proclaimed George. "It might hook it now; it might buy a mansion. All I can say is they better hang on to it. They just don't love country music like they should. It's almost like selling your soul, the way I feel. It made me [what I am today] and I'll not deny it. It took care of me 'cause I loved it so much. Why should I want more than I can handle?"

In 1974 George had become so adamantly opposed to what was happening to country music that he, along with about fifty others, formed a group called the Association of Country Entertainers. Their enterprise had been triggered by Olivia Newton-John's winning the 1974 Country Music Awards Show's Entertainer of the Year award. George joined to protest the increased acceptance of pop singers into the country music arena. Many of the traditional country music singers joined in with the effort. They included Dolly Parton, Hank Snow, George Morgan, Jimmy "C" Newman, and Tammy. The group caused quite a stir and was severely criticized. The raging controversy was described in Patrick Carr's *Illustrated History of Country Music:*

> Critics [of ACE] pointed out that many of the founders of the ACE were former pop or rock singers who had made a rather complete transition into country, and that earlier giants like Jimmie Rodgers and Bob Wills had incorporated pop elements into their music, but [ACE member] Johnny Paycheck argued that the music content was only part of the issue: "Our chief complaint is that if an artist gets a crossover record that is played on both country and pop stations, that artist has an unfair advantage in the CMA awards."
>
> Another ACE member, Billy Walker, was more candid about the group's purpose: at a Nashville press conference he explained that many members were concerned that "outside influences" and the attempts to take country music to a wider audience would dilute country music "until it no longer exists." He continued, "We are mainly people who made country music what it is today, trying to protect our business because we see it flaking off in thousands of directions. We're trying to keep it at home."

But progress can't be stopped. Ironically, one of the early members of ACE, Dolly Parton, went on to be one of the crossover trailblazers. The Association of Country Entertainers never did have any real impact. Its membership dwindled and the group was eventually forgotten. George dropped out when his personal troubles began. But in his heart he felt the same. "I never have thought I was anybody other than I just love to sing," George revealed. "I was aware of having a hit ever' now and then, of having a good record that people liked. That's why I never could understand how anybody shouldn't be so thankful to have a hit, yet they become so conceited and stuck up. My goodness, how can they do that? Even have the time to feel that way? Do they love the music or do they love the money? I want to be around people who love to sing."

George continued to make his point known the only way he knew how, by singing "good country songs." Sherrill obliged. And even though George still occasionally bad-mouthed Sherrill's use of strings and backup vocals, Sherrill was actually creating a format through which George Jones, the purist, could remain true to himself and still be commercial. Critics would later point out that the elaborate orchestrations seemed only to augment George's traditional vocalizations.

George's recording was greatly hampered throughout the mid-1970s by his sadness. He stayed drunk much of the time. But still Sherrill got him in the studio long enough to record a series of incredible hits that would become George Jones classics. " 'Once You've Had the Best' is an example of a song based on George's real-life problems," analyzed Diana Johnson and Kyle Young in *The Greatest Country Music Recordings of All Time*. "Recorded in 1973, the song is illustrative of what columnist Jack Hurst calls George's 'much-noted ability to wring suffering, sorrow, and rebellious joy out of himself through tightly clenched teeth.' 'The Door,' a monster hit recorded the next year, clearly shows George's vocal capabilities and his ability to interject great feeling into his songs by accenting certain notes and lyrical phrases. The song contains other added effects, including the actual sound of a door slamming, followed by a rousing chorus with George's voice surrounded by tumultuous background of vocals and strings.

"Within four months after cutting 'The Door,' George recorded 'The Grand Tour,' another major hit and, in George Jones's opinion, one of his greatest songs," the analysis continued. "The theme is a good marriage gone bad, and George becomes the guide through a house that was once filled with love and happiness before the wife left 'without mercy, taking nothing but our baby and my heart.' "

As George's singing became richer and more poignant, perhaps because he had more hurt and pain to draw upon to create the mood in his songs, his fame mounted. Tragically, he was to receive his recognition and glory at a time in his life when he felt most undeserving. George Jones was fast becoming a dinosaur, a creature from another time, trapped in a world he no longer understood or cared to.

20
It Sure Was Good

HE **TAMMY WYNETTE** and George Jones union was something akin to the passing of two comets in the heavens. They came from their respective pasts, collided, then spun apart to travel again in separate directions. But both were greatly affected by each other. They had been attracted like magnets, drawn together with each anticipating that the other would fulfill dreams. And when it was over and the dreams had dissipated like fog penetrated by the light of the morning sun, they were plagued by thoughts of what could have been.

After their split their lives took a downward slide, both personally and professionally. Tammy's was to be a slower, more consistent tumble. She was never to return to the popularity that she had enjoyed in the late 1960s and throughout the early and mid-1970s. Personally, she was to continue reaching for her illusive dream. George's private life, meanwhile, rolled, twirled, and tumbled like a roller coaster. But strangely enough, his career, which was to be plagued by dips (primarily because he virtually stopped singing at times) continued to draw listeners.

He struggled through the divorce proceedings, a hodgepodge of charges and countercharges. Tammy filed the papers in January 1975 on grounds of cruel and inhuman treatment. Following the advice of his attorney, George filed a suit against Tammy and Shorty Lavender (who was a friend as well as the booking agent for the couple) shortly thereafter, charging both with "conspiring to damage his career."

Tammy was not to be outfoxed or outmaneuvered. After all, she had an image—of a woman who stood by her man for as long as she could—to uphold. Subsequently Tammy released a pleading announcement to the Nashville press. "George is sick," she proclaimed in blaring headlines, "and badly needs help. Many of my friends in the music business have tried to help him over the last several weeks. It is painful for me to endure this, but my real concern is that George get some help to protect him against his own worst enemy—himself. Everybody who is in the music industry knows that George and Shorty Lavender are like brothers. Everybody is aware that George, when he is normal and rational, loved Shorty. He wouldn't say a thing about Shorty Lavender if he was well. I want to ask George's friends and the lawyers he is talking to not to take advantage of him or manipulate him.

"I do wish that the lawyers and the press would not try to use George's illness as a means of hurting him or needlessly airing our personal problems," Tammy concluded. Later, Joan Dew, who lived and traveled with Tammy for several years during their joint writing of *Stand By Your Man*, reflected that as insensitive as it may have seemed at the time for Tammy to have released such a statement, Tammy's motivation was sincere. "She was saying, 'Give me sympathy,'" Joan observed. " 'I stayed with him as long as I could.' She was getting attention with sympathy." But by making the annoucement, Tammy had created a strong public impression that George, a man who had great difficulty separating his public and private images, was a drunkard.

The property settlement was quickly resolved. George kept the Tyne Boulevard house; Tammy maintained residence at their Franklin Road abode. George kept the houseboat and she took the tour bus. He also was obligated to make $1,000 a month child support payments for Georgette. But none of the material possessions were important to him. George had already lost the things that had any value to him. "What good is it?" he asked. "It's not what you were seeking to start with. Once you get love, you don't turn loose of that, no matter what you do. You can go buy a car, you can go buy a house, you can go buy anything, but you're never satisfied. You're not settled without love."

In the days, weeks, and then months that followed his divorce, George drove up and down the highways like a lost man. He seemed to have nowhere to go. "It was kind of sad," recalled John Lentz, Tammy Wynette's attorney at the time. "After the divorce I was at Tammy's house one night and George was circling the driveway. She was living on Franklin Road, and the driveway had a circle front. He would just drive around and just keep driving around. Once he did it like five times, then he would drive out."

George was looking for a companion and retained a flicker of hope that he could make good his ways and win Tammy back. "He loved her for years there," mused Helen Scroggins. "I was even hoping they would try and get back together because I thought they really loved one another. They looked like they had enjoyed one another, and I don't know, I always thought they would get back together. 'Course they didn't."

But that was because Tammy had lost interest in George. She quickly started dating again, first New England Patriots football player Tommy Neville, then singer Rudy Gatlin. Then, just six months after her divorce from George had become final, Tammy began dating movie star Burt Reynolds. George had long been dismissed from her mind, but he hoped it wasn't true. "Tammy was trying to be nice to George," recalled Lentz, "but there was no love left for George other than as a friend. There was no romantic love left as far as Tammy was concerned. And George still had a romantic love for Tammy. He was like a schoolboy in love with some girl who didn't want him. He was being rejected. But it was always an uncomfortable relationship for George, more so for him than it was for Tammy because he was the one that was being rejected. Then, she was the dominant member of the relationship. If he had left her, it would have been different. The fact that he'd always gotten what he wanted and the fact that he was George Jones and nobody had ever done that to him before made it like Tammy was the forbidden fruit and he wanted her back all the more."

But the more tragic reason George kept going back to Tammy was that he didn't know where else to go. He was like a puppy dog snuggling up to the cold body of its dead mother. Tammy was gone, but the memory of her was better than nothing at all.

He saw no future without her. His respite was the whiskey bottle. "Often I'd go four or five weeks at a time and hardly eat nothin' at all," George said. "By then my stomach would be so small that maybe half a hamburger would be all I could take. I'd wake up the next mornin' and want to vomit, but even so, I just had to have a drink. You get so far down and your mind gets so screwed up, you just don't care."

In the meanwhile executives at CBS Records were trying to figure out a way to salvage the individual careers of their two artists. Since George seemed determined to continue his self-imposed drinking sabbatical for a while longer, they directed their initial attention toward Tammy. "We were very concerned," admitted Mary Ann McCready, a marketing director at CBS. "Their duet career had been so strong and their ability to draw [crowds] had been so strong that everyone was concerned that neither one alone would have the strength of the two of them together.

"We started a major campaign on Tammy." she continued. "We got the cover of *Family Weekly* and covers of other magazines. Then we arranged for her to perform at the White House. We promoted her as 'The First Lady of Country Music performs for the First Lady of the Country.' " Tammy went and sang in the summer of 1976 for then President and Betty Ford along with Ella Fitzgerald and Roger Miller. Her magazine articles and the White House visit succeeded in getting her name back out into the public eye as an individual. Other divorced women across the country identified with her plight, and they responded by going out and buying her records. They empathized when Tammy woefully sang ' 'Til I Can Make It on My Own.' It became a hit in 1976 along with the poignant 'You and Me.' But her comeback effort following the divorce would not compare with the kind of attention George was getting.

By the early part of 1976 George seemed to be a little like his old self again. He had new management and was performing again. According to reports received by CBS executives, George was singing better than he ever had before. In an effort to test George's appeal they booked him to appear at Willie Nelson's annual July Fourth Picnic in Gonzales, Texas. Scheduled to sing along with Kris Kristofferson, Jerry Jeff Walker, David Allen Coe, Leon Russell, and Asleep at the Wheel, George was a straight man in the midst of longhairs. Willie, Waylon (Jennings), and Kris were leaders of the so-called outlaw movement, one of the groups that George had campaigned against only two years earlier when he had helped form the Association of Country Entertainers. Willie had started his annual picnic celebration in 1972 after leaving Nashville, weary of the town's bureaucratic ways. "The people I had been involved with had done things their way for years and years and had been successful," Willie had said when asked why he had left to return to his home state of Texas. "They didn't want to change their way of thinking, and I didn't want to change mine. I had definite ideas—things I wanted to carry out . . . and according to regimented bureaucracy, I wasn't doing it right."

So Willie had left and was now somewhat of a guru to hordes of southern young people who liked to wear their hair long and smoke marijuana and who took pride in snubbing tradition. One of their favorite events to attend was Willie's annual picnic, and they turned out in droves each year; thousands of them packed into a field like sardines, jumping, screaming, jiving, dancing, fainting, throwing up, yelling, and getting crazy. Into this format CBS executives booked George Jones, not knowing how the singer would be received, but curious. Never in their wildest forecast could they have predicted what happened.

"I can remember George was so nervous that day," recalled Mary Ann McCready. "We met him and his group at a private airfield and drove them to the picnic, which was a good ways. The closer we got, the more nervous he became. Cathy Cronkite was with us, and she was a great distraction for him. He couldn't believe he was sitting in the same car as Walter Cronkite's daughter. We finally drove up to the grounds, and there were more than one hundred thousand people there who had their shirts off and were rowdy. Everything in the world was going on. George was in this polyester suit and he looked out and said, 'These aren't my people. I'm not supposed to be here.' Then, when George got onstage, he was a nervous wreck and scared to death. He was the only performer who had a little outfit, and the band had matching costumes, and he was such an oddity in the show."

But George knocked them dead. "Before George could get halfway through the first song he was hit with a wave of adulation that nearly knocked him over, literally making his knees go weak above his triangle-toed lizard cowboy boots," reported Joan Dew. "They screamed, applauded, and cheered him on for 45 minutes that became a passionate, lusty love affair between one man and a multitude. George Jones cut a whole new set of notches on the pearl handled pistol of traditional country music that day, and he rode out of Gonzales a hero. Reporters and disc jockeys picked up the fever, spreading the word, until Jones was the new 'in,' the dude to be reckoned with, the reborn LEGEND, if you please."

Later the same year George's album, "Alone Again," was released. It was a return to basic, traditional country music and his first album since the 1950s to feature a "passable five-piece band, and it was cooked easy on the syrup, heavy on the corn," recounted journalist Patrick Carr. None of the singles were big hits for George, including one of his all-time favorite songs, "Her Name Is," which featured electric guitar with wah-wah pedal filling the vocal voids. But the critics went wild. *Newsweek* called the work "an unassuming masterpiece." The *Village Voice* said that George "should be on a list of America's all-time top ten best singers" in any category—country, pop, rock, or opera. In the *Chicago Tribune*, longtime country music analyst Jack Hurst noted that George puts "more feeling into single bars of music than many other singers manage to get into whole albums." *People Magazine* listed Jones as "the best country singer in the world," and *Penthouse* named him "the Holy Ghost of Country Music."

The outpouring of praise did not stop with the critics. As though a gate of silence had been opened, George's admirers came tumbling forth. "I've never talked to a country music person whose favorite singer wasn't George Jones," announced country music singer and songwriter Tom T. Hall. Willie Nelson and Waylon Jennings both went on record as thinking George was one of America's greatest singers. Bob Dylan listed George's rendition of "Small Time Laboring Man" as one of his favorites. Kris Kristofferson named George as among music's all-time heroes. Singer Emmylou Harris admitted that she had twenty-three George Jones albums in her possession and once remarked, "When you hear George Jones sing you are hearing a man who takes a song and makes it a work of art—always. He has a remarkable voice that flows out of him effortlessly, and quietly, but with an edge that comes from the stormy part of the heart. In the South we call it 'high lonesome.' I think it is popularly called 'soul.' "

The outburst of praise and admiration for this skinny man from Texas took almost everyone aback. Some, who had not seen George in concert or heard his new record, asked why all this attention was being given to this man who had been virtually ignored by everyone outside of the country music world.

Jack Hurst of the *Chicago Tribune* provided the answer. "Because of the overpowering emotion and intuitive skill Jones brings to music. His records are so quintessentially and excellently country that they rise above the form, attracting the attention of connoisseurs from every other popular-music field. In lyrics that are often banal in black and white, the great voice surrenders itself to working class despair, elation, confusion, and rage. Songs affect him so strongly, Jones says, that he loses himself in them."

Nashville's CBS executives were ecstatic. "We were practically jumping up and down," recalled Mary Ann McCready. George Jones, they predicted, would be country music's icebreaker. He would be the one who would carry country music out beyond the honky-tonks and bars into Carnegie Hall and convince the entire nation that country music had something to offer everyone.

Try It, You'll Like It

EORGE HAD NEVER felt quite as distraught as he did during those months following his divorce. He was broke, drinking constantly, performing rarely, and in desperate need of someone to lean on. He sold his Tyne Boulevard house, its walls resounded of earlier, happier times. And he moved to Florence, Alabama, where his buddies, songwriter Peanut Montgomery and his wife, Charlene, lived. They were folks he could chum around and drink with. They loved singing and writing songs, and they provided some semblance of a family life. "Peanut is my best friend," George said gratefully at the time.

George recalled that those days ran one into another. "I'd get in the car, drive to Nashville, drive around, and drive back," he said. He frankly didn't know what to do. Billy Wilhite, who had been George's road manager since 1971, when George had parted ways with Bill Starnes, tried to get George to do as many dates as possible, but they were few. Mostly George drank, got depressed, then drank some more.

Then one day in the early spring of 1975, while George was

sitting in Nashville's Hall of Fame lounge, a tall, burly man was introduced to him. His name was Shug Baggott and George remembered, "I had been messed up for two or three months. He just came along and brought hope and bright lights into my mind."

Shug Baggott was in the nightclub business and had only recently shut down a rock and roll club called The Electric Circus. "Business had gotten bad, and I shut it down, and I had decided I had done rock and I had done pop and I had done soul [previous clubs], and I had decided to do country music. When I told people I was looking for a country music name they told me that the best was George Jones. So I met George there at the lounge and we started talking. But every time we started talking he would be drunk before we would get through. This went on for two or three days, and then I said, 'George, I can't continue to do this.' And he said, 'You're right. I'll be here at noon on Monday and I will be sober and we will make our deal.' Sure enough, noon Monday, he was there. We made the deal. The deal involved him putting up the money. I was broke and didn't have any money. But when I met with George's CPAs I found out he didn't have any money. So I borrowed $15,000 from First Tennessee Bank to open up. It ended up taking about $35,000."

Baggott's club was renamed The Possum Holler and opened up in the summer of 1975 to a receptive audience. According to Baggott, the club was a smashing success. George was impressed and recalled that he felt Baggott was someone he could trust and lean on. They quickly became constant companions. George's friends, including Peanuts and Charlene and his booking agent Shorty Lavender, recalled later they had their suspicions about Baggott. But they had nothing specific about which to be critical. Baggott was a college graduate and claimed even to have nearly gotten a law degree from Nashville's YMCA Law School. He had been an executive with Nashville's Werthan Industries, a manufacturer of plastic bags. But they feared Baggott might turn out to be nothing more than a smooth talker telling George what he wanted to hear so as to take advantage of him. Baggott waved away the criticism as nothing more than "sour grapes." "They were all living off of George," said Baggott. "They didn't like me because I was taking away their free ride," pronounced Baggott.

The Montgomery's real concern was the way Baggott took over all of George's business and financial affairs. "Shug moved in and pushed everybody else out," observed Peanut, a tall, thin, and balding man with bushy eyebrows and a thick mustache. Billy Wilhite, George's road manager, was one of the first to go after Baggott entered the picture.

"Billy Wilhite was one of these good-time guys that just hangs on and he had managed to get George to say he was his manager," charged Baggott. "But he was like a $200-a-week yes-man that didn't have the ability to do anything as far as managing was concerned. But he would get George, lead George by the hand, get George on his dates and things like that, at that time what little dates he was doing."

So Baggott moved in, took hold of George's psychological and emotional reins, and virtually told everyone else "to get lost." George was mesmerized and content. Baggott was making all the decisions that he was too weary to make. And besides, George thought Baggott was trustworthy. "I've been took by just about everybody I've been associated with in my twenty-one years of professional music business," reflected George in the fall of 1975. "But I can assure you I'm associated with some very fine people right now."

Shortly thereafter, George asked Baggott to be his manager, convinced that Baggott would make his life easier. "I had gotten closer and closer to George as a result of the club operation, and we opened that on a shoestring, and he saw me pull that together and more or less perform miracles getting that place open and doing well," bragged Baggott. "And the club at that time was almost supporting George Jones's road show. He didn't have the money to actually go out and do his dates, and the club was more or less supporting him. So after seeing me do that, he asked me to manage his career. I told him I would if I could get a percentage."

Baggott knew George was in dire financial straits, badly in need of cash. "Jerry Jackson [George's accountant] had given me a list, and he said George was $297,000 in debt," recalled Baggott. So

Baggott went to a man from whom he knew he could get up-front money—Bob Green, who owned the Executive Inn (a hotel and restaurant/lounge) in Evansville, Indiana. "Bob Green gave George a guarantee of three quarters of a million dollars [for one year] and also gave George a $150,000 advance," claimed Baggott.

George was impressed and signed a management contract with Baggott. But the $150,000 plus an additional $100,000 that Green advanced a little later went quickly. Part of the money went to pay off George's debt. Another portion was spent on what Baggott called "high living." "For instance, George wanted Tammy to have a brand-new car sitting in her driveway when she got back from the road for her birthday that year," Baggott explained. "This was on a Saturday. We were sitting out there on the boat, and we didn't have any money in the bank, and I had about two, three thousand dollars cash, and he had about five thousand dollars cash, and he wanted a brand-new Mercedes sitting in Tammy's driveway when she came driving in. You know, you can't give a present to someone unless it's paid for; you can't say here's your present, and we're paying the payments for you. It had to be paid cash. So I talked him out of the Mercedes and talked him down to a Thunderbird, which was still then thousands, which we didn't have.

"So I wound up buying a gold Thunderbird, and the guy took a check that he knew wasn't any good, and he knew we would get it taken care of eventually. . . . [I told him] give me a couple of weeks and I'll get it taken care of for you. But we went ahead and got that gold Thunderbird, and it was sitting in her driveway when she got back."

George was still trying to win back Tammy's affection, Baggott recalled, not understanding why the singer was continuing to try. He had recorded several duets with Tammy, two of which ("Golden Ring" and "Near You") had become number one hits for them during that year. The music and the memories kept him going back to her, again and again. "We would be out on the road, and George would decide he wanted to go see Tammy," reflected Baggott. "We'd have a date, we would be winding up like Saturday night, and he wanted to go wherever she was. It was call the Lear jet and zoom over to see Tammy. That got to be real expensive."

By the early months of 1977, Shug Baggott and George Jones

were practically inseparable. This allowed George to break his ties with Tammy. "I lived, breathed, ate, drank George Jones twenty-four hours a day, seven days a week," recalled Baggott. But much to his chagrin, Baggott still had not been able to bring George under his control. Baggott would later admit that he had gotten into the arrangement with the idea of turning George into a money machine. But he was having to spend so much of his time just comforting and being with George that he had little time to sit in his office and actually pursue business deals. Baggott had also discovered that George had no aptitude for understanding the business aspects of his profession.

"George had no idea how to read a set of books," observed Baggott. George's lack of interest in his career, his sporadic windfall purchases, his trips to see Tammy, and his continuing drinking problem all began to weigh on Baggott. But he kept quiet. At this stage of their relationship he did not want to alienate the singer who, more and more observers were saying, could be the Elvis Presley of country music.

It was mid-March of 1977, and George had been on a real drinking binge. He was in no mood or condition to go to the Executive Inn in Evansville and sing. He was pleased to hear Shug say that he agreed. "But we owe it to Bob to at least show up and let him know we're trying," George recalled Baggott saying. "We have a personal service contract with him, don't you remember? Can't you at least go to show him it's not because you're drunk?"

The argument was convincing. Green had given him a lot of money, and he did want him to know he was trying. So, with Baggott's help, he got up and dressed and they took the next flight to Evansville.

"We got up there, and we had a doctor come by," recollected Baggott. "This doctor told me, 'If you can get George dressed for the show and get him downstairs, I can promise you he can do the show.' I said, 'It's impossible.' He said, 'Will you do it?' And I said, 'OK, I'll do that, but he can't do the show.'

"So I told George," continued Baggott. "I said, 'All I want you to do is walk out on the stage and tell the people that you're just not feeling well and then they will see that you're not drunk.' At that time we hadn't missed a date in months. So we got George downstairs, backstage, and this doctor gave George a shot. George said, 'I'm just going to walk onstage and try to do a couple of songs.' He was just so weak, and I said, 'George, don't try to sing. I know you can't. Just go out there and tell them you're sorry.' 'No,' he said, 'I'm going to try and sing one or two songs.'

"They announced him, he drug out on stage, just barely drug out there," continued Baggott. "He started singing the first song, 'Ragged But Right,' and about halfway through that song, boy, he kicked in and did one of the best shows I've ever seen. He finished the show, and we got him back up to the room, and he was totally exhausted again. The doctor said, 'I'll give him another shot before the next show.' That went on all week. He did the best shows ever. I've never seen him so full of pep and everything. When I asked the doctor what the shot was he said, 'I gave George the shot to help his sex life. There's medication we have to do these things.' I didn't know anything about drugs, so I said 'OK.' "

When two weeks passed and George was in a similar state of exhaustion, Baggott said he called the same doctor, offering to send a Lear to pick him up so that he might again administer the "miracle shot." This time, however, the doctor refused. "I even asked him what medication he had used so we could get it somewhere else," recalled Baggott. "The doctor just wouldn't talk to me about it. About three months later I was in Evansville, and I happened to be at a table with this doctor, and we got to talking, and he told me what he had given George. 'It was liquid cocaine,' said the doctor. Then I made the mistake of telling George.

"George had always been antidrugs, totally antidrugs," continued Baggott. "But [the incident in Evansville] took the veil down. Right about that time George started running with Paycheck, and at that point Paycheck was heavily on cocaine. One night when we was at Possum Holler I went looking for George and couldn't find him. I found George and Paycheck downstairs. When I came in they were real secretive and everything. I don't know for sure, I can't say for sure, but I believe that was the first time that he actually did snort the cocaine."

Even though George would later say that Baggott was the one responsible for getting him addicted to cocaine, Baggott claims he was merely drawn into an already existing situation. Nonetheless, Baggott admits he did nothing to deter George's use of the drug. "At first I thought it was heaven-sent," admitted Baggott. "George was killing himself drinking. He was going to die. The doctor told me there was no question. His liver had swollen. You could see it when his shirt was off. And in the beginning he handled it [the cocaine] real well. I'd see him order one drink and just let it set there. I asked a doctor later about cocaine, and the doctor told me, 'It's not going to kill George.' So I felt pretty good about the whole thing."

In the initial stages of his use of cocaine George snorted only before shows. "He always had to have something to get him on the stage," proclaimed Baggott. And for a while George used the drug minimally. Then Baggott heard about George's trying to buy cocaine on the streets of Nashville. "He would just go up to somebody in Printer's Alley and just walk the streets and ask somebody to sell it to him," recalled Baggott, with a chuckle. "One time he bought some stuff that had a lot of quinine in it, and it really hurt his throat. 'Course they cut that stuff with various things. Being in the club business, I had an acquaintance that I knew was a big dealer. So I started getting it for George." Before long, George was a regular user. He snorted before his shows. It gave him enough courage to go on.

22

Same Ole Me

FTER THE WILLIE NELSON picnic CBS executives were convinced that George could be a superstar. "We frankly had no idea how much George was loved by his cohorts," admitted Rick Blackburn, head of CBS's Nashville division. "After all those people started talking about him the way they did we starting gearing up."

The task they had at hand was a difficult one. It was late 1976, and country music had not yet gained mass popularity. In New York, country music was still considered the music of the redneck. Few New Yorkers, especially those who ran in the prestigious print and media circles, had any appreciation for the musical form. The crossover hits of Dolly Parton and Kenny Rogers were still half a year away. Dolly hit with "Here You Come Again" in 1977 as did Kenny with "Lucille."

But even in the face of overwhelming resistance, the record executives were convinced that George Jones was the fellow who could turn the snobbish New York skeptics around. "Country music was not readily accepted by the New York media then," recalled Mary Ann McCready. "Asking the New York media to go out and review a country artist was virtually impossible. To my recollection, there were only a couple of people in New York who cared anything at all about country music. We thought George to be the epitome of a country music stylist. So we decided to gamble on him. We figured that if we could get the Andy Warhols and the Susan Wans and all those people [the trendsetters] out to see him, we thought that once they were there, they would love him. We thought these people would consider George hip, a stylist, and get their endorsements. And then we figured once they had seen George, they would be open to everybody else [in country music]. We were hoping that George Jones would break the barriers. And we knew at that point if there was anybody who was capable of doing that, it was definitely George Jones."

So they decided to showcase George in the Big Apple, right smack in the middle of their acknowledged cynics. They worked on the project for nearly a year, anticipating one of the great musical coups of all times. "We were about to accomplish in one night what would have taken months really to accomplish otherwise," observed Mary Ann.

They booked George into one of New York's hottest and trendiest nightclubs, the Bottom Line, on September 6 and 7, 1977. Then they proceeded to invite the town's kingpins to the show. "At that time no country artist had ever performed at the Bottom Line," said Mary Ann. "Over $30,000 was spent on promotion and for flying reviewers in for George's performance." A lot was at stake, not only for George's career but for country artists in general. For many of those attending, George would be their first taste of country music. "Walter Cronkite, Dan Rather, *Time* magazine, *Newsweek*, and *The New York Times* were going to be there," recalled Mary Ann. "We were flying in representatives of newspapers and publications from all over the place."

Odd as it may seem, the record label executives knew little of George's mounting emotional problems. The quiet, corporate offices of a record label are a long way, both physically and spiritually, from an artist's life on the road. George's communication with the label executives was usually limited to contractual and financial discussions. In turn, George knew little about the New

George's family of women in 1973. Tammy is holding Georgette. The other girls are Tammy's children from former marriages. Left to right are Gwendolyn Lee, Jacquelyn Fay, and Denise. (Photo by Jill Krementz)

George loved playing with Georgette. Here they are together in her room at their Franklin Road house. (Photo by Jill Krementz)

George and Tammy alongside their tour bus. (Photo by Jill Krementz)

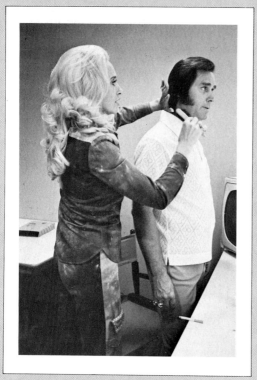

Many times Tammy primped
George's hair before a show.
This scene was typical. (Photo by
Jill Krementz)

The wall of George's and
Tammy's awards and momentos.
(Photo by Jill Krementz)

Tammy said that Georgette had singing in her genes. So it wasn't surprising that George and Tammy encouraged their daughter to sing with them. Here they are in 1973 on the Grand Ole Opry stage. (Photo by Jill Krementz)

George and Tammy's bed in the Franklin Road house. (Photo by Jill Krementz)

George with manager Shug Baggott. (Photo by Slick Lawson)

George recording with Johnny Paycheck. (Photo by Slick Lawson)

Photo of George with good pal Merle Haggard. (Photo by Alan Messer) Records)

Rick Blackburn, vice-president of CBS Records, in his Nashville office.
(Photo by Jill Krementz)

George with Tammy and her husband, George Richey, after their professional reunion in 1981. (Photo by Slick Lawson)

George Jones and Tammy Wynette making their first appearance on "The Tonight Show" together in February 1980. This was their first professional appearance together after their reunion. (Photo by Kathy Gangwisch)

George's first appearance at the Wembley Festival in London in February 1981. (Photo by Kathy Gangwisch)

In February 1981, George got together with (from left to right) Hank
Thompson, Vern Gosdin, Tammy Wynette, the late Marty Robbins, and
George Richey at the Royal Garden Hotel in London for a little
impromptu harmonizing. (Photo by Kathy Gangwisch)

George taping "Hollywood Squares" with other country music stars in February 1981. (Photo by Kathy Gangwisch)

George, with famed British rock star Elvis Costello, backstage at the Wembley Festival in 1981. Elvis recorded a duet with George in 1979, "Stranger in the House." (Photo by Kathy Gangwisch)

George sings for a crowd of 10,000-plus on his opening day (Labor Day, 1983) at Jones Country. The woman on the left is Leona Williams. (Photo by Jimmy Bryant)

Happy at last, George is with new wife, Nancy, and sister and brother-in-law, Helen and W. T. Scroggins, on his "Jones Country" property. (Photo by Slick Lawson)

George and Nancy. (Photo by John Yarwood)

York date that CBS personnel were so vigorously planning except that he was supposed to be there. Not once did the record label executives think that George wouldn't show up. The idea was too preposterous. Artists begged for that kind of promotion. "We thought George would want to be there," concluded Mary Ann.

In the late summer of that year George and Shug had a temporary falling-out. And in the meanwhile Nashville attorney John Lentz and booking agent Shorty Lavender had signed on as George's management. But the relationship was to be short-lived. By then George had become dependent on Baggott, the man who controlled the drugs.

"I remember that CBS Records had gone to great lengths to get George an appearance at the Bottom Line in New York," recalled Lentz. "He was to be the first country act ever to appear there. CBS was sending a lot of us to New York. George was living in Alabama, and Shug was down there with him. George was to meet us at the Nashville airport, but he didn't show up. So I just went on to New York. Then I got a call at the New York Hilton from Shug Baggott. He told us his brother Sandy [who was George's road manager] was with George and George was going to be up on the next flight.

"Well, the next flight came and went and George still didn't appear," continued Lentz. "This was the day of the show, you understand. Then we got a call from Shug, and he told us that George was not coming because he didn't think the folks up there would like his music. So he wasn't going to come. Well, CBS had booked the Bottom Line for two nights, and they were rightfully upset. A lot of influential people were due to come to his premiere performance. So the CBS people in New York wanted Shorty Lavender and myself to leave New York and go to Alabama and try to find George and get him up there for the second night even if he missed the first night.

"So we left all our stuff, our clothes and everything, and flew back to Nashville," Lentz continued. "Then we got a private plane and flew to Alabama. We flew into this small town in a small airplane, rented a car, and started hunting for George. We drove all around, went to his house. I remember it was spitting rain. Shorty camped out at his front doorstep, and I took off in the car looking for George. Finally I went to his barbershop, and George had just left. I had missed him by less than five minutes. We searched for George all the rest of the day, and it became obvious that we weren't going to find him. So it was my unpleasant duty to get back in the plane in mid-afternoon and fly back to Nashville and then catch another plane to New York to tell the people that he would not be there for that show either. CBS spent no telling how much money to promote that date. It was his big shot."

No one, particularly the executives at CBS, knew what to make of George's no-show. "For about a week everybody was just horrified," recalled Mary Ann. "I think the general feeling was a deep sense of disappointment because it had been built up to such a high level of anticipation within the company and outside the company with the press and media. When he didn't show up it was a real disappointment. We had to call all those people and tell them that George wasn't going to be there. We couldn't find half the people because they were already on their way to the party. I remember thinking, 'What in the world is going to happen to him? What are those people going to say about him?' "

But again the CBS executives were surprised. Not only did the press forgive him; it seemed to have new-found respect for the singer. "I remember everybody at CBS thought George's blowing off a date at the Bottom Line meant the end for George," recalled Sue Binford, a CBS Records publicist at the time. "As it turned out, it was only the beginning. The love affair with George Jones spiraled after that. The press totally embraced him. And in retrospect I think there were several reasons they responded the way they did. I think the timing of what happened had a lot to do with the press's love affair with him. Music was pretty boring out there in the mid-seventies. Most of what was being done was a manufactured kind of sound, just various kinds of commercial, assembly line, regurgitated stuff. The press was looking for somebody out there who was still trying to deliver music with a grain of truth to it. Then they heard George, who did music that had a real purity to it. His music had a real depth and had an edge. So George struck a chord not only with the country press but with the rock press, too."

But Sue contended that not only did the press have a high regard for George's music; they began to respect the man. They had been snubbed by a singer whom previously they had snubbed. Ironically, George had created a mystique without meaning to. They could not understand a person who didn't want to be a star. And prompted by their curiosity, they began to seek him out. "They knew George was a survivor," continued Sue. "New Yorkers, being New Yorkers, love survivors. They love winners. By listening to his music, they knew George was a survivor. Plus, the press got wind of how much the people at CBS loved this guy. Press people can smell that kind of thing a mile away. If somebody in marketing is pushing somebody because it's been assigned, that's real different from pushing somebody because it's important to them personally. And that's what happened to George. Pushing George Jones became a part of them.

"An emotional ball started to roll on him," she continued. "The guy had a legion of brothers, sisters, mothers, and fathers there who were really pulling for him. I don't know why it happened, exactly. It's practically unheard of in the industry. I know why I felt the way I did about George. We've become a society where simplicity doesn't exist. And we've gone through the last ten years of people trying to get back to the simple things in life. There's been a return to the family and basics. And here you've got a guy who comes along and literally represents the return to simplicity.

"We live in the midst of so much bullshit, and then there's George," she concluded. "I know I related to him from that perspective. He represented something to me really basic. I felt like I had gotten caught up in a lot of the periphery and the glamour and the glitter of the music business. And here was this most unglamorous, unglittered man who wanted to do nothing more than sing songs. I thought that was great. And I think it was the same reason the New York press was drawn to him and eventually went nuts over him. None of the attention he got was manufactured. It was the press getting caught up in the same thing the CBS personnel had gotten caught up with. This guy was stripped down and down to earth and made no bones about it. They loved him for being that way."

You've Got the Best of Me

CTUALLY, **NO ONE SHOULD** have been surprised by George's no-show at the Bottom Line. George did not want to be a star. His desire had always been the same, simply to sing. "My music has always been the most important thing in my life," George once said. "When I started out I had no thoughts of being a star. I didn't even have thoughts about making a decent living. I didn't care if I made a dollar. I never thought where my next meal was coming from. I was at my peak when I had my guitar in my hand and I was singing, whether I was by myself, at my house, in a club, or wherever. I was really more concerned with my own pleasure than whether or not they enjoyed my singing."

Those who had worked closely with him were aware of his attitude. "Of all the people I've ever recorded in my life, I think Jones cares the least about ambition," observed producer Billy Sherrill. "He doesn't think like other people. The typical entertainer would say, 'I'm going to headline a show on this big TV thing, and we're going to make a big video and probably sell the album another 200,000, and I'm going to do "The Tonight Show," and I'm going to do a week in Las Vegas and make another $300,000, and this thing looks great, and I can't wait to do it.' Jones would say, 'They want me to do the damn "Tonight Show." I guess I'll have to. I need the money, so I'm going to have to do Vegas. I'd rather be out somewhere on a boat or on my farm or something, but I'll do it if it's got to be done.' George doesn't care about pushing himself on other people."

"In all the years I've worked with artists, I've never worked with one who had such little regard for the importance of interviews, press, and promotion," observed Kathy Gangswisch, one-time personal publicist for George. "I think if I had gone in and told him that I had lined up the cover of *Newsweek*, *Time*, *People*, and *Life* all in one month, he would have just gone, 'That's nice.'"

Another of his publicists, Susan Hackney, once remarked, "There is no differentiation in his mind between giving an interview to a *Time* magazine reporter or to a local newspaper reporter. In fact, most of the time, he'd rather give the interview to the local reporter."

The crux of George's attitude was a carry-over of the Big Thicket mentality. "George proved that he could not only sing," reflected Big Thicketer Gordon Baxter, "but he had given the whole world finger. In the Thicket, that's style, that's classic, and the people down here thought George was really fine for doing that."

But George's natural resistance to making such appearances had been fueled by his ongoing concern over what was happening to country music. Only two months before his scheduled Bottom Line performance, George had explained to a reporter, "They're trying to bring country music too far uptown—to the big city— trying to modernize it too much. Country music is in your heart. It's in your soul and the sound of your voice. You don't walk out onstage with a thirty-six piece orchestra if you're gonna sing country music. You walk out there with a pedal steel guitar, basic instruments. They used to make fun of us, call us hillbillies, wouldn't have a thing to do with us. Now some of the biggest businessmen in the world out of New York and the West Coast have taken over Nashville. It's nothing but a syndicated rat race now. Not a thing like when I first came to Nashville."

George certainly did not want to give the impression that he had compromised like everyone else. So he didn't go to the Bottom Line. But more importantly, George wasn't sure that New Yorkers would appreciate his brand of music. "They," he said later, "weren't his people." And when given the choice of performing at a local Texas club or the prestigious Bottom Line, George would have chosen the former any day. His people, George knew, loved music the same way he loved it. Above all else, George did not want to run the risk of being rejected in New York.

"You know, I never did understand George not showing up for that date," John Lentz reflected. "I came to the conclusion that George would like to be smaller than life rather than bigger than life. I realized he'd rather be at that barber shop in Florence, Alabama, than being cheered at the Bottom Line in Manhattan. Here he was, the first country performer at the Bottom Line, and he chose to be with his buddies in Florence. I would have preferred to have been in New York if I had been George. I decided then I didn't have enough hours in the day to spend them on people like George Jones."

Whether George knew it or not, he was now a member of the entertainment industry, an organization that had been spawned for the very purpose of creating stars. He had begun as a simple singer in a simple business. In the early and mid-1950s country music had no stars, just good ole down-home singers. Now the country music executives, in their efforts to compete with pop music, rock music, and Hollywood, were making use of strategies that had long proven successful in these other arenas. Hollywood filmmakers bragged about their roster of movie stars; rock record label executives compared notes on their new starlet singers. Now country music was developing its own lists of stars. George was to have been one of them, but he didn't want any part of the promotional gimmicks and supersophisticated marketing tactics. He wanted to remain "just ole George."

The man in the middle was Rick Blackburn, vice-president of CBS's record division in Nashville. On one side he had the corporate hierarchy to report to. A few of them wanted George out. Not only had George jeopardized his own career, but he had embarrassed the corporation and all those involved with the Bottom Line project. Egos had been rudely stepped on. George's no-show and his subsequent personal troubles had perturbed even the most tranquil of CBS New York executives. "There were people in our company who really thought it best that we would not loan or invest in him," recalled Blackburn. "I understood. That's a corporate way of looking at things. If you're a banker, you're looking for strong collateral. We were not looking at a very stabilized person. But I went to bat for George. I love the guy and think he's the greatest country music singer alive. Now that's the bottom line. I knew he was going through all these changes, and I wanted to keep the pressure off.

"Frankly, I was baffled by the fact that George was being successful in spite of his attitudes," admitted Blackburn. "All he wants to do is to sing records and play some dates. He really doesn't understand the whole entertainment umbrella that we work under. But I admire that. You know, 85 or 90 percent of the artists we have on the roster or who are on any record label view this profession as a way to gain success. Jones ultimately doesn't want any part of it. I respect that he's his own person."

Ultimately, Blackburn won out. George was kept on the CBS roster. And luckily for Blackburn, George's talent prevailed. For in spite of the personal problems and trauma that George was to endure in the ensuing months, George's popularity as a singer remained strong. "George is so talented in his phrasing, of the way he sings, that he's had it real easy," observed Billy Sherrill. "In that way, he's never had to prove anything. George Jones has always been a great singer."

By the early months of 1978 the drug that Shug Baggott had originally thought was "heaven-sent" was causing real problems. At first Baggott thought George's cocaine problem was the result of a weak nature. "George had no control," Baggott complained. "He had no willpower. I'd see him take that bottle of cocaine out and do it, then we'd be sitting there talking and he'd be screwing the top back on. Then he would get it right back out and take off the top and do it again. I would say, 'George, you just did it.' He'd say, 'No, no, I don't believe I did.' I'd say, 'George, you did; you just did it.' But he'd do it again anyway. You can only get so high with cocaine, and George kept trying to get higher. He thought if he kept taking the cocaine, he'd get higher."

Eventually, however, Baggott began to realize that he was losing control of his own cocaine habit. "It was all so simple," Baggott recalled. "If I was sitting there and feeling depressed and felt bad, I knew all I had to do was take a bottle out and open it up. That's all you had to do to feel as good, the best you have ever felt in your life. I knew I could feel that way anytime I wanted to with that little bottle in my pocket. Of course, afterwards, I found out it led to disaster.

"But before it did, we had a great time," continued Baggott. "We were out there on a boat with a bunch of women and drugs, and we were partying and having a big time and going to Vegas and doing all these things. It was fun; it was a lot of fun. Why else would I have spent $500,000 on anything that wasn't fun? But I found out it's like taking a jump out of a plane without a parachute. It may be fun, and it may be an extremely exhilarating experience, but it, like cocaine, leads to disaster. If nothing else, it leads to financial disaster, because when I started out it took me about $30 for a forty-minute high. By the time I finished it took me about $150 to $200 for a fifteen-minute high. You build up a tolerance to it so that nobody can afford it. But while you're on it, it makes you think you're invisible and that you're ten feet tall. You cannot have a negative thought when you're on cocaine. Since George was depressed all the time anyway, he was especially vulnerable."

During the months that followed, many wondered why George did not leave Baggott, the man George repeatedly accused of "getting me on cocaine." It would have made sense for him to leave. And George did, frequently. For a while he teamed back up with his former road manager, Billy Wilhite. Then for a period he signed with Shorty Lavender and John Lentz. There was a brief union with Texas tycoon Carooth Byrd, son of Rear Admiral Richard Evelyn Byrd, the man who helped discover the North Pole. But each time he returned to Shug Baggott. For by then George was so paranoid as a result of his drug-taking that he didn't know who to trust or where to turn. "Every which way I turned I got more flabbergasted," recalled George. "I was paranoid. It seemed whatever way I turned, it was the wrong way. He [Baggott] knew my weakness, and he just walked all over me. It was almost like a science fiction movie. I didn't believe those things could happen in real life."

By the time George's troubles began in the summer and fall of 1978, the nature of Shug's and George's relationship had changed. For by then Baggott had become a drug supplier for much of Nashville's music community. "George had told other artists who used it [cocaine] that Shug could get you some," recalled Baggott. "Then the first thing you know, I was buying it for a number of people in the music industry. That's the main reason I didn't go to trial and was willing to plead guilty after I got caught. I was guilty, but the main reason I didn't try to fight it was because there was a number of major artists and people in the music industry who were involved. We just had this little buying cooperative. This friend of mine would buy it and then bring it to us.

"We were getting the best," bragged Baggott. "And everybody liked the arrangement because the people who were getting it from me were people who didn't want to deal with just anybody."

From time to time George proclaimed he was going to the law and tell all. But he never did. For by then George was scared, frightened that he was going to be killed for what he knew. And Baggott did little to soothe his fears. For instance, there was the little matter of the $650,000 life insurance policy that Baggott took out on George. "After he got me started on coke he came to see me about making each other the benefactor of a $650,000 life insurance policy," divulged George.

Baggott would later laugh about George's paranoia. "Yeah, I took out the policy," Baggott chortled. "There was a guy here in town who was writing insurance policies as a deal on a lot of stars. The company was paying him 120-percent first-year commission. So he had a man put up some money for the first year's premium. Then he would take out insurance on named people, and the company would pay the guy 120 percent for the first-year commission. So he would get back 20 percent more than he had put in. Then he and this guy that was backing him would split the 20 percent. The insurance company's deal was that they assumed they could keep some of it on the books and make it worthwhile. So they came to me and wanted me and George to do that. It sounded like a good deal to me, and so George and I went over and took the examination. George was real paranoid, but the policy went both ways.

"I heard later George even took some cocaine that I had gotten for him and had it analyzed," Baggott continued. "But you know what? He still used it," Baggott pointed out. "Later, I told George that I couldn't believe he had thought I was going to kill him. Lordy, have mercy."

But George could not be convinced otherwise. Furthermore, he didn't know what to do about his fears and premonitions. "George kept thinking he was going to die," Baggott said, shaking his head. "I couldn't believe this guy." So the saga continued. "It was hard to cope," George later admitted. "I was trying to do my own guiding, and everybody was leading me left, then right. And I'm the type of person that I believe in anybody in the world and will do just about anything they wanted, which was a lot of the reason I was in the position I was. I was a fool and kept going right back and doing it again the next time and the next time and the next time. I didn't want to lose faith. I kept thinking that there had to be somebody good around here somewhere. I still wanted to give him the benefit of the doubt. I almost come to the point of losing faith in mankind. I said to myself, 'Well, the whole world must be like this.' But I know it isn't. I believe in love and trust. And I think once you get in that state of mind [of losing faith], you're just gone. You'd have to give up. I thank God that I never lost that trust and faith in people. I kept athinking, 'They just can't all be this way.'"

24

These Days I Barely Get By

HE FIRST INKLING of George's personal problems began to surface publicly in the fall of 1978. In August Tammy sued him for nonpayment of child support for Georgette. She claimed that George was $36,000 behind on his $1,000-a-month schedule. Then, shortly thereafter, John F. Lawhon, a Nashville furniture store, sued for money owed. Then the Internal Revenue Service followed suit. When asked why he hadn't made the payments, George answered simply and meekly, "Shug was supposed to have done that." When asked why he hadn't, Shug asserted the money had gone for "office expenses."

So George's nightmare began. In September he took a shot at his best friend, Peanut Montgomery, with a .38 caliber Smith and Wesson. "He knew the problems I was havin'," protested George. "But the wrong night, he called me, knowing the shape I was in, drinkin' more, because I didn't know just what I was goin' to do and worried to death.

"Well, I don't know why I thought about it, but I always go down to the river bottom [Cypress Creek, a tributary of the Tennessee River] and sort of meditate. Just sit down there, you know. So I told him I'd meet him at the riverbank. So I took off, and I was there before he was. And I was just boilin' over. I was already messed up in my mind, drunk and agitated. And he pulled up beside me in his car and said the wrong thing to me. [George later claimed Peanut said something about him not being saved.] I'm very sorry for what I done, because I'm not the sort of person to do that. I just had my finger on the trigger and had my thumb on the hammer to pull it back, so that's when the gun went off.

"I thought it went off to the right, in the back of the car, and up in the air," George told a reporter. "But it didn't do that. They showed me a picture where the bullet was just about an inch below the chrome at the top of the door, just where he was sittin'. I'm just thankful he's still alive and that it didn't hit him, because it's just not in me to do that. But when you get all these things in your mind you really become a crazy person."

Peanut filed charges against George, assault with intent to murder, but later dropped them, saying, "I just wanted to teach George a lesson and hoped the charges would bring him to his senses." Instead, the publicity seemed to make George only a little crazier and more confused. Shortly thereafter, Peanut's sister-in-law and George's girlfriend, Linda Welborn, pressed charges of assault and battery. Again, the charges were later dropped.

But by then the lawsuits were literally raining on George, most of them filed when he had reportedly not showed for scheduled performances. Shorty Lavender, who was still booking George, claimed Baggott had been double-booking the singer, making it impossible for George to be available for all his dates. Baggott ignored the charges, claiming that Shorty was the one who had no right to book George. "In the booking contract that George had signed with Lavender, Shorty Lavender put in a clause in it that says 'this contract is contingent upon George Jones obtaining releases from previous contractual bookings.' Well, I had proof, because I was involved in them, that George had never received any of those releases. So Shorty's contract wasn't valid. I wasn't concerned about Shorty Lavender's claim or argument that he had a contract because I didn't recognize his contract as valid."

Meanwhile, George claimed part of the reason he wasn't making all of his dates was because, "It costs a lot of money to move my band and equipment from place to place. I need three nights in one city to make it worthwhile. But these people are more interested in getting their commissions." Regardless of the reason, George was ultimately and legally responsible for being at his scheduled dates. He was also responsible for either being in court when the cases were scheduled to be legated or having a lawyer there to represent him. In many instances George did neither. He was either in no shape to go himself or had no money to pay a lawyer. Many of the cases were won by the opposing side simply because George failed to appear in court.

By the end of that year Shug talked George into filing for bankruptcy. "I didn't want to do it, but Shug talked me into it," George said. "He filed bankruptcy at the same time I did to save his ass." But again Baggott denied responsibility. "Carooth Byrd had started the procedures," Baggott said in his defense. "They had made this decision that George was in such bad shape financially that his only escape was bankruptcy. They had already started the research to file when George came back to me. But George didn't want to file because of the embarrassment."

News about George's bankruptcy flooded Nashville and national TV and newspaper headlines. George had now become a one-man soap opera with a new episode unfolding nearly every week. The bankruptcy was to be one of the media's most detailed chapters of George's troubles. For, by looking at what he owned and what he owed, the media was able to take a peek into the personal life of a mysterious and flawed man. His assets were listed as a mobile home; a lot in Lakeland, Florida; twenty acres in Marion County, Alabama; and personal items, including guitars, stage clothes, furniture, boots, and jewelry. They had a total value of $64,500, according to the bankruptcy papers. And on the other side of the column were listed his debts, some $1.5 million worth.

He appeared to owe everyone with whom he had any association. He owed nearly $400,000 to CBS Records, $100,000 to Carooth Byrd, $50,000 to Baggott, another $135,000 in various forms of personal and bank loans, but the bulk of his indebtedness was to the thirteen individuals who had filed because George had not shown up for his scheduled performances. Many of these suits were later dismissed or found to be excessive in their amounts because of the promoters' laying claim to potential profit rather than to direct losses.

But in the cold winter of 1979 only the sensational and lurid details of his disintegrating life seemed to be in the news. George oftentimes wondered why the reporters didn't tell the public why he was in such bad shape, rather than just that he was.

"The thing about the fans is what bothered me so much," admitted George. "To read things like he's not going to be here to sing because he's drunk. When the truth was those promoters didn't even ask why I wasn't going to be there. They had read that I was drunk, so they'd just go out onstage and say, 'George is drunk and won't be here.' I was sick. But I knew that those fans, say maybe a lot of them, had saved and walked out of the woods to see me, maybe two or three miles. Crippled old grandmothers, little brothers. I guess that bothered me more than anything in the world.

"I remember when I was a kid that I would have gave anything in the world to go to one of those shows to hear Roy Acuff or somebody like that," continued George. "I knew the fans had nothing else to believe; they had heard it so much. 'George is drunk, drunk, drunk, drunk.' So many of them dates was canceled by me ahead of time but never one because of the money that was deposited. Those promoters didn't want to lose that. What the hell would they want to give it back for, because what the hell, George was going to get the blame anyway. They figured it wasn't their problem. What I should have done is went anyway, even if I had to crawl. 'Cause God only knows what the fans went through to save enough to get there."

George's horror story continued throughout 1979. He began to drink again, sometimes snorting and drinking concurrently. Rumors were milling around Nashville that George Jones was living out of the back seat of his car, that he was broke and had nowhere to go. Even Nashville hotel personnel were refusing to admit him into a room, especially after he and Shug got into a fistfight in the lobby of one. "I think he had decided he was going out like Hank Williams," recalled singer Diane Sherrill who sang backup for George for a short period. "My father had a life-size picture of Hank that was given to him by Ernest Tubb. It meant a lot to my dad because Ernest gave it to him. But George came in here to our house one day and asked for it to keep a few days, just to keep in the car with him. I told my dad he'd never see it again. I heard later that George drove around for days with that picture in his car talking and singing to it. George wanted to go out, but it just wasn't his time. I don't think Hank was trying to kill himself when he died. I think he was overworked and troubled, and it just got the better of him. But I think George was trying to kill himself."

"I kept having this fear that George would get too drunk or under the influence of drugs and that he would actually kill himself in a car," recalled Rick Blackburn. "George loves to drive a car, and I had bad dreams that he would either kill himself in one or somebody else. That was my biggest fear. I knew that, if he hurt somebody, he wouldn't be able to live with himself. I think something like that would have destroyed George Jones. Billy Sherrill and I talked about it a thousand times."

Throughout that year George's friends begged him to get help, to check himself into a hospital. "George has got to get help and get himself straightened out," Shorty Lavender said at the time. "You can't stay off the coke without medical help. You can try to stay off for a couple of weeks, and then your insides start eating at you. George can stay off for two weeks, then he just can't take it anymore."

But George was paranoid, afraid that if he checked himself into a clinic or hospital that he would be declared "insane." "A lot of people would like to see me do that so they could say I was crazy," George said. For by then George had decided to testify against Baggott. "I want to be subpoenaed," he declared. "I'm gonna say he's a crook. I want the truth to come out." But sadly, George was in no shape to do much of anything. The months of continuous tension, pressure, and financial collapse had taken their toll. In the summer of that year it became obvious to everyone that George Jones was not himself.

He seemed to have lost his perspective on everything. This once proud man who refused to ask anybody for a penny was now going from friend to friend asking for money, like a child asking for candy. "Waylon and Cash were willing to give him nearly any amount he asked." recalled Baggott. "They paid $20,000 so George could get his bus fixed and get back out on the road. Another time I went to Johnny and told him George and I needed $40,000. Johnny wrote the check and said, 'I thought you were going to need $250,000 and was prepared to write it' if we needed it. But I told them the worst thing they could do for George was to give him money.

"But Waylon gave George a sack full of money, $60,000, $70,000, $80,000 in cash," continued Baggott. "George drove around with it in his trunk. Then he got down to where he had only $25,000 and went back over to Waylon and told Waylon, 'I need some more money.' Waylon gave him more money, and George went back again, and Waylon gave him some more money, but all this time George wouldn't do any work. Waylon had told George he'd give him money as long as he tried to sing a little. But he wasn't. Then one day George walked in, as hot as a firecracker. I said, 'What's wrong, George?' George said he'd walked in to see Waylon and told him he had to have $5,000 and that all he had left was an old guitar. So Waylon got out his checkbook and wrote out a check for $5,000 and told George to leave the guitar on the couch and made George leave. George came over to my office just in a rage. He kept saying, 'I can't believe Waylon kept that guitar.' I said, 'George, you took it over there for that. Besides, you still have $25,000 of Waylon's money in your trunk.' Then George said, 'Yeah, but he don't know that I don't need that money.'"

But the worst was still yet to be. With the passage of each week George seemed to be losing his ability to differentiate reality from fantasy. His manner was erratic, his actions unpredictable. Charlene told of George calling in the middle of the night, saying he never wanted to see her and Peanut again, only to call the next morning, having no recollection of the earlier conversation. "One day he came into our store [she and Peanut had an antique store in Florence] and started acting crazy to entertain the women in there," recalled Charlene. "Then he started telling me to do something or he was going to have a heart attack."

The worst moments for George's fans and associates in those

dreary months of 1979 were when he went onstage. For there, regardless of what was happening in his personal life, he had always reigned supreme. His performances were like no others. He emitted emotion in a show, touching even the most cynical and hardhearted. In the words of country music authority Bill Malone, "George's voice would sometimes drop into a low register, then sweep into a high wail, often enunciating his words with rounded, open-throated precision, but occasionally moaning them through clenched teeth and with the classic pinched-throat delivery of the southern rural singer. Jones would demonstrate why many people consider him to be the greatest country music singer of all time."

But in those months the old George Jones was gone, and in his place stood a pitiful shadow of his former self. A George Jones admirer was left with only the hope that somehow God would see fit to give country music's greatest singer another chance.

"George had now reached the point where he stayed high all the time," recalled Baggott, who was caught and charged with trafficking in illegal drugs shortly afterward. He subsequently pleaded guilty to possession of cocaine and served one and a half years at Maxwell Penitentiary in Montgomery, Alabama. "He was having periods where he went crazy and didn't know what he was doing. It was about this time that 'Donald' appeared on the scene. George has always been afraid of me and my brother Sandy. George never talked to us in the same way he talked to everyone else.

"George could talk like Donald Duck and did so at times to amuse children. But one day when George and I were having a heated discussion George began to cuss me in the Donald Duck language. I was shocked and asked him, what did he mean talking to me like that? George immediately started warning Donald not to talk to Shug like that. George and Donald became engaged in a real argument. Every now and then he would say something nasty to me as Donald Duck and then apologize as George Jones.

"He would look at me and say, 'Shug, I told him not to talk to you like that,' " continued Baggott. "George began to use Donald to talk anytime he was afraid to say something as George Jones. He had always been rather shy around the girls, but Donald knew no such shyness or fear. Donald could say anything he wanted to, and

George would reprimand him and say, 'I'm sorry about that, but I just can't control Donald.' This statement was becoming more true all the time. George was losing control of Donald.

"Around this time George was beginning to forget the words to his songs. His shows were spotted with forgetting the words, but Donald never forgot any of the words. George would be onstage singing, and hesitate; then Donald would take over and finish the line. At first the audiences would laugh and think it was funny. But after a while they became irritated because George was messing up every song. This went on for months until everyone realized that George had lost control of Donald. George even confided in me that he could not control Donald any longer. He told me he had been riding around town talking and arguing with Donald and had stopped the car and actually ordered Donald out of the car. George said he was afraid he was losing his mind.

"Then one night when George was supposed to be making a comeback appearance at the Exit In [a club in Nashville], everybody knew," concluded Baggott. "Most of the people in the audience were music industry people. George came onstage and announced that George Jones was washed up, a has-been, but that on that night a new star was born who was going all the way to the top. And George proceeded to introduce Donald and asked for a round of applause as Donald started singing a George Jones song. As George stood onstage, face drawn, with his pants falling down because he had lost so much weight and looking ridiculous singing like a duck, you could see tears in most of the people's eyes. George continued singing like a duck until they carried him away in a straitjacket."

Mercifully, Peanut Montgomery had George checked into a psychiatric hospital in December. That George was not corralled sooner was an indication of just how alone and friendless the singer really was. No one had wanted him to stop. Stopping meant an end to the party.

25

My Elusive Dreams

**IRACULOUSLY,** and much to the credit of producer Billy Sherrill, George's music continued to flow throughout his troubled years in the late 1970s. "You wouldn't believe how many times I've recorded George Jones when he wasn't here," Billy Sherrill recalled, with a chuckle. "I'd go into the studio hoping that I was picking a key close to what he'd record a song in, and then we'd [musicians] cut the tracks. Then sometimes, when he was just hanging around, I'd say, 'Let's try this song. I've already got the track cut.' I've cut a whole bunch of records on Jones when he was somewhere else. But I'd rather spend three minutes with George than three hours with most other singers."

In 1977 George recorded his album "Bartender's Blues" with a single by the same title that had been written specifically about George by singer James Taylor. Taylor did backup on George's single. The song was a hit. Off the same album came "I'll Take It Out in Love," another self-revealing song about a man who wants nothing more than love. Later that year CBS released what was predicted to be one of George's all-time big sellers, "George Jones and My Very Special Guests," a product of many hours of commitment on the part of such musical heavyweights as Linda Ronstadt, Willie Nelson, Elvis Costello, Emmylou Harris, Waylon Jennings, Johnny Paycheck, and even Tammy Wynette. The album featured several excellent duets, but none were big hits, perhaps because George was disappointed in his own effort on the album. "I'm proud that I was lucky enough to have such fine, beautiful people to agree to do it," reflected George at the time. "But I'm not proud of my work on it. In other words, it wasn't up to par. I'm not proud of what I did."

Much of George's lack of enthusiasm for the album may have been because George knew that regardless of how much money the album made, he wasn't going to benefit personally. Earlier that year, George's bankruptcy petition had been denied (it would later be granted on appeal), leaving George financially vulnerable to any one of the promoters who had sued him. "I'd rather donate the profits from that album to a crippled children's home where it would do some good rather than see a bunch of crooks getting every nickel out of it. If it sells ten million or one, I won't get a dime from it. The debtors and my ex-manager Shug Baggott have seen to that."

As if George didn't have enough problems on his own, he was additionally grieved with what had been happening to his former wife, Tammy. Throughout 1977 and 1978 Tammy was in the news almost as much as he. During a single nine-month period intruders reportedly broke into Tammy's house fifteen times, once scrawling "SLUT" and "PIG" on her mirrors and television screen.

"Tammy was dating Rudy Gatlin at that time," recalled George Richey, who would later marry Tammy. "Rudy and myself had taken her children and my children to Skate Land (in Nashville). My ex-wife and Tammy were alone in Tammy's Franklin Road house. I got a phone call at Skate Land asking that we get back over to the house. They thought somebody was in the house. I thought, and I think Rudy did too, that this was a typical female overreacting to some kind of noise. When we got back Rudy and I went through every crevice, nook, and cranny in the house. We had no gun. I had a butcher knife and a fireplace poker. Rudy had a fireplace poker. We went through every inch of the house and found nothing. Regardless, we took all the kids, [along with] Tammy, and all of us went to my house. We locked Tammy's house up and we all spent the night at my house.

"The next morning, which was a Sunday, there was to be a band rehearsal at the Franklin Road house," continued Richey. "When we got there, we opened the garage door and on the door going from the garage into the house were six or seven x's smeared in lipstick. We went in and on every TV screen, and on the smoked mirror that was over her canopy bed were words like 'slut,' 'pig,' 'whore,' 'bitch,' and 'kill.' "

A few weeks later, a wing of Tammy's house burned down. Then still later, her tour bus went up in flames. Rumors abounded that Tammy had created the public furor to garner publicity.

"This is a conjecture on my part," reflected Joan Dew, "but the harassment that went on for so long—the hang-up phone calls and the little harassments around the house—were all done by her as a way of getting sympathy and attention. Because every time something like that happened, she was going with somebody who wasn't available to her. They wouldn't commit themselves. And Tammy wants total commitment and if that's not forthcoming, then she will connive and scheme to do things to get that. One of the ways she feels that you can get that is if a guy thinks that you're a woman in danger, he'll protect you and come and save you."

But in late 1978 Tammy's unobserved attackers took to more drastic and dangerous tactics. First her eight-year-old daughter by George Jones, Tamala Georgette, was supposedly the victim of an attempted kidnapping. Then in early October Tammy was kidnapped. "It was the most terrifying experience of my life," Tammy said, describing how she was abducted from the parking lot of a Nashville shopping center. "[A man with a stocking over his head] opened the door, held the gun in his left hand, and dragged me out of the car. Then he hit me with his fist." The gunman then supposedly drove her out into the countryside and dumped her.

In Nashville, Tammy's abduction caused quite a stir. The music community didn't know what to make of her supposed kidnapping. Most were skeptical. A few wondered if Tammy had gotten involved with the wrong group of people. A few members of the press even speculated that George Jones might have played a role. But George denied any involvement.

"I happened to be at a friend's house that night," George later said. "I went to see a friend, and then a little later I went back to my apartment. My son was living with me, and when I walked in he said, 'Hey, Daddy, did you hear about Tammy? She got kidnapped. It was on the news a little while ago.' I was very disturbed because her new husband, George Richey, told me that a week before someone had tried to kidnap my child, Georgette. Right away I got on the phone and tried to get a hold of someone up there, but nobody answered.

"Naturally, I wanted to get right up there, so the next morning I drove to Nashville and tried to get ahold of somebody, but I still couldn't. Then I heard it was all over town that there was the possibility [I had kidnapped her]. But anybody who would say anything like that about me don't know George Jones the way they think they do. Because that's the woman who gave me quite a bit of happiness and was a good mother." George Richey later cleared George's name, and even laughed that someone could even conjecture that George Jones had been involved. But the police found no suspects and the fanfare gradually subsided, leaving Nashville to wonder what really happened.

As late as November of 1983, the mystery of Tammy's kidnapping had not been solved. George and Tammy Richey were adamant that the subject would never again be opened for discussion. "I think I have some idea of who was responsible for the kidnapping," said George Richey, while sitting on a sofa in his Jupitor, Florida, living room. "But if I talked about it, I wouldn't be living to tell you about it."

"We were better off not saying anything more than we did," added Tammy. "We'll never say anything more about it. But let me say that the rumor that I made it up is ridiculous. I couldn't. How would I go about cracking my own cheekbone? There were things that happened in the case that were never published and that will never be talked about. It was definitely not done for publicity or sympathy. That was a terrible ordeal that I went through that will frighten me and scare me and that I will dream about for the rest of my life."

Still, the suspicions regarding Tammy's abductions remained, possibly because her career had faltered badly by the late 1970s. Some thought she had become desperate for attention. And then there were the other aspects of her life that seemed out of control. By the fall of 1983, Tammy had undergone 13 major operations on her abdomen alone. In 1976, she had married and divorced a handsome, young Nashville real estate broker, Michael Tomlin. The marriage lasted only a few months. Joan Dew speculated Tammy married Tomlin to make Burt Reynolds, whom Tammy had been dating, jealous. If she had, the ploy didn't work.

In July of 1978, Tammy married once again, this time to George Richey, a successful songwriter and producer and former husband of Tammy's best friend, Sheila. On the surface, their relationship appeared ideal. At least professionally, they complemented one another. Richey had produced musical giants like Tex Ritter, Roy Rogers, Sonny James, and Freddy Hart. He had been head of Capitol Records and was working as the musical director for the popular syndicated country music comedy show, "Hee Haw," when he married. In addition, he was a prolific songwriter and had even written several of George's and Tammy's individual and duet hits.

Richey went on the road with Tammy, playing the piano and assuming the musical director role for her shows. Eventually he became Tammy's record producer after she left Sherrill in 1981. "We just stopped having fun," said Sherrill of the breakup. "So we each decided to do something different." In her book Tammy proclaimed she had never been happier after marrying Richey. "I look back on the time we've had together as the most contented I've known since I was a little girl, when Daddy was always there to take care of me," she said. "Richey is like that. No man had ever done for me as he has."

But friends worried about Tammy, noticing that she was becoming increasingly dependent on painkillers and drugs, particularly Demerol, and, as a result, had undergone a personality change. "Tammy used to be fun," claimed Joan Dew. "She was a great person once. Now you'll never know what kind of mood she'll be in because of all these drugs she's taking. Look, the only reason Tammy stayed with Richey this long is the drugs," asserted Dew in the summer of 1983, although Richey strongly denies the accusation. "[Otherwise] she would have never stayed with him this long. Once he moved into her house and divorced Sheila and married her, once that was done, she had his commitment. Then what was she to do? That was OK for a year, then she's bored again."

But Tammy claimed her new-found happiness and contentment was based on her feelings toward Richey, not on a drug-induced dependency. However, she did admit to a prolonged and frequent need for certain drugs.

"I've depended on Demerol plus a lot of other medications," Tammy reflected in November, 1983, just a few weeks after being released from the hospital once again, "to get me through an awful lot of shows and a lot of pain. There's been many nights when I thought I would die if I had to go on stage and I depended on pain pills to get me through many times. I don't care to admit that because I've had enough operations and enough illness that have been real that I don't use it as an excuse. It's just the truth. I've depended on pain medication many times.

"I've had physicians tell me many times that I was dependent on painkillers. In the same sense, they would turn around the next week and do surgery and use Demerol. I don't know what the answer is. I just had my thirteenth operation on my stomach. The first one was when Georgette was ten days old. Then I had an emergency appendectomy. The next year I had a complete hysterectomy. I form scar tissue very quickly and very badly. I had adhesions very bad.

When they started this last operation, they had no idea they were going to run into what they did. They knew I had enough to operate on like it was. But when they got into the stomach, the doctor told Richey and me that he had to work for the first two-and-a-half hours to cut away adhesions before he could even begin the surgery he was going to do. I form adhesions every time I'm cut upon. He said he still didn't touch the adhesions in the bottom part of my stomach. He just couldn't. They couldn't keep me [anesthetized] any longer. I was under six hours like I was. I scar very badly. I have adhesions very badly. They don't show up on x-rays, so they've had to do exploratory surgery on me twice to remove adhesions. And I've had total intestinal blockage three times from adhesions."

Tammy's dependency on Demerol and other painkillers came about because of adverse reactions to most other drugs. "I've always known that Demerol was very addictive," admitted Tammy. "But I always knew too that there were so few things that I could take for pain. Morphine cuts off my respiratory system immediately. Codeine I can't take. Naline I can't take. It never bothered me that Demerol was addictive because I always felt that I was a strong enough person that if I didn't have to have it, I wouldn't want it. When I have to have it, I took it and other things. There were other things I could take at times. When I didn't have to have it, I didn't take it. But I couldn't have worked these seventeen years the way I've worked without having to depend on something because I've had too many things happen, too many illnesses.

"I do deny that I was addicted," she continued. "Maybe I see addiction different [from most people]. I see addiction to Demerol or morphine or whatever as like somebody having to have it like on a daily basis or if they don't, they go through withdrawal. I've never done that. But I don't deny that I've used it and I've used it an awful lot."

According to Joan Dew, doctors along the way had requested that Tammy check herself into a hospital to overcome her addiction. Each time Tammy refused. "She wouldn't admit that she had a problem." noted Joan. "She'd just go to another doctor."

On that November day in 1983, Tammy claimed she had found happiness in her life. And perhaps she had. But there was no question that the frail, thin woman who sat in a room overlooking the vast ocean was a mere shadow of the young woman who had come to Nashville fifteen years earlier to prove to her family and hometown folk that she could become somebody. The singer who had warbled "Apartment No. 9" and "Stand By Your Man" had been bursting with life, hope, and energy. The Tammy Wynette of 1983 was tired and weary, struggling to maintain a career and public image. But at least she was content with one aspect of her life. She had at last found a man who could take care of her in the manner she had always wanted. George Richey was truly the prince who had charged in and swept her away. Tammy Wynette was at long last living in the white cottage.

CHAPTER
26
I'm Not Ready Yet

PEANUT MONTGOMERY** had not wanted to have George committed to a hospital's psychiatric ward. But he felt he had no choice. "He had become addicted to cocaine," Peanut told the psychiatrist at Florence's Eliza Coffee Memorial Hospital in the winter of 1979. "And over the last month both alcohol consumption and cocaine consumption had been markedly increased to the point that he would be stuporous and then would awaken and make threats of shooting the people that were closest to him." Feeling that George was not only a threat to himself, for he had started talking about committing suicide, but also to others around him, Peanut signed George over as a ward of the state of Alabama. Peanut Montgomery, one-time drinking partner of George's and now a reformed preacher, probably saved George's life. Peanut had hesitated as long as he had because "I didn't want to make George mad at me."

George was checked into the hospital on December 11. Hospital records reflect that George was "suffering from an acute paranoid state with suicidal and homicidal potential to a high degree. He

205

was suffering from delirium tremens, secondary to chronic and acute heavy intake of alcohol, and his admitting diagnosis also included the suspicion of chronic use of cocaine." Florence's Eliza Coffee Memorial kept him for a couple of days, and then the hospital authorities reported that the best place for George was at Birmingham's Hillcrest Hospital, under the care and attention of a Dr. Joe Nuckols. "He is highly trained and skilled, as is the hospital, in the treatment of narcotic addiction and alcoholism in addition to his other psychiatric conditions," hospital records note.

George was promptly transferred, even though, at the time, Peanut and Charlene didn't know how the hospital bill was going to be paid. "Hillcrest was a real fine place," recalled Charlene. "It's where a lot of rich people went. George didn't have any money, and we didn't know if they'd admit him without a deposit. Amid a flurry of phone calls, Peanut reached Paul Richey, Tammy Wynette's brother-in-law. "Tammy had told me, if there was ever a time George needed help, to call her," explained Peanut. "So I did and got Paul. I told him the problem, and he said he'd be right down with the money."

As it turned out, Hillcrest accepted George without a deposit. But because of Peanut's phone call, Paul Richey was now involved in the rehabilitation of George Jones. "I had a great empathy for what George was going through," Paul later revealed. "I'm an alcoholic, too, and had just gone through getting myself straightened out. In fact, I had just checked myself into Cumberland [a drug and alcohol rehabilitation center near Nashville] a few months before and had called my wife and had told her to call George Jones. I wanted him to go through the program with me. She suggested that I wait until I went through and then maybe I could help him. It was about four months after that when I became associated with George Jones. I was real happy to hear George was going to get some help."

Early in his stay George was resentful and bitter that he had been checked into a hospital against his will. But he was far too exhausted to do anything except mouth his protest. For five days he slept, waking only to go to the bathroom and feed himself. On the sixth day hospital reports note he began socializing with the other patients, taking his meals in the dining room, and showing signs of recovery. By then his initial anger had subsided and he seemed intent on getting well. George was already on a pentobarbital withdrawal regimen to overcome his cocaine addiction. Now George's psychiatrist was anxious to find out the underlying disturbances contained within the troubled singer's psyche.

Nothing George told Dr. Nuckols was new. "The patient blames all of his problems on the fact that all of the income is tied up to pay his debts," the doctor reported. "The patient states that he has felt that everyone is against him. The patient's history further indicated that he feels he is unable to perform. He is a top star in his field, and his inability to function in this capacity has been extremely depressing also to him." But George never had been one to seek comfort from doctors. Instead, George revealed later, most of his help during his stay in the hospital came from God.

"I started doing a lot of communicating with the Good Lord," George reflected. "I had chances to see down hollers I'd never seen down before. I hadn't wanted to see down them. I hadn't taken the time to see them. I think that sometimes the Lord has to hurt you, which is no hurt at all when compared to what He's hurt. When you see His love you know it. You can almost hear Him say, 'Now, you know why I gave you the choice.' I believe that if you don't take it, and you know it, you later wonder why you gave it up. You keep fighting it, and it's such a beautiful thing. You've got to be nuts because there ain't nothing that you've witnessed so far on earth that can equal it.

"A mama's love is about the closest thing that you can say that real love is, 'cause she'll sit up all night with you, she'll rock you, she'll doctor you, she'll take up for you, she'll hurt for you. That's like God's love," George continued. "God is not like when you command somebody to do something. God is love. The word love came from when He gave His only begotten Son. God showed what love really is then. He favors nobody. This world is full of the worst people in the world, and he loves them just as much. He made man in man's image, not God's. That was another strong love, unselfish. So we could have our own way of thinking, two choices. That's the reason Adam took the bite of the apple. And he thought it tasted so good. That's like me; I didn't want to give up something that tasted so good. But I found out it don't taste nowhere good as all that."

Sitting in the controlled stillness of his hospital room while reading his Bible and praying, George became convinced that he could now control his drug and drinking consumption. He even began to think about his future and how he could reestablish his career and resume singing. "I've always been called 'Mr. Instant,'" George admitted. "If something sounded good, I'd do it right then and get going with it. But I got to going with the wrong things. I made up my mind in the hospital that I was going to start thinking things out before I took the first step and try to do everything right this time. I knew that the most important thing was to get the right person handling my affairs. I decided to be careful and not to jump into anything like I used to. I asked God to help me."

His recovery at Hillcrest was nothing short of miraculous. Peanut had been told George might be there for as long as "sixty to ninety days." The doctors pronounced George "well" after only twenty-one days. They released him with the warning "that George was to limit his stress."

George's recovery was so incredible, in fact, that some wondered if George had not been as bad off as they had earlier thought. He had long before acquired the nickname of "possum" because of his uncanny ability to "play dead" at his convenience. W. T. Scroggins had witnessed George feign drunken stupors many a time to avoid singing. Sometimes even George wasn't sure if his condition was real or pretend.

What was real when George walked out of the Hillcrest Hospital on January 2, 1980, was his desire to begin anew. He felt better than he had in months. To celebrate his release, George asked a friend to take him to a liquor store. "You know how it is just getting out of the hospital," said George, having convinced himself he could control his liquor. "I just have to have a little drink." But perhaps George suspected that he might not be able to control his drinking after all. Perhaps he knew he was going to need help. Because by the evening's end, he had asked Paul Richey to be his manager.

"I had gone down to greet George when he got out," recalled Paul. "I had a lot of good news to give him. After the doctor had said George was going to need to stay in the hospital for sixty to ninety days I came back to Nashville and called my brother [George Richey]. I suggested to him that we call several producers, publishers, writers and ask for donations so that George's expenses while he was in the hospital could be paid. I went down and opened an account at my bank with my banker and myself signing. And we started paying George's expenses. He was two months behind on his house payment, two months behind on the car payment. Then we paid the utilities, everything that George had needed paying while he got well.

"So, when I went down the night he checked out, I showed George the books and the checking account records so he could see everything had been paid. I had written him a letter while he was in the hospital letting him know everything was being taken care of. So I had taken him the records. That's when he asked me to be his manager. He said that anyone who had done for him what I had done for him was the kind of person he wanted managing him.

"So I told George I would [be his manager] on two or three conditions," said Paul. "I said, 'first of all, there could be no more drinking or snorting coke.' Then I told him I would manage him as long as his career didn't interfere with my publishing business or my business didn't interfere with his career. George agreed, and we signed a management contract."

Paul moved quickly into his new role. In March, he staged a press meeting during which George made two major announcements—his own comeback and his professional reunion with Tammy. The gathering was held at the home of George Richey and Tammy and was reminiscent of the old days except that Tammy was now married to another George. George Jones squirmed and seemed uncomfortable but jokingly referred to Richey as "my husband-in-law."

"I'm just sure I'm on the right track this time," George said to the dozens of press persons gathered around him that day. "I don't plan to work quite as hard, maybe ten to twelve days a month. I don't want to overdo it, but I want to get back in full swing. I'm very happy, and it just seems wonderful to be able to sing again. I think singing with Tammy will help the both of us. I need their help to get my feet back on the ground again. They have been very good friends, being concerned and wanting to help. That's encouragement that I need bad, and I really appreciate it."

George and Tammy recorded "Two-Story House" immediately. It was their first duet together in more than two years. Both needed the career boost of their mutual appeal, but some thought Tammy was in need of it more than George. "I think that reunion was as much Tammy's idea as it was Richey's," recalled Joan Dew. "How long had it been since Tammy had had a real hit, two years?" "Two-Story House" glided up to the second slot on the *Billboard* charts. They followed that tune with another, "A Pair of Old Sneakers."

Paul wasted no time reestablishing George's career. He signed him with Jim Halsey Booking Agency, perhaps country music's most prestigious and successful booking agency. The company was already booking Tammy. George returned to the road, appearing primarily as a solo act and occasionally showcasing with Tammy. They went on "The Tonight Show" together, then they appeared on the daytime game show "Hollywood Squares" together.

George returned to the recording studio, finally finishing up "He Stopped Loving Her Today," a song he had attempted to record before he had gone to the hospital. "It took over a year to record that song," Billy Sherrill revealed. "The intro was recorded nine months before the recitation. Then the last verse was recorded three months after that. He did the first part in 1979. George'd come in, and he would be tired and hoarse, and we would have a fine first verse, but he wouldn't know the melody. He kept singing it to the melody of 'Help Me Make It through the Night' all that year, 'til I finally beat the other melody into his head. George would say, 'This is a better melody.' I'd say, 'Yes, George, it is a better melody, but it's "Help Me Make It through the Night." You'll be sued. We'll all be sued. You can't do that.' So finally he got the right melody and we released it."

In October of that year, during the Country Music Awards Show, George was presented the Male Vocalist of the Year award, and his song "He Stopped Loving Her Today" won Best Single and Best Song. George's comeback had been nothing less than spectacular. Against all odds and expectations, he had made a startling recovery. For months he didn't miss a show and he even made surprise appearances with Tammy. In addition to his CMA Awards, George was also presented a Grammy by the National Academy of Recording Arts and Sciences for best male country vocal performance.

It was to be one of the best years of his career. "He Stopped Loving Her Today" was a classic country music tearjerker, taking advantage of George's full range of vocal versatility. It was to become one of his biggest sellers, garnering first gold and then platinum status. From all obvious appearances, George seemed back on top.

Then there were rumblings of trouble in paradise. George appeared on a Nashville newscast, making strong accusations about Paul Richey, comparing Paul to Baggott, who by now was serving time in prison. "They both stole my money," George charged. But Paul said the accusations were ridiculous and should be ignored because of George's condition.

"When George said those things on Channel 2 he was messed up," declared Paul. "Four days earlier he had gotten out of a hospital in Beaumont, Texas, where his family had him committed. We had been at a date, and when we got on the bus he asked me to have him committed to a hospital. He said that with the heavy schedule ahead of him that he would never make it unless he checked himself into a hospital. So we drove up and checked him in on a Sunday afternoon and checked him out at Tuesday noon.

"Then we drove to Beaumont," continued Paul. "A day later he went crazy, and his sisters had him checked into a hospital down there. They had brought him back [to Florence], and then for two days the Channel 2 reporters were after him. They told him that they had interviewed me and that it looked real bad on him. They followed him around. So finally, after he was backed into a corner, he said, 'Well, if that is the case, then here's this.' I don't think that's fair for reporters to do that because George was sick. Then they lied and cornered him into saying something."

Nevertheless, George stood firm in his desire to leave Paul. George wanted out from under Paul's management for several reasons. First of all, he was again exhausted. "I've been working harder than I ever have in my life," declared George, who had been under doctor's orders to take it easy. Second, George felt he was being taken down the same path as he had been under Baggott. Paul was booking him into fancy New York clubs and building him up into a star, something George wanted no part of. Paul even booked George back into the Bottom Line for a return performance. This time George showed up, but he was miserable being there.

But what hurt George more than anything was his growing belief that the Richey brothers and Tammy had used him. "They got me to work with them to show people that they were concerned about me, that they were trying to help me," reflected George. "They even started this recording thing. They came to me with that. You know why they did that, don't you? So the fans and people will believe the lies she's told about me and forgive her because all that must be true, the fans will say. They'll say, 'Look how she's still trying to do something to help him.' I don't need no more of this help. I'm not putting her down. But I'll not change and do things for the almighty dollar. I didn't ask for that to start with."

Because of his inability to handle disappointment, George began drinking again. His old flashes of paranoia started reappearing. So, when his bankruptcy petition was denied and his cash flow became severely restricted, he assumed Paul was taking money. Try as he might, George could not understand how he could have been earning thousands of dollars each week and yet have only a few hundred to spend.

George told Paul he wanted out of the arrangement but Paul stayed firm in the saddle. He was sitting atop a five-year management contract with George and was not about to be toppled. "Nobody wants out of this deal more than I do," professed Paul in the summer of 1981. "But George owes me between $150,000 and $180,000. Those are the monies my brother and I loaned George to get started again. And there is no way I'm going to let George out of his contract with the money he owes us. I'm not just going to turn my back and say that's OK."

But about that time a tall Texan named Billy Bob Barnett entered the picture, arriving like the Lone Ranger out of the western horizon. He had heard George's plea for help and was there to offer assistance to the weary singer—for a price, of course.

CHAPTER
27
The Battle

EORGE HAD MET Billy Bob while performing at his Fort Worth club, Billy Bob's of Texas, in June. Even then George and Billy Bob discussed getting together professionally. In July, when George went public with his dissatisfaction with the Richeys, Billy Bob roared up to Nashville to discuss with George a takeover of the management of his career. George was agreeable. "I don't mean any offense to Billy Bob when I say this," admitted George. "I'm not putting him down, but any move would be better than the last two big ones I've made in these last few years."

Billy Bob was a big man who did things in big ways. George's entangled financial affairs prevented any kind of an immediate agreement between George and Billy Bob. George's bankruptcy was on appeal, and Paul was holding strong to his contract. So, needful of something to announce about their newfound friendship, George and Billy Bob proclaimed the intent to be partners. There was quite a hoopla about the whole affair. George, ever in need of having someone to lean on, announced that he was moving back to Texas to live near Billy Bob.

Subsequently Billy Bob threw two big parties in George's honor. The first was a farewell party, given in Nashville at a beer joint named Pee Wee's, which was owned and operated by George's longtime friend, Pee Wee Johnson. Much of Nashville turned out for it. Literally dozens were turned away at the door. Then, after putting George and his entourage on a Lear jet and flying them all to Fort Worth, Billy Bob hosted another party in his VIP lounge at Billy Bob's. This time it was a party to welcome George home.

For a few days, all seemed bliss. Then, as suddenly as the relationship had started, it all ended. At the last minute George backed out of his new arrangement with Billy Bob and announced he had decided to manage himself. "I felt that Barnett's people were heading me down the same road I had been down before," announced George. "Business people take all the meat in the soup."

In private, George admitted Billy Bob had been too flamboyant for his liking. Again, the paranoid George was afraid of being taken advantage of. "The business has changed so much since George started that he just doesn't understand a lot of it now," observed Tom Binkley, George's attorney. "When he was taking care of business the singer was paid his $2,500 from the club owner's take, and he pocketed that and went on. Well, now you have to pay payroll taxes and the overhead. With the Lear jets and all, he just didn't understand the costs. He's back to riding the bus now instead of taking those Lear jets so much."

George was criticized for splitting with Billy Bob, but he was determined to get a hold of his career. He wanted to keep it simple, the way it had been before he hit the big time with Tammy. He hired a road manager, Wayne Oliver, and tried to get his career back in line. "Billy Bob was just too big-time for George," sneered Wayne. "We're back down where we feel comfortable and in control." Finally, George got a lucky break. His long-pending bankruptcy was at last granted so that his finances became somewhat manageable. And in a grand effort to make a new start, he moved to Muscle Shoals where Peanut and Charlene Montgomery were beckoning him to come join them. They were the last semblance of family he had, so he went.

The Montgomerys had moved the few miles from Florence to Muscle Shoals so that Peanut could start a little church there. By now the converted Peanut had felt the calling to become a preacher. "Just call me Brother Peanut," offered George's former drinking buddy. But to pay the bills until Peanut built up a congregation, Charlene had started selling real estate. No sooner had George announced his willingness to move to Muscle Shoals than she was out hunting George a place. It didn't take her long to find one, get it furnished, and have it ready and waiting for George to move in. Her sister, Linda Welborn, moved in shortly thereafter. The Montgomerys made subtle hints that George and Linda might at long last marry, so as to make Linda "an honest woman." But George rebuffed those efforts and continued dating around.

Through Wayne, his road manager, George met one woman he started dating regularly, much to the dismay of Linda and the Montgomerys. But George was not to be discouraged, for he had a good time with her, a better time than he had ever had with the somewhat mousey Linda. Her name was Nancy Sepulvada; she was a divorced mother of two teenage children living in Shreveport, Louisiana. She was dark-haired, dark-eyed, and George described her as "pretty as a pup."

"I had a girlfriend who was dating his manager," recalled Nancy, who was working at a factory at the time. "He had invited her to New York and she wanted me to go, too. I had been working twelve-hour days and then going home to my two daughters who greeted me with 'Hi, Mom, what's for dinner?' I was worn out, and my kids had gone to visit their daddy. I almost didn't go, but at the last minute I thought, 'Why sit at home by myself and get depressed?' So I went. I didn't know anything about George Jones. I loved his music, but I didn't know about him skipping shows and all the rest. We just had fun. He sang real good that weekend, and I thought he was real nice."

Ironically, right after he started dating Nancy, George and Wayne parted ways. Neither, they discovered, was happy with the arrangement. But in the midst of their disputes they took time out to go to Nashville to pick up George's second Male Vocalist of the Year award. "He Stopped Loving Her Today" won for a second year in a row the coveted Song of the Year award. But as George watched songwriters Curly Putnam and Bobby Braddock accept the award, his heart wasn't in it. Once again, his personal life was in a shambles.

Soon after he and Wayne parted ways, George began having run-ins with Peanut and Charlene. He had grown weary of Brother Peanut's constant moralizing and sermonizing. At every opportunity Peanut quoted the Bible and talked of George's soul "burning in hell" if he did not change his sinful ways. But there was always Peanut's request that George give to his fledgling church until finally George was convinced that Peanut and Charlene were no different from the rest, that they too were more interested in getting to the change in his pocket than in his well-being.

"George has a different way of testing whether or not people are sincere," explained George's hairdresser and longtime friend, Jimmie Hills. "Like when I first started getting to know George, he came over here to my shop one day. We had a good time, talking and drinking coffee, and we talked. He wasn't drinking or nothing. He asked me to use the bathroom and went in and used the bathroom and come out. He told Danny, my boy, that there was a little shaving kit out there in the car seat that he wanted him to go get. Danny went out there and got it. George pulled out a whole sack of money. He must have pulled out $7,000 or $8,000 and handed it to me. I said, 'What's this for, George?' He said, 'I want you to have it.' I said, 'George, I don't want it.' I told him if he was trying to buy my friendship and things like that, that I didn't want to have a friend like that. I said, 'You're welcome here in my house, and I'll do anything in the world for you that I can, but I don't need your money.' Anyway, he was testing me out right there. They say he'll do that. That's why they call him the possum. He'll check you out. If I took it, I'd had the money, but he probably wouldn't have anything else to do with me. He expects a friend to be a true friend."

At some point during the fall or winter of 1982 the Montgomerys lost the "possum" test. Subsequently George fell into a deep, blue funk. He was terribly conscious that he was, yet again, alone. His already worsening drinking problem became chronic. And he started snorting cocaine like before his recovery. It had become increasingly difficult for him to resist. A couple of Muscle Shoals drug dealers were following him around like shadows. "They'd slip it in to him in every conceivable way," recalled Nancy. "George was too weak to resist."

Somehow, all through those long months of his decline in late 1982, Nancy remained, absorbing his rage and taking the brunt of his anger. He was convinced that no one really cared. He seemed determined to run her away, too. He threw her off the bus on several occasions, leaving her to fend for herself with no money in strange towns in the middle of the night. "She went through hell for him," mused Ann Hills, Jimmie's wife. He hit her in fits of anger, cussed her out for no real reason. Still she stayed. "I somehow knew if I left him then, it'd all be over," she recalled. "I thought he was well worth saving. Because when he was straight, he had a heart bigger than anybody I've ever known."

George wanted to believe. He hungered to have the strength to straighten up. "I can remember going over to Westside Hospital with him a year earlier," recalled Rick Blackburn. "I remember going over and sitting on the side of the bed. He said, 'Rick, you've got to help me.' He was choked up and teared and sincere, and he said, 'I just really got to get control of things. I'm going to be fifty years old, and I don't see the light at the end of the tunnel. I've made a lot of money in my day, and I've sung a lot of songs, and I just don't have anything to show for it all.' And then he says, 'I'm scared. You've got to help me.'

"It dawned on me that this guy doesn't work under any retirement plan, and all of a sudden he's trying to solidify his life a little bit, and he's thinking about his kids, and he's thinking about his family life," continued Rick. "He kept saying, 'All I want to do is just buy a house, and I want to settle down, and I just want to live normally.' "

But a year later he was still too weak to straighten up. "He's in this game, and he don't know how to get out of it," explained W. T. Scroggins. "George talks a lot about religion and all that. When you see a fellow do that who's doing bad, they really know what they're doing. He don't want to do it, but he's scared. That's what you call running scared. If the boy would just open up to somebody, he'd be all right. He's just like a lion in a cage. He ain't going to sit down. I think if George would sit down and just open up and talk and bring all this out, I think it would help him more than anything. I think it'd help him more than a doctor. We [Helen and I] try to let him know that somebody cares. But George thinks if he goes to talking like that, that you think he's crazy. In his mind he really thinks everybody thinks he's sick, but he ain't."

As the weeks passed, Nancy became more of a crucial figure in George's life. "He still don't trust her completely, but he's beginning," observed W. T. "He brought her down here to see what we thought, and I told him she was a fine girl." But regardless of her support and her strength, George seemed unable to stay off the drugs. "We had been trying to get George into the hospital for months," recalled Helen Scroggins. "I nearly got him in there twice, and he'd slip through my hands. We had him right down there at his son's house, and we didn't get him in the hospital then because his son wouldn't let us come down there to get him.

"You know, then Jeff really hadn't growed up about his daddy. Jeff is real tenderhearted, but I think the biggest problem was Bryan. He wasn't wanting George in the hospital. But when we had told them we might have to call the law there at Vidor to help us to get George in the hospital, they just throwed [the idea] plum out. Dr. Caskey had told us he would meet us and put him in there and take care of George. When we said the law, they didn't want no law. I told them, 'George is sick. I don't like it either; he's my brother. I don't like to have to get the law to escort him to the hospital, but had you rather for him to be dead?' I tried to talk to them, but they wouldn't listen. George got to where he wouldn't even come to my house 'cause they all told him I was going to put him in the hospital. If that bunch had kept their mouths shut, he'd have come to my house. He always trusted me, and we could have got him some help."

But there seemed to be no help to be found. Toward the end of 1982 Helen was scared, frightened that her brother, George, might not make it after all. "George is losing his voice," she said sadly. "The doctor told him if he didn't straighten up, he couldn't sing no more. I'm not sure George could live with that."

Still Doin' Time

GEORGE'S TURNAROUND came at the darkest hour, at that moment when he could play no more games with himself or anyone else, when he had to decide if he really wanted to live on. But it was to be more than his decision alone, for by the late winter of 1982 George was a very sick man. To survive he needed more than kindness or romantic love; he needed the love of a mother. George was lucky; he finally realized that someone cared after all. Most people are never really sure.

There was a series of happenings that occurred to make George realize he was cared about. Nancy had become totally frustrated to the point that she thought by taking her own life she might convince George to live. She tried suicide by taking an overdose of epilepsy pills. Fortunately, she was found in time to be saved. "The doctor told me that she wouldn't have killed herself," recalled Ann Hills. "That those pills would have messed up her mind. I asked her why she had done it. She was asittin' there on her bed crying and sayin', 'I don't want no house; I don't want no Lincoln automobile. I'll live in a shack down by the railroad track. I just want to be with George. I just want to fix black-eyed peas and cornbread for that man. If I thought that me dying would help make him see the light, then that's what I want to do. I've tried everything else, and nothing's worked. I thought maybe this would.' We talked, and I convinced her that killing herself would only make George worse. All I know is that she sure loved that man a lot to be willing to give up her own life."

Nancy had been trying her best to get George off the drugs, but to no avail. Nobody else, except the Scrogginses, seemed to understand just how difficult it was for George to pull himself away from the cocaine habit. Drug dealers were ever present around George, giving him the stuff either to win favor or to keep him hooked. In Shreveport, where they now had moved because it had gotten so bad in Muscle Shoals, Nancy was fighting everybody alone. She was trying desperately to get George to Texas, where she knew the Scrogginses would help. But everyone else, including George's children, seemed to be working against her.

"Then, one night, Jeff called me up crying," explained Helen. "He said, 'I know I done wrong when I let Daddy slip right through our fingers.' Jeff had went over there the night that George played at Orange. Then Jeff seen his own self [what was happening]. The pushers got ahold of George, one on each side, and carried him to the bathroom. Jeff went there and banged on that door and tried to get them to let his daddy out of there. George was begging for them to turn him loose and leave him alone. Jeff said, 'Helen, I told them if I ever caught them ever giving my daddy a shot or anything, I'd kill em.' That's when he went on with his daddy back to Lafayette and he got to helping him.

"I told them boys that their daddy couldn't get out of the cocaine by hisself," continued Helen. "I said, 'He's got to have help or he's going to die. He's going to take an overdose and that's going to be it,' I told them. So the boys started going over to their daddy's and staying a lot during the week and helping."

It was encouragement that George desperately needed. "They helped fix up his place," recalled Helen. "Mr. Bruce [a family friend] helped get George a satellite dish [for TV], and George was thrilled over that. Then George come in and the boys had helped Nancy get all the curtains up and the bedspreads and everything and put them up and that just tickled George to death. I talked to him the night the boys had done that, and George was telling me how happy he was about the boys helping out and about seeing the grandbaby [Jeff and his wife had a three-year-old girl]. I later found out George had made [Jeff's wife] go out and get a housecoat and some house shoes and what all. That's when he really started doing all right."

George's real turning point came, however, when he saw his son, Bryan, under the influence of drugs. "Bryan was strung out on cocaine," lamented Helen. "George seen his own kid. George told me about going to see him once. And when he seen his own son strung out like that I think it kind of opened his eyes. He told us, 'If I can get off of it, then Bryan could get off of it.' So, you see, George begun to hurt in two ways. He was hurting because he had to go without that cocaine, but the bigger hurt was watching his own son strung out. After that he began to do something to straighten hisself up, 'cause he couldn't say nothing to his son until he did."

Finally, after nearly seven years on the run from himself, George decided to stand still long enough to face his problems. His transformation did not take place overnight. To overcome the cocaine addiction he needed days and even weeks of solitude and quiet, away from the stress of the road and club life. So he and Nancy retreated to her house in Shreveport, holing themselves up for days. There, with her help, he began to get well again. She cared for him like a mother, spoon-feeding him when he was too weak to feed himself, holding his head while he was sick, comforting him when he thought the agony was too much to bear. "I think that's when he started trusting her," recalled W. T.

With the worst behind him, he began to talk again of the future. He started driving over to see W. T. and Helen Scroggins, at the same time looking over property to buy for himself and Nancy. "He was telling me he had seen this land," recalled Jimmie Hills. "He didn't say he was going to build a park then. He was going to buy the land and build a log house. He'd always wanted a log house. I knew by the way he was talking that he was better."

In early 1983 George and Nancy moved to Colmesneil, Texas, just a stone's throw from where the Scrogginses lived and less than sixty miles from where George had been born fifty-one years earlier in the middle of the Depression. As his confidence grew and the memory of his yesteryears faded into the dust of the dirt roads leading outward toward the East, George decided to build a park like he had always wanted, one where his people could come on Saturday and Sunday afternoons to listen to a few hours of good ole country music. No alcoholic beverages would be allowed; it was an evil drink. Playground equipment would be built so that the little children could play while their parents sat at picnic tables listening to the music. He could have his friends—Little Jimmy Dickens, Merle Haggard, Johnny Cash, and others—come down to join him. And the best part of it all was that it would all be right outside his back door. He began talking about coming off the road.

So Nancy, George, and the Scrogginses began work on his "Jones Country" project. They cleared the land, dug up stumps, seeded grass, and planned construction of the performing building. They recall that George was happier than they had ever seen him. He still had his difficult moments, however. He was committed to being on the road for at least another year or so to make up for dates that had been blown. Good road jobs also brought in the money necessary to begin construction of his park. Jones Country money was still tight. And from time to time a drug dealer drove to colmesneil to try to sell George a few snorts of cocaine. Usually they were run off before they had a chance to get to George. But all in all, George was happy. He was at last beginning to see the light at the end of the tunnel. "He said he was nearly fifty-two years old and that, if he was ever going to settle down, this was it," reflected Jimmie Hills. "He said, 'I'm through. This is my home.' "

"He don't have to dress up to go to town like he did when he lived in Nashville," explained W. T. "He'll put on those slouchy jogging britches and wear them into town. He goes into the stores just like he's a common farmer around here, just whooping and hollering. He acts like these folks around here, where if he did that in these big cities, somebody would try to send him to the asylum."

"I always told George that, if he would get to a small place like this and stay there long enough, people would get used to him and they ain't going to bother him," added Helen. "They don't bother him here like they would in a big city. You just can't be comfortable in a big city." "When he first moved here, we had a real problem keeping people away," interjected W. T. "Nancy'd call, and I'd go over and get rid of people. I had to get downright rude to get everybody in line. After a while, they got the message. Now they don't pay him no attention."

George and Nancy purchased a three-bedroom mobile home and bought nearly sixty acres of undeveloped timberland on which to set it. The acreage proved to be ideal. They were miles from their nearest neighbor, nestled in a clearing that provided both open space but with an overview of the surrounding wilderness. George needed the isolation. "George told me the reason he didn't want everybody coming around was that he was still going through these here aftereffects [of the drugs] and being depressed. He said, 'I still get like that. I can fight it better if I'm by myself, if I stay alone, just at home and nobody around me.' I said that showed he was trying."

And try he did, although there were a few setbacks and touchy moments. "Nancy said one night Bryan come in drunk," recalled Helen. "She had been trying to get some food down George so he could get to where he could eat again. She told George, 'Just go on to your room, and I'll handle it.' That night she got Bryan in bed, and then she said the next morning she went in there where Bryan was, and she told him, 'I don't want that to ever happen again.' She said, 'We love you and everything, but you're not going to go out and get drunk and come home and act indecent. That's not helping your daddy. He's trying to get straightened up, and we're not going to put up with this.' After that, Bryan started really trying to help hisself. Now they've been taking him on the road with them."

By the spring of 1983 George had not snorted cocaine for months. "If he can get through this next year like he is now, I think he's gonna be just fine," noted Helen. She credited Nancy as the reason for George's recovery. "I think the big difference is Nancy," observed Helen. "That little girl really works. She keeps their books and writes down everything he spends. She even got him to thinking about what he spends, and she don't write the checks. She makes him do that. He don't got no manager. He's just got a booking agent, bodyguard, lawyer, and like that, but no manager.

She and him take care of where his money is going. He's gotten to where he's real concerned with where his money is going. He never used to be like that. He even stands up better for himself now. He used to just let people walk all over him.

"Nancy's the biggest thing that's helped him," she continued. "He feels like he's got somebody who really cares about him, George, and not just what he can buy her. He doesn't want to have to buy anybody's love. All he wanted was for somebody to love him. He thinks the world of her. W. T. really likes her, and George said that, if he likes her, she must be all right. She went through a lot with George. He got off this here dope without any professional help. I think if he had been really hooked, he would have needed outside help. But he did it all on his own. I think he must have been playing possum a lot of them times to get people to leave him alone. Now, he went through some bad times, and Nancy stayed with him. I told George that anybody who stayed with him through all that had to be good. He'd hit her and do all sorts of bad things, but she stayed. She treats him wonderful. He doesn't know what he'd do without her. She has his food ready even if he don't want to eat. She makes sure that he gets off on time. He's done seventy-six shows in a row now without missing. All that credit goes to her. She told him that she would be with him even if he got rock bottom. All his life George wanted somebody he could trust and who would treat him like a real person. Now he's got in her what he always wanted."

George Jones took Nancy Sepulvada as his bride on March 4 of that turnaround year. The ceremony was brief and took place in the living room of W. T. and Helen Scroggins. The groom wore blue jeans and tennis shoes. The bride was attired in blue jeans, western shirt, and cowboy boots. Rev. Jack Minyard, pastor of Colmesneil's First Baptist Church, performed the ceremony. No official photos were taken, only a few Polaroid shots. Only W. T. and Helen Scroggins were in attendance. "We didn't fancy anything up," George told a local reporter later. George did not promise Nancy perfection. "He still drinks a little now and then," commented W. T. "That's to be expected." But he did promise to try to live the right way. Perhaps his willingness to marry was his seal of sincerity.

"George has got real good plans," concluded Helen. "If everything goes all right, he's going to build a studio here. He wants to quit the road and have his own place to perform. George is too old to keep going on the road. He wants all his family together. He considers his family our children, his children, Nancy, and her children. But before that can happen he's got to first get his two-story log house built. Then he'll get a performing place built. He's got one of his sons working for him, and he wants to have his other son with him, too. He won't go hardly anywhere without Nancy. She lets him be himself. I feel better about George now than I have in a long time. I think this time he's gonna make it."

CHAPTER

29

Shine On

HE DAY WAS A HOT ONE, even for June in East Texas. George Jones, clad in shorts, an open polyester shirt, and tennis shoes, stood in front of his nearly completed platform stage talking to a workman. It wasn't yet noon, but already sweat was heavily beaded on George's brow. The eight men scattered around the performing stage were drenched in their sweat.

A horn blew and, turning around, George saw his brother-in-law, W. T. Scroggins. "How you doing, boy?" exclaimed the old man as he rolled out of his navy pickup truck. Helen got out from the other side and went over to give George a hug. "It's a real hot one, huh, Helen?" said George with a smile as he took a sip from his beer can and wiped the moisture from his forehead. While W. T. and George talked about the progress of the men's work, Helen moved off to peep into the dressing rooms and loft of the fifty-foot-by-thirty-foot pine structure.

"Billy, our son-in-law, is building this place," explained Helen. "Him and his sons. We knew he'd do a fine job." Amid several men hammering and sawing, she strolled through the two dressing rooms, the two baths, a living area, and then pointed out the loft up above, where George had built a place just for himself and personally invited guests. The roofed stage area was behind a door, and when she opened it a forest of tall pines stretched out as far as the eye could see. "That's where George is gonna build his log house," Helen said, pointing to a small hill off to the right. "It'll be far enough away so he can have some privacy. They're gonna build them a wall around their log house with a seeing eye so nobody can walk up without being noticed."

Someone hollered from among the pines, then suddenly Nancy came thundering up across the needle-strewn forest bed astride a three-wheeler going as fast as she dared. A small, thin black woman, reminiscent of Prissy in *Gone with the Wind*, straddled the seat behind her. "Hi, Helen," yelled Nancy. "You remember Barbara, the maid, don't you?" Nancy asked after speeding around W. T.'s pickup truck and then screeching to a sudden halt.

Two young girls, both displaying the same dark good looks of Nancy, arrived shortly thereafter on another three-wheeler, sending squeals of laughter into the wind. They stopped alongside Nancy and Barbara. "Don't you want to come up to the house where it's cool?" Nancy invited, patting a spot next to her. Helen hopped on. "George is a tyrant on these things," Nancy yelled over her shoulder. "One time I jumped off; he was going so fast. We have races, but George always wins." Then with a giant guffaw, Nancy added, " 'Course, he gets mad if he doesn't."

The brown mobile home was just ahead, located directly behind the back-of-the-stage area up on a small hill. Nancy laughed like a kid, jerking the fast-moving vehicle from one side to another so as to avoid fallen tree limbs and stumps. Suddenly the three-wheeler stood straight up as if frozen in time. Then slowly, very slowly, it fell backward, finally coming to rest upside down. "Helen, are you all right?" shrieked Nancy, who was practically doubled over with laughter. "I forgot to tell you to lean forward when we started going up the hill." Still chuckling, Nancy jumped up from the ground, brushed her clothes, and then helped Helen brush hers. "Is Helen all right?" yelled George as he walked quickly from the house trailer. He and W. T. had decided to drive the truck back around. " 'Course, I am," answered Helen with a big smile, pleased that George seemed concerned. "Can't you drive no better than that?" teased George as he came up to hug his wife.

Already their newly seeded yard was lush and green. Rose bushes, peach saplings, and numerous plantings adorned the front yard. A porch had been constructed at the front step-up door, and various black aluminum figurines were perched around. Although the wooded area surrounding the home was breathtaking in its splendor, this wildness and ruggedness was in marked contrast to the neat, well-groomed yard flanking the trailer. The noise of the stage construction was muted by the distance and thick pine growth.

The trailer, tastefully decorated in shades of beige and cream, was nice but unpretentious. "I've seen George live in million-dollar mansions," reflected W. T. "But I have never seen him prouder of a place. I didn't think he would stay long in a mobile home. But he has. I've seen him walk through them there woods yelling, 'I'm so happy. I'm so happy. I can't sleep at night, I'm so happy.' It makes you want to cry to see him like this," W. T. added.

"Say hello to Shine On," Nancy said to W. T. while pointing to a six-week-old, black-and-white pug with a spiraled tail. "Shine On" was the title of George's latest hit single. "We call him Shine for short." Nancy moved the crew through the living room, kitchen, and then into the den, where Barbara was preoccupied with a TV program as she mechanically folded towels. "Let's go out back," said Nancy with an outward motion through the open sliding door. In the backyard set an old-fashioned swing chair, a wooden love seat, and a picnic table.

"I don't like horses," Nancy's younger daughter, Sherry, said with a pout while plopping ungracefully into the love seat. Adina rolled her dark eyes and mounted an albino Appaloosa mix and proclaimed, "Well, I do," while eyeing her mother, a signal that she wanted the horse.

After having run from person to person, turning flips, twirling, and chasing its tail, Shine On had captivated everyone's attention. "She's crazy today," observed Nancy. "She's doing things she's never done before. Quick, bring me a mirror," Nancy directed Sherry. "She's scared of herself," said Nancy, who, upon taking a mirror, set it on the ground in front of the little dog. Sure enough, Shine On started barking at its own image, then ran away. Everyone laughed. "If I looked like that dog, I'd run, too," W. T. hee-hawed.

"When you gonna put on the beans?" hollered George from inside the sliding glass back door. "Look at that; he didn't ask if I was gonna put them on, he told me to put them on," said Nancy, with a chuckle. "He's getting spoiled." Getting up, she turned and added, "Ain't that great?

"Why don't you all come back in here?" Nancy said after a few minutes of being inside the trailer. "It's cooler." She was already busy putting snapped green beans in a large aluminum pot. She added ham hock, small potatoes, and covered the mixture with a lid. "George is a real finicky eater," observed Helen. "When they're on the road he wants Nancy to fix him a fresh chocolate pie every night after he performs. So Nancy bakes him a chocolate pie."

"When we went here a while back on the road with them, George and I would eat pert near a whole pie every night," said W. T., as he sat and sipped hot coffee.

"Oh, you're exaggerating," retorted Nancy.

"What do you mean, woman?" responded W. T. "One of George's pieces is half the pie."

The sun had moved by now across the sky and was beginning to drop into the horizon. The temperature had cooled, but still the day was sticky and humid. A black man started mowing the grass in the backyard. The noise from the lawn mower totally drowned out the sounds of the construction crew working on the stage. They continued their "chewing of the fat" until dusk. It was a favored pastime of country people. Then W. T. stood up, stretched, and announced he and Helen had to go home. "She's gonna fix some dumplings," W. T. said, glancing around to see the reaction. Helen's dumplings were a family favorite.

Getting no reaction, W. T. and Helen moved toward the door, certain that they'd be talking to George and Nancy again before the night had passed. Even when George and Nancy were on the road, the foursome stayed in close communication with one another.

"We're real close-knit now," W. T. later observed. "This is the way George has wanted it for all his life. And I think he's learned enough to 'ppreciate what he's got now."

George had not asked for much all those years. He was a country boy who had wanted to stay country, who had the misfortune of living in a society that pushed him to change. "I would like to be left alone," George had reflected earlier. "Just let me do what I know I can do, what I want to do, what I love to do. God has given me so much strength. I should have been dead already. But I just kept believing. I've always said the truth will win, and if the Good Lord is willing, it will win."

On Labor Day weekend of 1983, just two weeks before his fifty-second birthday, George Jones opened his park, Jones Country, to a capacity crowd. More than ten thousand people—farmers, factory workers, housewives, and builders—turned out for the occasion. George had hoped for maybe five thousand or so to attend. He felt real pride that day and gave the crowd one heck of a performance as a show of his gratitude. At last, George Jones had found peace with himself. Amid the pine trees of East Texas, he was back home.

Discography

SINGLES

STARDAY	TITLES	DATE
130	You're in My Heart/No Money in This Deal	3-6-54
146	Wrong about You/Play It Cool, Man	5-29-54
160	Let Him Know/Let Me Catch My Breath	7-16-54
162	Let Him Know/You All Goodnight	9-25-54
165	Heartbroken Me (with S. Burns)/Tell Her	11-6-54
188	Hold Everything/What's Wrong with Me?	5-14-55
202	Why, Baby, Why/Seasons of My Heart	8-27-55
216	What Am I Worth/Still Hurtin'	1-14-56
234	I'm Ragged But I'm Right/Your Heart	4-7-56
240	Rock It/How Come It (as Thumper Jones)	5-5-56
247	It's OK/You Gotta Be My Baby	6-30-56
256	Boat of Life/Taggin' Along	8-11-56

STARDAY	TITLES	DATE
264	Gonna Come Get You/Just One More	9-15-56
279	Yearning/So Near	12-8-56
591	Boat of Life/Where Will I Shelter My Sheep?	6-16-62

D		
1226	New Baby for Christmas/Maybe Next Christmas	

MERCURY		
71029	Don't Stop the Music/Uh, Uh, No	1-19-57
71049	Just One More/Gonna Come Get You	2-15-57
71061	Yearning/Cry, Cry (with J. Hicks)	3-21-57
71096	Too Much Water/All I Want to Do	4-29-57
71141	Flame in My Heart/No, No, Never	7-1-57
.71176	Tall, Tall Trees/Hearts in My Dream	8-26-57
71224	Cup of Loneliness/Take the Devil Out of Me	11-11-57
71225	Maybe Next Christmas/New Baby for Christmas	11-4-57
71257	Color of the Blues/Eskimo Pie	2-3-58
71339	I'm Not the Wrong One/Nothing Can Stop Me (with J. Hicks)	6-23-58
71340	Wondering Soul/Jesus Wants Me	6-30-58
71373	Treasure of Love/If I Don't Love You	10-13-58
71406	White Lightning/Long Time to Forget	2-9-59
71464	Who Shot Sam?/Into My Arms Again	6-22-59
71506	My Lord Has Called Me/If You Want to Wear a Crown	10-5-59
71514	Big Harlan Taylor/Money to Burn	10-19-59
71583	Accidentally On Purpose/Sparklin' Brown Eyes	2-8-60
71615	Have Mercy on Me/If You Believe	5-2-60
71636	Family Bible/Your Old Standby	6-4-60

MERCURY	TITLES	DATE
71641	Out of Control/Just Little Boy Blue	6-20-60
71700	The Window Up Above/Candy Hearts	6-20-60
71721	Family Bible/Taggin' Along	12-19-60
71804	Tender Years/Battle of Love	6-5-61
71856	Did I Ever Tell You? (with M. Singleton)/Not Even Friends	9-4-61
71910	Aching, Breaking Heart/When My Heart Hurts No More	1-6-62
71955	City of the Angles (with M. Singleton)/ Talk about Lovin'	4-21-62
72010	You're Still on My Mind/Cold, Cold Heart	7-14-62
72034	I Want to Be Where You're Gonna Be/ When Two Worlds Collide (with M. Singleton)	9-29-62
72087	I Love You Because/Revenoor Man	2-9-63
72159	Are You Mine?/I Didn't Hear You	8-3-63
72200	Mr. Fool (with M. Montgomery)/One Is a Lonely Number	11-9-63
72233	The Last Town I Painted/Tarnished Angel	2-15-64
72293	Life to Go/Oh Lonesome Me	7-11-64
72362	I Wouldn't Know about That/You Better Treat Your Man Right	11-14-64

UNITED ARTISTS		
424	She Thinks I Still Care/Sometimes You Just Can't Win	3-3-62
442	Beacon in the Night/He Made Me Free	4-15-62
462	Open Pit Mine/Geronimo	5-12-62
500	A Girl I Used to Know/Big Fool of the Year	9-1-62
528	Not What I Had in Mind/I Saw Me	1-5-63

U.A.	TITLES	DATE
530	Lonely Christmas Call/My Mom and Santa Claus	12-8-62
575	We Must Have Been Out of Our Minds (with M. Montgomery)/Until Then	3-30-63
578	You Comb Her Hair/Ain't It Funny What a Fool Will Do	6-22-63
635	What's in Our Hearts (with M. Montgomery)/Let's Invite Them Over	9-21-63
683	Your Heart Turned Left/My Tears Are Overdue	1-4-64
704	Suppose Tonight Would Be Our Last (with M. Montgomery)/There's a Friend in the Way	3-21-64
724	Something I Dreamed/Where Does a Little Tear Come From?	5-23-64
732	Please Be My Love (with M. Montgomery)/Will There Ever Be Another?	7-4-64
751	The Race Is On/She's Lonesome Again	8-15-64
804	Least of All/Brown to Blue	12-19-64
828	House of Gold (with M. Montgomery)/I Dreamed My Baby Came Home	4-17-65
858	Wrong Number/The Old, Old House	4-17-65
899	Don't Go (with M. Montgomery)/I Let You Go	7-10-65
901	What's Money?/I Get Lonely in a Hurry	8-28-65
941	Blue Moon of Kentucky (with M. Montgomery)/I Can't Get Over You	11-6-65
965	World's Worst Loser/I Can't Change Overnight	12-25-65
50014	Best Guitar Picker/A Good Old-Fashioned Cry	7-2-66
50015	Afraid (with M. Montgomery)/Now Tell Me	9-10-66

MUSICOR	TITLES	DATE
1066	Wreck on the Highway (with G. Pitney)/I've Got Five Dollars and It's Saturday Night	2-6-65
1067	Things Have Gone to Pieces/Wearing My Heart Away	2-6-65
1097	I'm a Fool to Care (with G. Pitney)/Louisiana Man	7-24-65
1098	Love Bug/Can't Get Used to Being Lonely	7-24-65
1115	Your Old Standby/Big Job (with G. Pitney)	10-2-65
1117	Take Me/Ship of Love	10-2-65
1143	I'm a People/I Woke Up from Dreaming	2-19-66
1144	Take Me/Ship of Love	2-19-66
1165	Y'all Come/That's All It Took (with G. Pitney)	2-19-66
1174	Old Brush Arbors/Flowers for Mama	5-7-66
1181	4033/Don't Think I Don't	7-9-66
1204	Close Together/Long As We're Dreaming (with M. Montgomery)	10-15-66
1226	Walk Through This World with Me/Developing My Pictures	1-21-67
1238	Party Pickin'/Simply Divine	3-13-67
1243	I Can't Get There from Here/Poor Man's Riches	5-20-67
1244	Take the World but Give Me Jesus/Cries of Loneliness	7-18-67
1267	The Honky Tonk Downstairs/If My Heart Had Windows	10-7-67
1289	The Poor Chinee/Say It's Not You	2-3-68
1297	Well, It's Alright/Small Time Laboring Man	4-13-68

MUSICOR	TITLES	DATE
1298	As Long As I Live/Your Angel Steps Out of Heaven	7-6-68
1325	Milwaukee, Here I Come/Great Big Spirit of Love (with B. Carter)	9-28-68
1333	When the Grass Grows Over Me/ Heartaches and Hangovers	11-23-68
1339	Lonely Christmas Call/My Mom and Santa Claus	11-23-68
1351	I'll Share My World with You/I'll See You While I Go	3-29-69
1366	If Not for You/When the Wife Runs Off	7-19-69
1375	Lonesome End of the Line/Just an Average Couple (with B. Carter)	9-26-69
1881	No Blues Is Good Blues/She's Mine	11-15-69
1392	Where Grass Won't Grow/Shoulder to Shoulder	3-14-70
1404	Going Life's Way/Unclouded Day	5-6-70
1408	Tell Me My Lying Eyes are Wrong/ You've Become My Everything	7-4-70
1425	A Good Year for Roses/Let a Little Loving Come In	11-21-70
1432	Sometimes You Just Can't Win/ Brothers of a Bottle	3-20-71
1440	Right Won't Touch a Hand/Someone Sweet to Love	6-12-71
1446	I'll Follow You (Up to Our Cloud)/ Getting Over the Storm	10-2-71

RCA		
74-0625	A Day in the Life of a Fool/Old, Old House	2-12-72
74-0700	I Made Leaving (Easy for You)/How Proud I Would Have Been	4-12-72

RCA	TITLES	DATE
74-0792	Wrapped Around Her Finger/With Half a Heart	1972
74-0878	She's Mine/I Can Still See Him in Your Eyes	1972
AMBO-0123	Tender Years/White Lightnin'	1972
APBO-0135	Late Getting Home/For Better or for Worse	1972
PB-10052	I Can Love You Enough/Talk to Me Lonesome Heart	1972

EPIC		
10815	Take Me/We Go Together (with T. Wynette)	12-25-71
10831	We Can Make It/One of These Days	2-12-72
10858	Loving You Could Never Be Better/Try It, You'll Like It	5-20-72
10881	The Ceremony/The Great Divide (with T. Wynette)	7-8-72
10917	A Picture of Me (without You)/The Man Worth Lovin' You	10-28-72
10923	Old-Fashioned Singing/We Love to Sing about Jesus (with T. Wynette)	11-25-72
10959	What My Woman Can't Do/My Loving Wife	3-3-73
10963	Let's Build a World Together/Touching Shoulders (with T. Wynette)	4-7-73
11006	Nothing Ever Hurts You/Wine (You've Used Me Long Enough)	6-23-73
11031	We're Gonna Hold On/My Elusive Dreams (with T. Wynette)	9-1-73
11053	Mary Don't Go Round/Once You've Had the Best	11-24-73
11083	(We're Not) the Jet Set/Crawdad Song (with T. Wynette)	2-9-74
11122	Our Private Life/The Grand Tour	6-8-74

EPIC	TITLES	DATE
11151	We Loved It Away/Ain't It Been Good? (with T. Wynette)	7-27-74
50038	The Door/Wean Me	10-26-74
50088	These Days (I Barely Get By)/Baby, There's Nothing Like You	3-22-75
50099	God's Gonna Getcha for That/Those Were the Good Old Times (with T. Wynette)	5-17-75
50127	Memories of Us/I Just Don't Give a Damn	7-26-75
50187	I'll Come Back/The Battle	2-7-76
50227	You Always Look Your Best (Here in My Arms)/Have You Seen My Chicken?	5-22-76
50235	Golden Ring/We're Putting It Back Together (with T. Wynette)	6-5-76
50271	Diary of My Mind/Her Name Is	9-4-76
50314	Near You/Tattletale Eyes (with T. Wynette)	12-11-76
50385	Old King Kong/It's a 10–33 (Let's Get Jesus on the Line)	5-21-77
50418	Southern California/Keep the Change (with T. Wynette)	7-16-77
50423	If I Could Put Them All Together (I'd Have You)/You've Got the Best of Me	8-13-77
50495	Bartender's Blues/Rest in Peace (with J. Taylor)	1-7-78
50564	I'll Just Take It Out in Love/Leaving Love All Over the Place	7-1-78
50647	Maybelline/Don't Want No Stranger Sleeping in My Bed (with J. Paycheck)	12-9-78
50684	We Oughta Be Ashamed/Someday My Day Will Come	6-30-79

EPIC	TITLES	DATE
50708	Along Came Jones/You Can Have Her (with J. Paycheck)	5-26-79
50849	Two-Story House/It Sure Was Good (with T. Wynette)	3-1-80
50867	He Stopped Loving Her Today/Hard Act to Follow	4-12-80
50891	When You're Ugly Like Us/Kansas City	6-21-80
50922	I'm Not Ready Yet/Garage Sale Today	8-23-80
50930	Pair of Old Sneakers/We'll Talk about It Later (with T. Wynette)	9-6-80
50949	You Better Move On/Smack Dab in the Middle (with J. Paycheck)	12-13-80
50968	If Drinkin' Don't Kill Me (Her Memory Will)/Brother to the Blues	1-17-81
502526	Still Doin' Time/Good Ones & Bad Ones	10-3-81
502696	Same Ole Me	1-23-82
503072	Yesterday's Wine/I Haven't Found Her Yet (with M. Haggard)	7-24-82
503405	C. C. Waterback/After I Sing All My Songs (with M. Haggard)	11-20-82
503489	Shine On/Memories of Mama	1-8-83

ALBUMS

Title	Label	Date
Double Gold George Jones	Musicor	1970
Nothing Ever Hurt Me	Epic	1973
The Grand Tour	Epic	1974
The Best of George Jones	Epic	1975
George Jones	Epic	1975
I Wanta Sing	Epic	1975
Memories of Us	Epic	1975
Picture Me	Epic	1975
Crown Prince of Country Music	Power Pak	1975
Golden Hits	Starday	1975
The Battle	Epic	1976
Alone Again	Epic	1976
All-Time Greatest Hits, Vol. 1	Epic	1977
Bartender's Blues	Epic	1978
Sixteen Greatest Hits	Trip	1979
White Lightnin'	Chiswick	1979
I Am What I Am	Epic	1980
Encore	Epic	1981
Country Gospel	Gusto	1981
Still the Same Old Me	Epic	1981
Shine On	Epic	1982

Index